LITTLE RUINS

Rebuilding a Life

MANNI COE

CANONGATE

First published in Great Britain in 2025
by Canongate Books Ltd, 14 High Street, Edinburgh EH1 1TE

canongate.co.uk

1

British Library Cataloguing-in-Publication Data
A catalogue record for this book is available on request from the British Library

ISBN 978 1 83726 324 0

Typeset in Sabon Std by Palimpsest Book Production Ltd, Falkirk, Stirlingshire

Printed and bound by CPI Group (UK) Ltd, Croydon CR0 4YY

The manufacturer's authorised representative in the EU for product safety is Authorised Rep Compliance Ltd, 71 Lower Baggot Street, Dublin D02 P593 Ireland (arccompliance.com)

MIX
Paper | Supporting responsible forestry
FSC
www.fsc.org
FSC® C013604

LITTLE RUINS

Also by Manni Coe

brother. do. you. love. me. (with Reuben Coe)

For Jack and Reuben: my hobbits
And for Matt Brown Hair

My friend, Malele, was born in our house over fifty years ago. His father inherited part of the farm from his grandparents and then sold his share twenty years later. Malele is linked to the house's history and concerned for its future, much like I am. When we bought it, he was relieved that it had fallen into our hands. He has taught us about the house and the land that sits behind it. When I told him about this book, he paused thoughtfully, then said, 'We all have a little ruin inside us.'

I only wish I'd known how big his 'little ruins' were. Our beloved Malele chose to depart from this world before the publication of this book that carries his words, his culture and his inspiration. All who knew and loved him will always treasure his memory and honour his journey.

AUTHOR'S NOTE

I WAS BORN RICHARD EMMANUEL COE in 1974. I was known as Richard until I spent a year in Bolivia, aged eighteen. There, I started using my middle name and new friends began to call me 'Manni'. I told people it was because Manni sounded better in Spanish, but there was another, hidden reason. In Bolivia, something happened that forced me to leave my boy Richard behind. Claiming Manni as my new name was much more than a cultural adaptation. It was a way for me to walk into a renewed sense of self. What I didn't realise at the time, and for decades after, is that I left that little boy behind, forgotten and silenced.

I have always written, but the lockdown gave me the time to nestle down with my writing and craft my first book. It began as a jolly tale about our home in Spain, an inspiring place in a quiet valley lined with olive groves. Everything changed the day tragedy struck our quiet corner of Andalusia. I changed.

What happened left me raw and exposed. I felt haunted and could find neither peace nor sleep. During therapy, my younger self, Boy Richard, began knocking at the door of my soul. I needed to turn and face him. I needed to acknowledge his suffering and release him from his place of pain.

There began my journey back to the centre of myself, a path I describe as a labyrinth. At times, this process was excruciatingly painful. Some readers may find aspects of the content of this book triggering. I am with you as you read it. Our house has allowed me to return to the very core of me. As we began our restoration project, I, albeit unwittingly at the start, was embarking on my own restorative journey.

The book describes that path of healing and forgiveness, of people who hurt me and also forgiveness of myself, for those people I hurt. I faced the little ruin of me and realised that the cracks were beginning to show. I needed to retrieve my little boy Richard and introduce him to my adult self, aligning the two and making myself whole. Finally.

Arrow, by Manni Coe

Late November and leaves fall with memories of warmth.
The River of the Silent Ones runs with colder water,
Slow, rush, trickle, burble, down.
Colours mute as trees stretch their boughs into empty spaces.
A glimmer line of hope frames a cloud,
Darker than I am used to seeing.
Casts a light
Clearer than I am used to watching.
A chilled wind rushes past my face, tickling the very core
    of me,
And it is then that I hear the echo of him.
A lonely stag performs one final bellow
For his auditorium of wild barbarism.
Like an arrow searching its target,
The rasp echoes down the gorge and I listen
Until it peters out through the coarse fingers of the oleander.
I am weighed down by words as the sorrow leaves me.
Darkness creeps over the ridge as the shadows disappear.
Only the purity of aim and the immense vista of eternal
    green.
I reach into the nothing to catch the arrow on the wind,
Snapping it in two on the nearest boulder of blackening
    limestone.
It hit its target and I can now find my way home.

PROLOGUE

I T IS MARCH 2020. THE sun yawns its glow through thick clouds. All is quiet, except, that is, my thumping heart. I need to walk to shake off the residue of another sleepless night.

A female golden eagle glides into my field of vision and I watch her land on a leafless tree. We regard each other. It is out here, at the 'Final Fence' in the shadows of Midday Peak, that stands as witness, sentry and guard, where my mind is clearest. Our dogs settle, each one on their favourite boulder. I will sit here for a while and they anticipate the wait. Memories will lead me down the murky backwaters of my soul.

I know, ultimately, that if I don't turn around and face myself now, I will carry the weight of this for the rest of my life. I could shun the suffering, brush it aside and walk on, hoping to leave it behind. But I know it will eventually drag me down. This is too heavy to carry. Something happened, something bad, and it hurled me back to the younger version of me; that young damaged boy. If I don't walk back to meet him, I fear the future me will remain unresolved. As much as I have love in my life now, Jack cannot help me with this. Love cannot help me this time. Love is the distant promise of a warm fire, a bothy in a storm in the Scottish Highlands, an anchor, a gentle cove. But love cannot shield me from the pain of returning.

I thought I had dealt with it. The persistence of trauma. Wounds leave scars. Perhaps naively, I had assumed my wounds had healed. Perhaps the emotional therapy I had undergone was holding the wounds like surgical sutures, but what had happened recently had ripped those away and I am here, in tatters again. Am I ruined? Am I to remain silent?

I remember my friend Jacob's words about our Spanish home: 'The Corner is a place where birds with broken wings will come to heal.' Can I be the first? But healing hurts. Why is it almost more painful than the pain itself? Shouldn't it be gentle and simple? I suppose it's the hurt itself that forms the stepping stones to cross over to the other side. We stumble. We wade in our memories, sometimes up to our necks in rushing, freezing water. We enter the raging river. There is no other way. I can no longer harbour memories behind a break-water of silence so I begin to break the wall of secrecy and start to imagine the words, to commit my pain to paper.

Jack understands what I need to do and helps me reach the decision with his silent gaze. At first, I am reluctant to share this inner place of privacy, but I concede to the compulsion to tell him more. There is a need to go backwards before I can move forwards. There is time. Once my greatest enemy, time has now gifted me more than I need.

I want to honour this opportunity and fill notebooks with memories. The only way out of this impasse is to write myself out. Words will tumble from me in landslides. My handwriting will change like the weather; sometimes neat and compact in tidy lines, often so tiny I will squint to focus on the miniature handwriting and occasionally, vast letters, barely legible, will scrawl themselves onto the page. The emotions behind the pen will urge it forward. I will write in bed. I will write in the bath. I will write as I walk. I will order art pads and a tin of sketching pencils to enhance the idea that words are art. In the end, only art remains. I will scroll. I will sketch. I will scribble. I will no longer be silent. I feel the need to purge even if it is only to understand myself acutely, to find once more the centre of me. It is time to enter my life's labyrinth. I needn't be afraid because, unlike in a maze, it is impossible to get lost in a labyrinth. There is a single path from the entrance to the centre.

First, I need to remember. Then, I want to write my way back to the source of pain, reaching the younger version of myself. Only then can I forget.

But where can I go to write? Can I write at the table under the fig tree? What if it's too cold outside? I need a space where I can lock myself away, far from distraction, far from noise. The barn is too big and the rotting timbers are barely holding the roof up. No, it might be dangerous. Jack and our friend

Debs are in the house. They are not noisy but I need silence. I need the absence of noise if I am to untangle myself from the shadow that grips me. I suspect that silence can trigger me away from pain.

What about the little cottage at the back of the house, the one most badly damaged by the flood? No one has used it since Maneo the shepherd left over five years ago. I push the doors open and an air of abandonment rushes out. My vision pans around the main room – there is little that suggests its original beauty. It is, essentially, a ruin. The floor warps, the walls bulge, the ceiling dips in places it shouldn't. The mirror is tarnished, the tiles are cracked, the paint chipped, the wooden window dry and split. The plaster on the fireplace has peeled off in chunks and in the hearth, blackened shards from olive wood and ash from how many fires? The cottage has suffered years, decades of neglect. This depth of damage doesn't happen overnight. But still, it welcomes me with its perfect imperfections.

Could this be the oldest part of the farm? The dimensions are different here. The room is smaller and the ceilings lower than in the main house. I feel comforted by the scale of this room. And as I tune my ear to outside noise, I hear only a faint murmur of water as the river slips by and a single call of a distant bird.

'Here,' I pronounce. 'I can write here.'

Part I

1

OLD MAN MOUNTAIN

S IX YEARS AGO, JACK, REUBEN and I became a family. As I observe Jack and Reuben's antics, watching them tickle each other, quoting lines from *The Lord of the Rings*, I wonder which of them has the extra chromosome.

We are a family of three, a trilogy. Two poles can't stand up together but three can. We lean into each other and form a wigwam, a structure. We complete each other and time appears to stop when we're together. It feels like we can fast-forward and step into our dreams. We deserve that, don't we? Each of us has had our fair share of setbacks.

Reuben and I met Jack six years ago, on a flight from Málaga to City Airport in London. We were all flying home for Christmas and there was a festive cheer in the aircraft cabin. As we took off, the door to the cockpit flew wide open. We could see the backs of the pilot's heads and there was a murmur of concerned chatter as folk down the aisle began to shoot each other confused glances and couples grabbed for each other's hands.

'What the hell?' I mouthed to my new friend, as I admired his Alexander McQueen boots. 'That's seriously dangerous.'

He ignored me.

When we reached cruising altitude, the Cabin Crew Director made a beeline for me and crouched in the aisle. Her accent was heavily Scottish.

'Sir, am I right in thinking that you took photos of what just happened?'

'You would be correct.'

She made me delete them. I felt flushed and let out a large sigh which made my lips resound against each other like a horse's neigh. I smiled at my handsome companion who was trying with all his might to avoid my gaze.

'Did you get any of that?' I asked him.

And then the first words he ever uttered to me: 'Please don't tell me you're a fucking nutter.'

If there was a heaven, this match would have been made in it.

We chatted for two and a half hours and my head started to fill with notions of unity. But surely not. That doesn't happen in real life, does it? At City Airport I gave him my card and said, 'I don't have your details so the ball's in your court, Simon.'

'Just the way I like it,' he replied with his trademark grin and then added, 'And the name's Jack.'

I remember my seat number – 25B. I wear those figures around my neck, engraved on three heart-shaped pendants, like a talisman.

I pull myself out of my memories and refocus on Jack, who is waiting for an answer. He asks me again. 'Where do you want to live?'

'Well, not in Torremolinos. That much I know,' I reply. I decide to be brave and say, 'I would love to live in an old house made of stone, surrounded by olive trees, in the middle of nowhere.'

'Oh, you do come out with some shite,' he chuckles. 'Can I remind you that I need to be close to Málaga airport. No further than 45 minutes. I don't want to spend my whole life in the car. Right, I'd better pack. London calling.'

As Jack sleeps peacefully beside me I can't switch my brain off and dare to dream. I wake up with a fireglow in my belly and begin to trawl the internet looking for rural properties within an hour from Málaga. Before Jack's flight has taken off, I find part of an old *cortijo* – farmstead – that is for sale.

Mum flies out to be part of the search party. I suspect her desire for a true home is as great as mine. As we drive north from the coast I notice the temperature gauge in the car slipping down in numbers.

'In the summer it can be 10 degrees hotter. In the winter, 10 degrees colder,' I tell her. 'People don't live up here for the climate. There's the mountain they call Lover's Rock.' I point down into the valley. 'It looks like the profile of a man lying down, looking skywards. Can you see it?' I ask her. 'Tilt your head.'

'Oh goodness,' Mum exclaims. 'I've got him. That's uncanny. Look, Reubs. Can you see him?'

Reubs tilts his head slowly and peers out through the car window. I hear him say, 'Old Man Mountain. Need show that my Samwise Gamgee.'

We stop to meet Tito, the estate agent, at a petrol station alongside the motorway that links Granada with Seville. We're in the compass centre of Andalusia as we follow him into a valley sprinkled with neat white houses, gleaming in the flat light of late morning. As we zigzag past a little chapel and a children's playground, swept clean with civic pride, my mind opens to expectation.

'This feels promising,' Mum says.

Why does sadness always knock during my happiest moments? I try to block it as I drive between perfect lines of olive trees and a field planted with potatoes. Am I not allowed to be happy? Will it always evade me? Mum's left hand starts doing that thing she does when she's nervous: her ring finger flicks between her middle and little finger like a metronome. My mind shifts back to my percussion lessons when I was a boy. I remember practising my rudiments and hear a paradiddle in my head. The tips of my drumsticks beat out the sequence.

Left, right, left, left
Right, left, right, right

The percussive rudiments of my childhood never leave me. Those Saturday morning classes at Leeds College of Music made everything a paradiddle. I played drums in a concert band and our school orchestra. I then started to play drums in church.

'Look, bruvr,' Reubs says, pointing to the distant hills. I imagine the skyline reminds him of Middle Earth and he mutters something about Saruman.

The tongue of asphalt reaches only so far and then peters out into dirt. I might as well be in a film. Everything appears picture-perfect. Birds dart from olive tree to olive tree through the groves. Tiny leaves flash silver undersides like shoals of whitebait.

I feel like it has taken me too long to get here. Fear, rather than joy, floods my veins.

Tito takes a sharp right turn, down a cement ramp and fords a river.

'Mum, this must be the Guadalhorce, Málaga's longest river,' I tell her.

'And we have to cross it? Careful. Don't go too fast,' she says, slipping her hand through the handle above her passenger door, just like my nanna used to do.

In the rearview mirror I see Reubs repeating one of his favourite lines from *Back to the Future*. He places his sunglasses on his head and then flicks them off his fringe so they fall onto his little nose. 'Where we're going, we don't need roads,' he repeats in his best Doc voice. Without warning I start to cry. You know that secret part of you that imagines an alternate reality? Mum slaps my leg, 'Oh give over. You'll get me started.' She wants this as badly as I do. Not for her but for me, so fiercely does she love me.

And then I see it. First one chimney and then another, stacked over antique baked clay tiles, reaching out from the tree canopy. A building that claims this corner of Andalusia as its own, looking like it's been here since time began. A perfect vision of gleaming white. Only as we approach it do the imperfections glare. Barrel terracotta tiles strewn on the forecourt, clamped in moss and lichen, gaping holes in the roof and cracks tracing their lines across and down the main facade. It's an imposing structure, sitting fortress-like as if it is guarding the pass. Pediments divide the vertical, the straight lines softened by years of layers of quicklime. Wooden shuttered windows with wrought-iron faux balconies wrap the first floor and lead my eye to a single balcony beneath the neo-baroque main facade. The house sits perpendicular to a long straight section of the river. Behind the house, a scissor-cut gorge peters out into the flat valley. There is balance and harmony here. The house has a whimsical air that makes me smile. What on earth is it doing here? Who built it?

'When was it—?' I ask Tito, and he interrupts me before I finish.

'1870.'

The gardens now merge with the wild that has started to creep into roses that were once pruned, hedges that were once clipped. We are surrounded by nature.

It reminds me of a house we stayed in on the Isle of Mull for our friend Katie's twenty-first birthday party: handsome, isolated and flanked perfectly by a backdrop of inviting hills. We could be in a Scottish glen were it not for the olive trees.

I feel like I have been here before. I can hear Jack telling me not to be so ridiculous.

'Oh my goodness. What a place, Manni!' Mum gasps. I ask her to show no emotion to Tito. 'Keep your cards to your chest, Mother.'

Reubs' tongue protrudes as he steps down from the car. 'We're just here to look, Booba. This is the first house and we'll probably see loads more before we make a decision.'

'Just look,' he tells me. 'See how we feel. That's why.'

My eye follows the faux pillars up to a triangular pediment that has a *lauburu* carved into its centre, the symbol of the Basque Country.

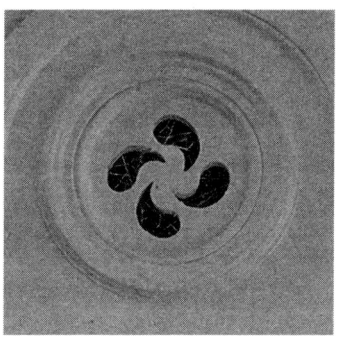

But it's the wrong way round, I think to myself, noticing that its four heads face an anticlockwise direction.

As we walk around to the part of the house that sits alongside the river, I look up and spot another lauburu carved into the main entrance. This one is even more primitive in its form and I notice that is faces clockwise.

Tito unlocks a padlock and slides open a barrel bolt lock.

Two heavy doors, the colour of a dull emerald green, swing open into the barn and stables that lie beneath the house.

'Oh, I say!' Mum squeals.

I scowl at her.

'So, I'll show you the half of the house that is for sale,' Tito tells us.

'Half of the house?' I ask him. 'I thought it was an apartment that was for sale.'

'It's more complicated than that.' He begins to explain as we follow him through a myriad of passageways, barns, patios and stairwells. 'Originally, this was one huge country estate and then it was inherited by two brothers, one of whom was my father.'

'Hang on,' I say. 'Un minuto. Reubs?' I backtrack to find Reubs taking photos of the mule stalls and the bales of hay.'

'Emmerdale Farm!' he says, his eyes sparkling.

I grab his hand and help him over the cobbles, up some steps and into the back patio where Mum is busy opening doors and peering into empty spaces.

Tito continues. 'I have lived here for most of my life but my father sold the other half about ten years ago.' His hand signals up and over a high wall that divides one of the back patios in two.

'So, behind all these dividing walls is the part that's not for sale?'

'Correct.'

'Then who owns it?' I ask.

'Two families from Málaga. They bought this place as an investment. But I can't show it to you as I don't have the keys.'

The knot in my tummy winds tighter. It is like walking into a dream tangled by complications. I spy a muddy water line in the downstairs rooms and make a wide-eyed gesture at Mum.

Tito notices, swallows hard and tells us about the terrible flood of 2012 and then changes the subject quickly. 'So, what is for sale is half this barn, half of this patio, half of these stables, half of upstairs, the carpark out the front, half the front garden, the pool and then the apartment upstairs,' he explains.

'Where's the apartment?' I ask him.

He takes delight in replying, 'All in good time, my friend. All in good time.'

I squeeze Mum's arm. I can't quite believe how big the place is. It's a TARDIS of stone and rubble. Parts of it lie in ruin. Roofs have caved in, their support beams rotten and hollowed out by termites. There is more than a whiff of abandon. I wonder if we've arrived too late to save it. Pillars pitch at peculiar angles, barely supporting sagging ceilings. The apartment upstairs waits for us behind its shuttered windows.

'I'll open them up now so you can appreciate the place in the light of day,' Tito says. There is theatre in his movements as light spills into the rooms, bringing hot air that pours into the fresh spaces, causing an instant rise in temperature.

'Wow,' I remark to Mum. 'Did you feel that?'

'Look at the thickness of the walls.' Tito widens the gap between his hands to half a metre.

The wooden panelled doors into the living room are painted an elegant grey and stand over two metres tall. One panel is bolted into the top of the door frame. A burst of rattles fills the room when Tito wrestles the other panel free.

Cla, cla, cla, cla, cla, cla, cla . . .

The house has its own noises. As we walk around, I do my best to not let my face give away my excitement. The place oozes with days-gone-by charm. The 3.5-metre-high walls are adorned from waist-to-ceiling height with tools, paintings, certificates, plates, religious icons and personal knick-knacks. It is a living museum of a family's past and present.

I spy Reubs' bottom sticking out of a wardrobe in one of the bedrooms.

'Find anything, Booba? I ask him.

'Nnya,' he replies. 'Not yet bruvr, but I will.'

For the next five days, I pace around inside my mind until Jack returns from London.

'There is another couple interested,' I tell him. 'But we have first refusal.'

'Agent's spiel,' he replies.

When Jack sees it for the first time, his poker face gives nothing away. Tito can't read him either and so starts to get a little edgy. I start to inflate with an air of disappointment. This is either a shared dream or no dream.

As we drive away, Jack turns to me and says, ' So, which bedroom is going to be ours?'

'Are you serious?' I quiz him.

'The place is amazing and if I drive, I can get to the airport in under 45 minutes,' he jests.

'Granny Manni,' Reuben quips from the backseat.

'Ah ha! Nice one, my Frodo.' Jack spins around and my two hobbits high-five.

'You're both so rude about my driving. I'm a careful driver!'

Reuben reaches through the little gap under my headrest and strokes my neck. 'Nah. I love you anyway, bruvr,' he says.

Jack suggests we go into the local village for some lunch. 'I want to get a feel for the place,' he says.

I know exactly where to take him.

'Champagne for everyone!' chirps Reubs.

I turn up the music and open the sunroof so Reubs can pop his hands out and bop in the back seat, feeling the hot air against his fingers.

Lunch is a rare moment of bliss. Bar Central is a classic haunt, bursting with locals enjoying their food with convivial natter. The walls are festooned with local colour and history. You can learn so much about a village in Spain from its most popular restaurant. Locals use it as an extension of their homes. Bar Central is the closest place to a British pub I've ever seen in Spain. I enjoy watching Jack relax into his surroundings.

Our offer on the house is accepted and we begin the paper-work. I only hope we can complete before administrative rigor mortis sets in. Menos mal (thank goodness) I speak Spanish otherwise the assault course of legal hoops we have to jump through might crush us. José Vicente, our lawyer, welcomes us into his despacho (office), on the first floor of his family home. He is a man of impressive discipline. His bookcases look like they are dusted daily, books ordered alphabetically by theme and not by author. We get the idea he's more interested in the law than the people who write it. He uncovers an outstanding tax payment for the exploitation and use of the land left over from the sixteenth century.

'Whatever next?' I ask him.

'Oh there are always surprises when we're dealing with old estates in Spain. It's positively feudal.' He beams, enjoying the convoluted purchasing process.

'And what do we need to do?' I ask.

'Go to the bank and withdraw 1,014 euros to pay the gentleman who's on his way down from Granada as we speak.'

He explained as I sat in disbelief, mouth wide open, that the tax was left over from a system called 'Emphyteusis', developed in Ancient Greece and used frequently on the Iberian Peninsula by the Romans. It gave tenants similar rights to proprietors. In our part of Spain, lands confiscated from Jews and Muslims were redistributed among Christians after the Reconquista – a series of wars to establish Catholic Spain and end Islamic rule – and the new owners held up these annual payments of Emphyteusis. It was surely a Christian aristocrat from Granada who was on his way here to collect his fee.

'It could have been worse,' I say with relief. 'When you said it was a payment leftover from the sixteenth century, I feared it might ruin us!'

'Oh no. Nowadays, the payments are merely symbolic but we still need to cancel it to ensure there is no outstanding debt against the house or land.'

'This will all be great content for your book,' Jack grins.

'What book?' I ask him.

'The one you're going to write about all of this! Keep writing!'

Reubs strikes a pose, arms splayed high in the air and chuckles.

José Vicente continues. 'Now, I've approached the owners of the other side of the house, on the river, but unfortunately they don't want to sell.'

I translate for Jack and he replies, 'That's a shame. Ask José if they might reconsider. I don't really want to be living next to an abandoned house. That's weird.'

On a recent visit to see The Corner for the third time, Jack distracted Tito with questions about the river's weir and ford just long enough for me to scale the dividing wall and see the other side of the house. Even though the house is located in the heartlands of Andalusia, the lauburu was not the only nod to Basque culture. The house was more akin to a *caserío vasco*, or Basque farmhouse. It lacked the grand central patio that gave onto the living quarters of the more traditional Andalusian cortijo where rooms for summertime were on the ground floor, kept cool by vegetation and water fountains. The winter rooms would be on the first floor with lower ceilings, in an attempt to trap the scant warmth of the winter sun. It was magical, barely renovated and full of character. I felt like I was running around an abandoned museum. Happiness seemed to sing down the corridors. The original features were intact: thick wooden doors painted the hopeful green of Andalusia's flag; hydraulic tile flooring with vivid geometrical designs; three fireplaces; windows and shutters with heavy iron crossbars; views; silence; light. The outdoors streamed in, sunlight chinking the edges of broken glass, nature and home coexisting.

'Do you want to buy it?' José asks us.

Jack understands the Spanish and we both reply on the same beat with a double, 'Si.'

'Leave it with me,' José replies.

Whatever he says to them works a treat and within three months here we are, at a notary's office on Málaga's rather grand main street, Calle Larios. We are dressed up for the occasion. Reubs has brought his MI6 briefcase as if he was on a Government mission. Earlier, I watched him pack his felt-tips and his 007 Aston Martin toy car, still in its box.

Thirteen of us sit around a huge polished mahogany table fiddling with pens and smiling inanely at each other.

'Don't light up anywhere near that one,' Jack says, gesturing towards a lady with a significant bouffant. Tito is puce.

The notary appears in the doorway, immaculately turned out, a watch the size of a mantel clock on his wrist, waving a Montblanc pen.

'Mr Coe,' he addresses me with a knowing look. 'My clerk

has just had a word in my ear. Could you please write your brother's name on here.' He hands me a piece of paper.

'I can do one better than that, sir. Here, Reubs. Get out your felt-tips and write your name on here.'

After a few idle minutes, the door flings wide open. The ceremony is about to start. 'Señores, good morning to you all.' The notary commands the room. 'Everything is in order for these gentlemen on my right to purchase a cortijo called El Rincón, in the vicinity of Archidona, from these ten people on my left.' Piles of paperwork pass from person to person to sign, some signatures more elaborate than others. The notary's signature is unfathomably complicated and reminds me of a surrealist sketch.

'And ladies and gentlemen, the most important part of this morning's proceedings is this document of ownership for Mr Reuben Coe.'

Reuben hears his name and says, 'That me.'

The notary has prepared a separate document, officiated and notarised for Jack, Reuben and me to sign. It states that the three of us are moving to Middle Earth and that we will be very happy in our new home. Reubs takes out a pink felt-tip and signs with untethered delight.

As we step out into the bustle of Málaga's Old Town, the señora who lived in the apartment takes my hand. 'I hope you will all be as happy there as I was. I wouldn't be selling it had my husband not died.' Her eyes glisten with memories. 'We lived our best and worst years there.' She speaks softly and then she is gone, her fur coat mingling with others as the Malagueñas begin their midday paseo (stroll).

José Vicente proffers his hand. '¡Felicidades chicos!' he says through a wide smile.

'Thank you for all your hard work, José. That wasn't easy,' I say, and then add, 'How did you convince them to sell to us?'

His face flicks with a wicked smile and he says, 'You'll have to get me very drunk if you ever want me to tell you that.' With a wink he spins on his heels and rushes off for his next appointment.

Reubs locks his eyes on mine and says, 'We are owners,' with a blossoming sense of pride. 'My boys,' he adds and pulls us in for a group hug.

We sit on high stools in a bar down a side street, drinking beer and munching on prawns, croquetas and octopus salad. Reubs orders 'Una clara por favor. Love a shandy, I do,' he tells the waiter.

Jack has to return to London for work, so it is just Reuben and I who drive up to The Corner the following morning. Beau, an English Cocker that used to belong to Jack's Mum, needs a playmate, so we buy BB from a breeder in Vélez-Málaga. She is a very intimidated Spanish water dog, the runt of a litter of nine nobody wanted because of the white socks and bib staining her black coat. She cowers under furniture but loves being cuddled. We sit them on the back-seat as we drive north. Reubs adjusts his scarf, making it a little tighter.

'Old Man Mountain, bruvr.' He points as we enter the valley. 'He always sleeps.'

'Do you think he will ever open his eyes, Booba?' I ask him.

'Hum. I don't know,' he replies, crumpling his face into a gesture of deep thought. 'What you think?' he asks me.

'Well . . . he's been sleeping for thousands of years and I think he'll sleep for thousands more,' I say.

I love it when Reuben's mind clicks through to a scene from his imagination. His eyes ignite with connection.

'Bruvr?' he asks me.

'What, Booba?' I reply.

'Will I happy here?'

'Hum. I don't know. What do you think.' I spin it back.

'I think I will,' he says emphatically. 'Our Corner bruvr.'

He grins as I swerve off the motorway towards our new home.

The delicate, desperate beauty of a place I begin to dare to call home. Is this a far-fetched yearning? Or can it be real? A crumbling ruin of a house with severe flood damage, gaping to the elements of bitter winters and burning summer days. But it is here that I start to hear myself more clearly. Or maybe I am simply starting to listen.

Light aligns along the earth's most secret contours. These bastion walls of stone and mortar are soaked with joy and

17

music and celebration and dance, but there is a melancholy too that clings to the cracks. There has to be. How can 133 years pass without tears? Life is stitched together with smiles and sadness.

It is here that I can find myself. It may be cold and old, but this is where my soul begins to sing.

Is The Corner the place I have seen in my dreams? There is only one way in, only one way out. The track leading here is a dead end. The Spanish call it a 'sin salida' – no exit. For half of my life, I have ached for this. It would appear I have found a way into my very own labyrinth.

2

PARADIDDLES

B RITISH PEOPLE THINK THINGS; SPANISH people just say them. It's a much healthier way of living – to speak the truth and in turn, learn not to be offended by it. My Spanish friends have often told me that my head is full of pajaritos (little birds), or that I have cosas de bomberos retirados (I am full of outlandish thoughts). The literal translation of the latter is 'traits of retired firemen', which is much more amusing. I have always dreamed. That much is true.

Growing up in Leeds, Yorkshire, I couldn't have wished for a more secure and settled childhood. My parents appeared happy and our lives were filled with friends and walks and holidays in caravans, BMX tricks, sledging in urban parks, knickerbocker glories, cream apple turnovers and dandelion and burdock fizzy drinks.

After church, Sunday lunch. After lunch, if it was fine, a walk in the Hollies. In rain or snow, Mum and Dad would drive us over the ups and downs to Yeadon Airport, where grown-ups sat in the cafeteria slurping mugs of tea while my brothers, Matthew and Nathan, and I sat on the hard floor, cross-legged, hands to the glass of the panoramic viewing platform. We would stare through the window, bulging rain-drops forming tiny snow-globe scenes of other families going on winter holidays. I accepted that their lives were different to ours. I never considered that my family could also go abroad. There were many things that I assumed weren't an option to me back then.

We wore second-hand clothes, hand-me-downs from a posh family who owned the BMW dealership in nearby Knaresborough, and took holidays in the seaside town of Whitby in borrowed cars. Matt and I delivered papers every morning before school. I was ten. He was twelve. Our rounds took us into the more affluent neighbourhoods of Headingley, where people read newspapers with posh names like *The Sunday Times* and *The Observer* in big houses. Sundays were a killer when the strap of my luminous orange bag, full of Sunday supplements and magazines, would dig into my scrawny shoulder. I teetered along, riding my bike at a 45° angle to counterbalance the weight.

I had my own room in the attic with a Velux window looking onto the grey Yorkshire skies. I remember the green wallpaper dotted with small white flowers and the polystyrene underroll my dad had pasted to the walls before the wallpaper, to achieve a smoother finish. I discovered to my delight (and to Mum's dismay) that I could press my fingertips into the wall and make little indentations. The area by my bed became pockmarked with my fingerprints. I suppose I desired to leave my mark, even then.

That's when the whispers began, the dull dampened echo of a non-voice. They always sounded the same even though the whispers had no sound. They were beyond sound, a muffled noise that broke the silence in my head and made me feel uneasy. They were my little ruins. If I paradiddled hard enough inside my head, they would leave me.

I enjoyed school, breakdanced on the recreation ground and tapped my percussion rudiments onto a black practice pad with my nylon-tipped drumsticks. The music teacher at Bennett Road Primary School put me up for a scholarship at Leeds College of Music and I won it. Every Saturday morning, I would take the bus into the centre of Leeds by myself, a little kid beginning to fill his head with big ideas. I suppose that's when the pajaritos flew in.

Left, right, left, left
Right, left, right, right

Paradiddles, double paradiddles, triples, rolls and the metallic cracks of snare drum rim shots beat inside my head. I used to tap myself to sleep (Jack will tell you that I still do). I learned to sight read percussion music and worked my way up to playing timpani and a full drum kit. How I longed for my own drum kit. One day. My teacher was my hero, but oddly I can't recall his name. He had blond hair, was always smartly dressed, and I was in awe of his flawless sense of rhythm.

Nathan and I developed a sense of wanderlust. From a young age we were both intent on discovering what lay beyond our city. The West Yorkshire Rover ticket gave us the opportunity to do just that. For one pound each, on Saturday mornings, we bought child tickets from our local corner shop. They were bookmark-shaped and yellow in colour. They came in their own plastic sheaf to keep them dry, rather like a comb pouch, and on our initial bus ride into town we punched them into the ticket machine by the driver, that day's date giving us licence to explore all of West Yorkshire on buses and trains until darkness fell.

Our favourite excursion was taking the high-speed train from Leeds Central to Bradford so we could visit the sparkling new Photography Museum. We both started to dream. Nathan is now a Fine Art Photographer with three galleries in the United States. Funny how those seeds were sown when he was so young. I remember his six-year-old cherubim face, wide-eyed in wonder, staring up at the world's beauty captured through the lens of photographers from around the world.

When my youngest brother Reuben was born with an extra chromosome on his twenty-first pair, everything changed.

Mum stopped baking bread.

The Coe family pivoted on a penny. Without ever wanting or intending to, Reuben David Coe set our family on a different course. Before Reuben was two, Dad felt a religious calling into full-time work with the mentally and physically different. He felt drawn to care for others. We swapped Yorkshire for Berkshire, a big house for a small one, friends for strangers and northern accents for southern ones. I was twelve.

Our new home in Tilehurst, Reading, was an end cottage. The gable end was only one brick thick. It had rising damp and the bathroom was downstairs through the tiny dining room and the even tinier kitchen. Mum used to say it was like living in a draughty railway carriage. Dad worked night shifts three days a week, leaving Mum to sit with her four boys in the front room, trying to make sense of it all. There was only enough space for a small two-seater settee and an armchair, so I always sat on the floor, my back against the sofa, a cushion beneath my bottom (I still like to sit like that now). My parents tried very hard to make it a happy home but things were different. In Leeds, we were happy. In Reading, we had to work at being happy and it wasn't easy.

Mum passed the time buying KFC Family Buckets or taking us to Pizza Hut for a family pizza and a large salad. Matt, Nathan and I devised a technique, using slices of cucumber to extend the edges of the bowl, allowing us to pile the salad-bar offerings a whole lot higher. Mum would clutch her handbag and stare into Reading's High Street, balancing Reuben on her knee, pretending not to be embarrassed as we tiptoed back to the table with a teetering tower of the tallest salad you ever saw.

Twelve was a strange age to move home. All-new everything and a bewildering confusion just as my skin erupted with pimples and growing pains ensured that my body cast an unfamiliar shadow. At our new school, the girls thought I was cute. The boys thought I was weird. I was that kid who cycled home in our school lunch hour, twenty minutes each way, just so I didn't have to spend sixty minutes walking around the playground by myself. I loved those twenty minutes of alone time in the house. I felt all grown-up. I would make myself a sarnie with crunchy sandwich spread or scoff a scotch egg with a packet of Monster Munch and a Penguin biscuit. If I watched the end of the lunchtime showing of *Neighbours*, I would have to pedal extra fast in order to make it back to school before the bell rang for the start of afternoon classes.

I found a way through when I won all my five events in the school's sports day. In my class, I was a hero. For them, the emotion only lasted for one day. For me, it lasted much longer as I glimpsed a sense of belonging.

Reading did not treat us well. Nathan got mugged in the toilets of Burger King. Matt got badly bullied by one of the city's gangs. One evening when Dad was at work on a night shift, three members of the gang tried to get into our house. They were banging on the door screaming Matt's name. Reubs was fast asleep in bed. Matt turned off all the lights and made Mum, Nathan and me lie down on the living-room floor. We lived through the acrid taste of terror, breathless and silent, as they made their way around the back of the house and tried to get in through the bathroom window. Mum was too far away from the phone to call the police. Who knows how long we lay there, pinned to the carpet like fear stains. It seemed an age before they left and none of us ever felt safe in that house again.

That depth of fear changed us. I'm sure it changed Matt. As a family we shifted our focus away from the city, in part to protect Matt from danger. But those shadows lurked. We will always remember them.

We began to spend more time out of the city in a more rural community, close to a church that Mum and Dad had discovered. They got on well with the dynamic vicar and preferred his more charismatic approach to Christianity to the traditional values of the grande-dame Anglican church in Reading town centre.

I was offered the opportunity to play drums in the worship band, so I dusted off my drumsticks and used my savings to buy my first-ever drum kit. I found it in the classified section of the *Reading Chronicle*. It was made by the brand Pearl and had red metallic shells and Remo drum skins. Its hi-hat cymbals were old and battered and sounded like two dead weights when they crashed together. I coveted the crisp, clean sound of the Paiste hi-hats I had played in a music store in Reading's town centre and started to save again. With my own kit, I felt like a proper drummer. I bought a drummer's kit bag and began to collect different kinds of drumsticks and brushes: wooden tips, nylon tips, nylon brushes, metallic brushes. I started to believe I knew what I was doing. Buying birthday and Christmas presents for me became easy – all I wanted was more drumsticks.

A prominent member of the new congregation tried to dissuade my parents from joining. Mum took it as a personal affront but in hindsight, this person was trying to warn us. She knew things we didn't. Regardless, we settled in to our new church, felt welcomed and celebrated, drawn into a sense of community. A year went by and then another before Mum and Dad decided it was time to move into the village. And so, the Coes upped sticks again. In the rural idyll, house prices were beyond our financial reach, so Mum and Dad rented a house with three bedrooms on the main road, by a petrol station. Friends gave us a caravan which became a fourth bedroom in the front garden. The lucky lot fell to me: I named her Yasmin after Yasmin Le Bon and kitted her out as best I could. I revelled in having a tiny place to call my own. We loved the name of our new village, but Reubs found it difficult to pronounce – *Tutting Clamper* was a mouthful for any of us. Matt stepped away from his place of fear. No one knew at the time, but I was being moved closer to mine.

pa–ra–did–dle
pa–ra–did–dle

I managed to keep it all a secret. I locked it away and never told a soul until I was far enough away that it seemed to hurt less.

When you've got four sons, it's hard to keep all of them safe and happy, all of the time.

3

OUR FIRST CHRISTMAS

Our first Christmas at The Corner is cold. We don't have a Christmas tree. We can't work the oven. We don't have any stockings for Santa. We couldn't find a turkey and there are no crackers to pull.

It is perfect.

We huddle around the fire cuddling each other and the dogs for warmth. It's the most isolated the three of us have ever felt and we lack for nothing but warmer clothes. It feels as if we are embarking on an adventure. All is wide-eyed wonder. At night, the temperatures plummet below zero and in the mornings, when we dare stir from our beds, our breath plumes in the air.

Friends arrive to share the fun armed with thermal underwear. Tamara is a painter, born in Georgia. She sees the world through a gentle and skilled gaze. Her most recent art collection is very angular – *Triangular Life*. She depicts everything in triangular form. I hope she sees us as a triangle. I rather like that idea. Maybe she should paint us.

She arrives with her two Russian daughters, Tonia and Maria. They tower over six feet tall and fill The Corner with their spirit of joy and discovery. They are Jack's friends but, like everything else in our relationship, the process of Jack's people becoming my people and my people becoming Jack's is pure pleasure.

Together, we drive to the local supermarket and fill the car with all manner of goodies, both healthy and otherwise. Tamara works out how to light the oven.

'What doughnuts,' Jack says with self-deprecation.

Reubs rasps a laugh and repeats, 'Doughnut,' as he gently whacks Jack's arm with a tea towel. 'What you like, Samwise Gamgee.'

I lock myself in our bedroom to sit on our bed and cry. Is that really laughter coming from the kitchen of our house? Why do I still have this deep, niggling sensation that I don't deserve to be happy? Am I really that damaged? I pull myself together. Not even Jack notices. I need to learn to live more in the moment like he does. It's just that the past pulls at me. It won't let go.

We cook up a feast and the calories heat us from the inside out. Bottles of Matarromera, Jack's favourite wine, flow as the living room ricochets with stories of old. It feels like these new friendships already have history.

On New Year's Day, we decide to summit the hill behind the house. It's a thorny scramble to the top. Reubs makes a valiant effort but halfway up, he decides he can go no further.

'Half,' he says and plants his bottom on a flat rock. 'I'm done.'

Tamara stays with him, not because she doesn't want to reach the top, but because she wants some alone time with Reubs. Later, she tells me that he was so kind to her, fussing over her to make sure she was comfortable. 'We had such a special time together,' she tells me, smiling.

When we heave ourselves on to the ridge that connects two craggy limestone peaks, the view forces us to sit down and take it in. We have a clear vantage point of the entire valley. The hilltop village of Archidona lies to the east, like a white brush stroke on a vast canvas of olive green. Everything is a huge grid of olive groves. In the distance, the brand-new high-speed train line cuts through the landscape like a necklace draped across a polka-dot dress. My eyes follow the river until it meanders out of sight, onwards to lakes and reservoirs, through forests and over waterfalls until it reaches the Mediterranean Sea beside the shiny city of Málaga.

Maria points to a cluster of boulders behind us. 'Let's climb up there,' she challenges.

After a couple of minutes Tonia breaks the silence we are all pulled into. 'I can't believe this place is on your land,' she says,

'Neither can I,' I agree.

'It's wild,' Jack adds. 'Let's go down and get that fire roaring, eh?' He hollers, 'Frodo!' into the breeze.

We can't see Reubs, but we all hear an elongated, 'Samwise Gamgeeeeee!' and giggle. I squeeze Jack's hand before beginning the descent down the steep flank of the hillside.

'Trickier going down,' I remark.

'Often the way,' quips Tonia.

As we approach the house, we see our new neighbours, Antonio and Esperanza, in their olive grove.

'There's Tony and Hope,' I tell Tonia as I wave.

Antonio lifts his cap and says, 'En diciembre, no hay valiente que no tiemble.'

'What was that?' asks the ever inquisitive Tonia.

'An old Spanish proverb,' I explain. 'In December, even the brave shiver.'

Food and fireside peace ensues. Tonia and I snuggle on the sofa. There is a crossover of purpose and plan. I can feel it and so can Tonia.

'I'm so glad you and Frodo found your Samwise Gamgee,' she says.

'It's magic,' I reply.

'It really is. I get it now,' she says. 'We all had our concerns. It all seemed too quick. You guys meeting, Reubs, and then this – The Corner. Don't get me wrong. Just seemed a lot for Jack to take on.'

'I can imagine the alarm bells,' I say. 'But there haven't been any doubts, Tonia. We haven't forced anything. It just happened.'

'Jack seems different somehow. Calmer. Happier. There's an unusual purity about you three. Anyway, enough emotional drivel. Can you fill my hot-water bottle, please?'

4

A SKIP AND A VIRGIN

I T IS TIME TO MAKE this house our home. Every single room is filled with the belongings of strangers. The late husband was an artist; Cubist-style still-life paintings of waves, fruit, coffee mugs and wine glasses boldly decorate the walls.

'How odd that la señora didn't want to take them with her,' I comment to Jack.

'She was finally able to admit how bad they are,' Jack says.

Does the family intend to come back? I decide to call Tito.

'Tito, buenos días. Are you well? We just want to mention something to you. We really don't think the family has left.'

Tito chuckles down the phone. 'Why? Have they left a lot behind?' he asks.

'A lot?' I reply. 'They've left everything! There was food in the fridge, shoes in the hall, dirty dishes in the dishwasher, clothes in the washing machine. Unopened post, paintings, photographs, tools, alcohol, plates, dishes, curtains, rugs, bed linen, blankets, lamps, books, beds, wardrobes, children's toys . . . '

'Hang on. Let me stop you there,' Tito interrupts me. 'I assure you. They have left. They have taken everything they wanted. All the rest is yours. Every knife and fork.'

In other parts of the world, this would never happen. In a house sale, homes are stripped clean of their contents, unless of course, an agreement is reached between the two interested parties. Clearly the owners would have preferred us to buy what they had left behind. In the sale negotiations, they had sent us a price list.

Old key on wall in living room – 50 euros.
Hand-painted spice rack – 30 euros
Early nineteenth-century mahogany wardrobe – 300 euros
IKEA sofabed, nearly new – 100 euros

On and on went the list.

Shoe rack by the back door – 50 euros.

'Bargain,' said a thrilled Jack. 'Thank goodness we didn't pay for it all!'

In exchange for a house full of goods, we now had the work of sorting through twenty years of clutter.

The main room is the largest, with an enormous casket fireplace, a double window facing north and double doors opening out onto a Juliet balcony with views of the surrounding peaks. Hidden in a corner, I find a painting. Well, it's not a painting but a photograph of a painting that someone has begun to paint over, like a painting by numbers.

The original depicts the house in its glory days: manicured formal gardens with stone walls and terraces, lined with wrought-iron balustrades and rose bushes lead up to the front of the house. Most striking for me is the colour. It's not white but a distinct Basque-farmhouse red. It looks transplanted from northern Spain to the south, a Basque soul far from home. I wonder when they painted it white.

The facade with its decorative architectural details – faux pillars, quoins, pediments and edges painted an earthy beige stand out against the imposing red of the walls. An ornamental garden, with clipped hedges and balustrades, looks onto the river. The terracotta tiled roof stands out against the clear blue sky. A crown is painted in the bottom right-hand corner of the canvas.

All I have is a name that I find engraved into a ceramic tile at the back of the house: 1901 Cayetano de Alvear.

'If his name is important enough to carve into a ceramic plaque,' I say to Jack, 'then I need to know who he was.'

How long did he live here? Did he build the house? What I wouldn't give to find a box of his belongings. The crown on the canvas looks like a nod to nobility. After some research I learn it is the insignia of the noble title of San Félix. So, he was titled! But why, I ask myself, did Count Cayetano – Cayetano de Alvear – build this home here, in this particular spot, tucked out of sight of the harsher plains of Central Andalusia? Did he find peace here? Was he running away from something? How did he come to be here?

Something must have driven him to build such a house on the other side of the river, with no access, far from the village. First, he built the bridge, opening the way to build the farm, with the bridge being the threshold between the civilised world and the call of nature. He brought the Basque culture with him, and not only the lauburus emblazoned on the two facades attest to his nobility.

I pore over bookcases and flick through an entire filing cabinet of documents in the hope of finding clues to his life, but find nothing of interest – details of Count Cayetano elude me.

When we mention the house's past to the few elderly neighbours who remember it, they spill their memories of its grandeur.

'Ay, Dios mío. ¡Qué belleza! ¡Qué maravilla! Oh you have no idea what it was like. It was like something out of a dream! How they kept those gardens!'

'We used to stroll along the riverside avenue on Sunday afternoons with our would-be suitors and chaperones,' another señora told us.

Anita, a lady in her eighties, who lives by herself in a house in the valley, remembers the house and farm in its days of glory. 'There wasn't a rose out of place. The place looked like something you'd see in a dream,' she tells me.

The Corner proves to be a time warp where hours, days and weeks mould into each other, and the one thing we don't notice is the passing of time.

Days go by without seeing another human or hearing a car. It feels as if we are far from civilisation. Jack and I both tend to connect to our wilder sides: longer walks, fewer showers, long days synched into sunlight hours and temperatures. We prepare meals until the pantry runs low, then look at each other as if disaster has struck and make ourselves leave.

'Looks like we'll have to go into town tomorrow.'

We begin to ignore The Corner's blatant imperfections: the missing tiles, the broken steps, the fallen tree branches, the collapsed fences. Normally, it's only when a visitor's arrival is imminent that we react to our surroundings.

'Right, you sweep and I'll mop behind you.'

'Reubs, make your bed, babes.'

'Put all the rubbish and recycling in the back of the car and I'll run it to the bins.'

First-time visitors are always the most fascinating. Few hide their surprise. Some call it 'the Palace'. One stands there with a huge grin and says, 'Are you actually serious?'

Most ask, 'How did you find it?'

Everyone asks, 'Who lived here before?'

If I had a euro for every time I have heard 'It has so much potential', we would already have the funds for restoration.

It's true; its possibilities are endless. It's time to call for a skip. We call Toledo, our neighbour. The lorry unloads it directly underneath the main facade. The Juliet balcony becomes the launchpad for all manner of toys, chairs, books, blankets, plates, papers, files and furniture. Reubs enjoys flinging items from the balcony, 'Up, up and away!' he says each time something leaves his hands. He follows every single shoe, curtain, box and packet with an arc of his gaze. 'Fun, bruvr,' he beams. 'Where skip go after?' he asks.

'We'll call the neighbours for them to help themselves to anything they might like and the rest will go to the dump,' I explain.

'Dump,' Reubs repeats, enjoying the sound of the word. 'Pluuuuuunge,' he says remembering one of his favourite TV shows, *Miranda*. 'We could watch that later, bruvr,' he suggests. 'I got DVD of that.'

Every now and again there is a wee tussle between me and the more minimalist Jack.

'But it's an old *bracero*! They used to burn open coals in them, to keep warm.' I plead. It remains on its hook on the wall.

'But it's a sculpture of the Virgin, Our Lady of Grace. She watches over the village,' I argue.

'She'll be watching over you in a minute if you don't let go of her,' Jack insists.

She falls to her fate in the skip, but after dark, when Jack is in the loo, I rescue her and hide her in the shoe box by the front door – she is still there.

Reubs gets up early every day.

'Morning, Frodo,' chirps Jack. 'How are you today?'

'Good, good,' Reubs replies as he moves in for his morning

cuddle. 'My Samwise Gamgee,' he mutters between squashy kisses on Jack's cheek.

'How does it feel to be adored?' I ask Jack.

'Oh, quite normal,' he replies. 'You know how it is. Right, who's for eggs? How would you like them, Frodo Baggins?'

'Hummmm,' Reubs considers. 'Scrambled today, I think.'

We all pause and smile.

Jack is in London for two weeks at a time and then spends long weekends with his boys. Reubs and I muddle through together. Most days I give him tick sheets with jobs he needs to do and he slowly works his way through them. He has never liked the word 'work', so turns work into 'play'.

He chooses different songs for different tasks: 'Shine Jesus shine' is his emptying the dishwasher song; he tidies his room to 'I will follow him' on repeat and he hangs the washing out to 'Chitty Chitty Bang Bang'.

In one of the barns downstairs, he finds a piece of wood that resembles Saruman's staff in *The Lord of the Rings*. He is now convinced that The Corner is Middle Earth and he embraces his hobbitdom even more fiercely.

It is unlikely there is a more fitting human representation of a hobbit than Reuben: short, stocky, flat-footed, with an innocent aura. He could have been born in the Vales of Arduin. So, it comes to pass, that Frodo and Samwise take walks together, through the valleys and hills of Middle Earth and happiness falls upon us. Frodo develops a new interest in the natural world: how things grow, where birds come from, how olive oil is made and the ingredients of jams and chutneys. He laughs when he learns that eggs come out of chickens' bottoms and then proceeds to tell us his favourite joke from *The Vicar of Dibley*.

He coughs and then begins, 'Santa go doctor. Say I got mince pie stuck my bottom.' His eyes are shining as he builds up for the punchline. 'Doctor say I got cream for that.'

We laugh and Reubs scratches his neck just below his hair-line, gently smacking his lips against his tongue in proud satisfaction. He loves making his boys laugh.

From a young man who, just a year ago, thought that cheese-burgers grow on grapevines, I am delighted by this newfound passion for nature and flavour and taste. It seems like The Corner is connecting him to his five senses. He looks radiant, clear-skinned, strong-boned and full of cheer.

This morning, he is organising his belongings in his room, finding homes for his framed drawings, cuddly lions, 007 memorabilia and his dressing-up costumes.

'My little room,' he says when I pop my head around the door to check on his progress. 'How long we been bruvrs, bruvr?' he asks me.

'How old are you?' I ask him.

'Ummm, thirty-two, I think. Am I?' he says.

'Then we've been brothers for thirty-two years,' I tell him.

'Wow! Long time, bruvr!' he sparkles. 'And how long me Spain?'

'Four years now. Time flies, doesn't it! Thank goodness we got you out of that home, eh?' I like to remind him of how far he's come.

He tuts and raises his eyes, remembering what we called it, that Mencap home in Berkshire. 'Dirty sheets, bruvr.'

'How are you getting on in your room, Booba? Do you like it?'

'Love it, bruvr. Lovely flew,' he says pointing out to the empty, cracked swimming pool and the olive groves beyond.

5

THE LONG ROAD TO ANDALUSIA

T HE DARKEST YEARS LOOM IN my memory. We will get there, but I'm not quite ready to return. For now, the year was 1992. I was eighteen. I had always dreamed of travelling far away. In my teens I saved up for a smart Karrimor rucksack. It was burgundy and navy blue with yellow stitching and smelled of adventure. I held on until I got my A-Level results, then bought an Interrail ticket and waved goodbye to Mum at Reading train station, who kissed me into my future. It wasn't her I needed to get away from. I suspect she might have wanted to come with me.

That was my first visit to Spain. I hated it and I don't use that word lightly. I witnessed a shooting in Madrid, got gassed and robbed in Pamplona and found Barcelona full of Olympic mania and greed. It seemed that everyone only wanted money, and my shoestring budget kept me far from the fun. The Catalan capital was eating away at my month's budget. I lurked in the outskirts, waiting for my parents to send me emergency travellers' cheques, then caught a train over the border to France.

'Good riddance! Hasta nunca!' I uttered as the second-class carriage shunted onto the French gauge.

I turned my back on Spain. Thankfully, Spain did not turn its back on me, but it would be several years before I returned.

A university degree in German and Drama awaited me at Aberystwyth, Wales. I loved getting my tongue around the name, but honestly, I had chosen the university because I had liked the matte finish of their prospectus brochure. As I stepped off the train to throw myself into Fresher's Week, I was gripped with the undeniable feeling that I was in the wrong place. Nothing appealed. I had an icky feeling in my stomach so I did a U-turn. I had learned, or so I thought, to read those small signs, those tiny tremors of intuition. I returned to base to decide what to do. Mum and Dad were very supportive. They have always trusted me and known never to stand in my way. Together we tried to find a solution. I deferred my university entry to give myself some thinking time.

'Well, you can't just throw away a year of your life,' my parents told me. 'You need to do something worthwhile.'

I applied to do a 'Year for God' with a missionary organisation called Youth With A Mission, and work on a rehabilitation project for street kids in Bolivia. Mere weeks later I was living in a community compound on the outskirts of Santa Cruz de la Sierra, feeling more at home than I'd ever felt anywhere. I learned Spanish almost by osmosis and became fluent within three months. I fell deeply in love with South America and its people.

Returning home after a full year away, a layover in Madrid confirmed my earlier impressions of Spain. In South America they call Spain 'La Madre Patria' (the motherland), their impression of the country tainted by the annals of social, political and religious history. The Spanish people seemed abrasive and haggard to me, particularly the women, who looked cheated by life, sucking on cigarettes for consolation. I was struck by the sharp edges of these Castilian speakers: pointy chins and angular noses, so different to the round, gentle and curvaceous personalities of the Bolivians. I followed signs to my departure gate through the badly lit and unwelcoming Barajas Airport to board my flight home . . . well, back to England.

For the second time I experienced reverse culture shock. Soon after arriving, I took a bath and cried when hot water came out of the tap. I cried even harder when it dawned on me that there was carpet on the bathroom floor. Bolivia had changed me further still, so much so that my life didn't feel like it belonged to me anymore. The familiar seemed peculiar. The everyday seemed foreign. I was back home with my family but I felt oddly alone.

On a whim, having never visited Scotland, I accepted a place at Edinburgh. I have my old school friend, Simon, to thank for this. He had started uni the year before me and had fallen head over heels in love with the city.

'Don't even think about it,' he told me. 'Trust me on this one. You'll love it up here.'

I trusted him. He was right. I did love it. I still do. There are few cities in the world that create so many heartfelt memories for everyone who visits. I think they store them in the vaults under the Royal Mile for safekeeping. Those years in Edinburgh linger and never leave me.

I arrived in George Square, the main university campus, wearing my alpaca poncho and stripey trousers that I'd bought in La Paz. One of the first things I did was sign up to the Christian Union to find my home amongst fellow believers. Looking back, I can hardly believe that I totally missed out on the debauchery of Fresher's Week as I was a teetotaller. What a waste!

I entered the PVC-floored, strip-lit, French department for my first-ever tutorial. French. Hang on. As I walked into the room, I was struck with blind panic when I realised that the only foreign words my mouth could produce were Spanish.

A beautiful, tanned girl sat next to me and smiled. 'Hello. My name's Sophie. I like your outfit.'

She must have seen the horror-stricken look in my eyes and I replied in Spanish: 'I can't remember a word of French. You're going to have to help me.'

And help me she did. During the tutorial, she passed me the answers on little pieces of paper under the table and spoke in my silences.

When the tutorial finished, I hugged her with relief. 'Thank you, Sophie. Can I take you for a coffee?'

We've been soulmates ever since. Her love for Spain drew me in. Having grown up on a cork farm in southern Andalusia, she talked about her adopted country in a way that inspired me to visit.

So, it was with trepidation that a year later I returned to Spain, to spend a summer in Andalusia at Sophie's family home. The south seemed altogether different. Nobody robbed me. I did not see anyone get killed and I could afford the most delicious café con leche. The speckled light and vibrant characters of southern Spain surprised me with their authentic allure. I had never expected to feel so at home so far away from South America, and there began my love affair with this land of contrasts.

That summer, time seemed to stretch and take on a new dimension. The hours of each day hung suspended in the buzz of the still, hot air. My conversations took on a fresh focus as I felt invigorated by peaceful sleep. Sophie's parents' house was unlike any place I'd ever seen. It had a name rather than a number. The combined passion for art, antiques and music of her parents, Malcolm and Ana, created a unique style that communicated their breadth of human experience.

I passed a fingertip across the spines of the books in the drawing room, glimpsing many names I recognised, but more that I didn't. The quicklime-whitewashed walls reflected the sun's harshest rays so that even in the afternoon, when everything outside was languid and listless, the house remained comparatively cool, the hot air rising to the rafters of the high ceilings, as an Arabic-style irrigation system burbled water along channels through the central patio. I remember wondering what it might feel like to live in a place like that.

Barefoot in the silence of the siesta hours, I sat and enjoyed the stillness. A contentment arose in me, one that I had not known so close to home. I was aware of textures and filtered sunlight. I knew I had found a place that marked the metronome of my soul. It was within the old stone walls of that house, on a cork farm in southern Spain, that I knew Andalusia and I were going to be soulmates for life. It happens rarely, maybe only once in a lifetime. I made a commitment to return. Sophie started telling me repeatedly that I needed to go to Seville.

Meanwhile, life's twists and turns took me back to South America, not once but twice. I was close to making Buenos Aires my base, enamoured by that sprawling city on the Río de la Plata estuary, but one panicked trip back, when Mum fell ill, gave me a thirteen-hour flight to realise I didn't want to be that far away from home.

London beckoned instead. Everyone should give London a try once in their life, right? I found a great job but was reckless with love – oh so reckless. If life is made up of ebbs and flows, then one of my very lowest ebbs happened when I was living in the Big Smoke. I broke somebody's heart. He didn't deserve it. He called me 'duplicitous', and I had to look the word up in a dictionary. Even today, I get hot flushes thinking about it – the guilt comes back to scald me. I did try to contact him once to apologise but didn't get a reply. I was being selfish, my need for forgiveness greater than his need to forgive.

I started a relationship with an artist, ten years older than me. He was my Picasso. I was his Dora Maar. Much like a Cubist painting, it was two relationships twisted into one. I got to see both sides of the moon. I got burned by both sides of the sun. We could see the best and worst of each other – like a shattered mirror, the shards were dangerous for both of us.

It was his mother who warned me. She and I would sit in the kitchen drinking cups of tea and smoking Silk Cut cigarettes.

'He's the most amazing person I've ever met, my son,' she told me. 'But you're too sensitive. You need to leave.'

The only logical outcome was for us to walk away from each other. I remember the phone call.

'I can't do this anymore,' he told me. 'You have to let me go.'

'Is that what you want?' I asked him.

'No. That's what I need,' he replied.

We have never spoken since. At first it took heroic amounts of self-control, but as the days and weeks passed, the impulse to call him waned. We were finally free of each other.

The only item I have from the whole affair is a black and grey towelling bathrobe from Marks & Spencer. His mother gave it to me as a thank-you gift. Quite what she was thanking me for, I will never know.

Karma dealt me a heavy blow and I was left with a broken heart. I have never been unhappier. London was a mirror to my misery and I couldn't shake it. I remember the soul-crushing sadness. I moved into a bedsit in Clapham, sharing one bathroom with nine other people. An Italian lived on the second floor. His name was Luca. I tried to befriend him but he was closed to contact. London didn't seem the sort of place where you talked to your neighbours.

Mum drove to London to help me settle in with a car full of practical, loving gifts. She has always loved to shop (in our family we have always joked that she props up several local businesses with her inability to resist a bargain). I helped her empty the car and carry everything upstairs: a red washing-up bowl, dustpan and brush, a flip-top bin, pillows, blankets, coat-hangers, a small rug, a mug tree, cleaning products, a potted plant and a bottle of fizz.

'Thank you. You've excelled yourself, Jenny!' I joked.

'I is good girl, I is,' she replied. I had been missing her. I imagined how difficult it must be for a mother to see a son so unhappy, so I tried to appear cheerful.

The fridge wasn't working, so I ran cold water in the communal bathtub and left the bottle of fizz to cool so we could enjoy it after our grafting. The place was covered with the last tenant's filth and, as we swept, scrubbed and sweated, we were careful not to look at each other.

'Oh, it's fine,' she said, just one time too many.

'Stop saying that!' I replied harshly. 'We both know it's awful. It's a dingy, miserable, north-facing shithole. I'll try and make it work, and if I can't, I'll get out.'

I felt the edge of anger and it saddened me that my body pulsed with it. 'I'm sorry, Mumsie. I didn't mean to snap. I'll go and fetch the fizz and we'll have a glass to celebrate.'

There was no fizz. One of my new neighbours had stolen the bottle from the bathroom.

I know she burst into tears as she drove away. My own tears stung. I didn't know where to turn. I didn't know who to ask for help. I'd taken so many wrong turns that I felt backed-up and trapped. Weight fell off my bones and I started to look ill. I became addicted to cigarettes. I remember the last thing I did at night and the first thing I did every morning was smoke a Marlboro Light. At one point my weight plummeted to 67 kilos (I now weigh 90 kg and then some!).

Nathan came to stay with me, trying to convince me I was okay. We both knew I wasn't. We spent the weekend doing what we've always done best together – creating. We started a photography project of London icons: mugs of tea in greasy-spoon cafés, pillar boxes, black cabs and streetscapes. I know Nathan was trying to help me shift my focus, but it's hard to help someone who is so low. He wanted to give me my smile back, but the only person who could find my smile was me. And I was miles away from happy thoughts.

Writing a diary helped quell the fears that I hid from most people. I hid from my friends. I hid at work, just like I had tried to hide at school. I promptly lost my job. I signed up to a temporary employment agency for a while and ended up working as a receptionist for an American bank near Piccadilly. I travelled on the Tube, head down, pushing along in the crowd with thousands of other people doing the same. I wasn't talking to anyone. I wasn't seeing friends. In my lunch break I would buy a meal deal from Boots and walk around St. James's Park until the hour was up. I could feel myself being forgotten, or was it simply that I was forgetting myself?

I started to feel the insides of me slipping, slowly but constantly, like lava carving its way down a mountain. It was one of the scariest feelings I've ever had. I know now that I was depressed and I should have sought help. I remember taking myself for an HIV test and crying when it came back negative. The clinician who gave me my results, kindly sat with me while I wept. He must have assumed I was crying from relief. I was crying because I was so desperately, heavily and unreservedly unhappy. My tears had finally found an outlet.

The all-time low came when the temping agency ended my contract and, as I was scanning a local newspaper, I saw an ad for a 'get rich quick' scheme. I knew it was a scam but I was pulled in by a fatalistic urge. I turned up to a warehouse in Victoria and joined a throng of other people with brave faces and empty bank accounts. The flashy company director's rousing sales pitch gave my soul a slow puncture as the life blood ebbed from me. He then led us through to a back room where we were given a huge black holdall full of goods to sell door to door. My assigned catchment area was a place called Neasden, part of the borough of Brent.

I couldn't muster the confidence to sit at the front of the upper deck of the double-decker bus. That would have been a statement and I didn't feel strong enough for statements. I chose a middle seat and tried to hide away. I thought I'd better open my holdall to inspect the contents. I unzipped it and 150 vibrating hairbrushes revealed themselves to me like a cluster of spiky cacti vying for light.

It is no small wonder that *HiddenLondon.com* has identified Neasden as the loneliest village in London. The North Circular severs it into two parts, leaving it devoid of any character it might once have possessed. I began with the businesses on Neasden Lane, an eclectic mix of launderettes, greasy spoons, sex shops and beauty parlours. I was spat at. I was physically removed from a supermarket. I became brazen and reckless. I was beyond caring. By some miracle, I sold one brush to a kind hairdresser who took pity on me and handed over five of her hard-earned Great British Pounds. I used the money to buy a sandwich and sat in the doorway of a boarded-up tenement.

When I tried to get up, I couldn't. A force worked against my inertia and kept me down. I gave up and let out the sadness I had been hiding for months. I was all the way down at the bottom of the pit. I realised I had lost my grip on happiness. I was the loneliest person in the loneliest village in London. It was a type of loneliness no one should ever feel. I mustered the courage to return to the depot early and tell them where to stick their vibrating hairbrushes.

I knew sinking any lower would be dangerous. I knew I had to get out of London and take myself to a quiet place to lick my wounds and heal. A radical change of environment might help me shift this boulder of sadness, or so I hoped. I decided to trust Sophie and go to a place where I knew I might be happy.

I left the bedsit, stored all my stuff at Mum and Dad's, and flew to Seville to convalesce. Within four hours of landing, I had rented an apartment. I sat on a polished marble floor in an empty flat, feeling happier than I'd felt in months. I gazed at an orange tree that basked in the building's central Andalusian patio and realised that I was a colourist. The azure blue of the Andalusian sky that turns indigo just before dark, the ochres of the painted facades, the mustard-coloured sandy paths of the parks and plazas, the Sevillians' dresses, the bougainvillea and jacarandas. Everything, everywhere was colour. It helped me to start a brand-new conversation in my own head.

I was still me and I was free to make a fresh start in this city of colour. If the stork drops you in the wrong place, there is no obligation to stay. We are free to roam and find a new home. Mine was to be Andalusia, but where exactly would I put down roots?

I made a pact with myself that if I ever felt shadows of a similar sadness, I would react quickly and change course without hesitation. I was hoping that the fear of those bleak memories would lead me to a happier place. I also needed to make friends with myself again, forgive myself and gently begin to unfold myself to the outside world. I took long walks and wrote every day in the gardens of the Royal Palaces – los Reales Alcázares. It is a place of rare beauty. As a new resident of the city, all I had to do was show my rental contract at the ticket office to gain free access. It was there, in the cafeteria, dappled by Sevillian sunshine, probing through the dense foliage of the jacaranda trees, that I began to write myself back to a restored sense of self.

I did not have a face-to-face conversation for four months and yet calm crept up on me until it took hold. I felt like a huge vessel of chilled, colourless water. Time syringed a cast dye of calm into me and it gently infused, sadness dissipating until I began to feel whole again. Nothing I did could speed up the process.

All my life I have longed to belong, to be able and allowed to put down roots. It became an obsession for me. I tried several times to reach a sense of belonging through somebody else's life – my first boyfriend in London, then the artist. It seemed plausible at first, but my place in their world was wholly dependent on the success of our relationship. When that faltered I was cast off and had to cling to what was truly mine to stay afloat, and that was a tiny life raft.

I remember the feeling of utter dread I felt every morning in that bedsit in Clapham, when I would light my first cigarette before getting out of bed. Looking back, perhaps it was cowardice that sent me to Seville. Maybe it was easier to start afresh in a city where nobody knew me. Sometimes I wish I could have stuck it out in London and proved myself and my critics wrong.

It was simply a matter of time. I was not happy, but I knew I would be. I needed to spend quiet time with myself, to listen and learn, to find once more the core of me.

6

THE RIVER OF THE SILENT ONES

ON THE SLOPES BEHIND THE Corner that lead up to the olive grove, lies a carpet of wild iris. I could swear they weren't there yesterday, explosions of purple and yellow like tiny paint bombs. I realise that it's going to take a long time to get to know The Corner – it's Basque after all. It's not going to let us in easily. The Andalusians are more effervescent in their offering of friendship, unlike the more reserved Basques. Ultimately, or so they say, once you have a Basque friend, you have them for life, but that they are a little like the British and take a while to prise open. The Corner doesn't want to reveal too much too soon. I feel we need to gain its trust.

But with every passing day and week, I discover more of her secrets, shards of her past that I find amid the rubble: a Roman roof tile in the olive grove, a ceremonial death mask down by the river, old keys with no doors, old doors with no keys. Each time I climb to Topknot, the cluster of boulders that crown the peak behind the house, or venture a little further to the Pinnacle, the highest point on the land, potsherds appear like tiny clues, parts of a broken whole.

The inhabitants of the land begin to peer over the parapet. Jack spots a fox on a patch of land in the middle of the river – Fox Island. Or so he says. I miss it as I am looking the other way.

'Oh come on,' I protest. 'You're having me on.'

'The sun shines on the righteous.' Jack grins.

There is talk of otters. Victor, our nearest neighbour, who lives in the first house on the left once we reach the tarmac, tells us crayfish and trout can be pulled out of the waters upstream. Badgers, polecats, rabbits, hares and birds of prey spy on us from vantage points as we begin to explore.

On paper, we knew that the house came with 82 acres, but I have no idea what 82 acres look or feel like. We suspect that none of the locals were interested in the land because the land produces no crops. Olive trees were only planted en masse in the 1960s, but Andalusia's dependence on them now seems intergenerational. The local mindset seems to be 'No olives, no income'. Apart from the olive grove and the levelled field behind the house where the sheep used to be corralled, the ground is rocky and untenable, making it nearly impossible to cultivate. Beyond the house, the land is a wilderness. I tread carefully as I feel as if I am intruding on nature.

Tito calls to see how we're settling in. 'Have you walked along the river to the Final Fence yet?' he asks.

'We walked along the river the other day but there is no

fence, Tito. It must have disappeared in the flood waters or have been taken down,' I reply

'No, no, no. I saw it there myself the other week. It's still there. Did you go past the spring?'

'Yes, we found the spring. Is that our spring? In the undergrowth under the fig tree? We found a dead badger there this morning.'

'And what did you do with it?

'Jack pushed it over the drop.' I giggle as I remember him naming the spot Badger's Drop.

'I think their set is down there by the riverbank. Right, that's the spot,' Tito assures me. 'That's the spring and it comes with the deeds of the house. It is for your sole use and don't let anyone tell you otherwise. That is worth its weight in gold. Water in Andalusia is treasure. And yet managing it has its challenges. So,' he recaps, 'you walked past there and carried on?'

'We didn't go any further,' I tell him. 'We stopped there as we thought we'd either gone wrong or we'd gone too far.'

I can hear him smiling.

'I envy you,' he says, 'with healthy envy, mind. I live in the city now and it bores me. You are never going to get bored up there, let me tell you that. That place will fill you with joy. It will also almost break you. We lived our best and worst years up there. You will be ruled by the rhythms of nature and the rules of the wild.' I linger on that thought, trying to work out the prophecy, before he continues with a snap. 'Anyhow, you didn't go far enough. You need to clamber over the boulders, down the mound into the flat meadow until it leads around a bend in the river. Carry on for another 500 metres or so and then you'll be in the shadow of Midday Peak. Past Midday Peak, you enter another valley where the river has settled into little pools where bamboo and oleander grow. A little further and you'll find the fence. That's the end of your land.'

When I return home after a guiding trip, I round up the dogs and head out to find where our land meets the neighbour's. As I walk, my steps beat out the shape of a giant question mark. Sure enough, beyond the promontory at the bend in the river that is covered in wild thyme, the path continues as the valley narrows. I stride into a space so wild it feels untouched by the outside world. The only vestiges of civilisation are the high tension cables that stretch above my head, taking power to the village.

How annoying, I think. *How amazing would it be if they weren't here.* We are never satisfied, are we?

The limit is marked by the flood-damaged remains of a metal wire fence. The path forms the riverbank and narrows as it negotiates piles of toppled boulders before it opens up into a flat sandy beach. It is the perfect cove and feels entirely hidden and secret. I look around and am struck by a new conviction of solitude. I don't think I've ever felt this alone. It's a feeling that could easily become an addiction.

The boulder in the middle of the river invites me to leap. It has an indentation in the middle of its bulk, like a giant's thumbprint pressed into plasticine. The hole is just wide enough for my frame. I squeeze in and lie like that. I enjoy the feeling of being hemmed in as I dangle my head over the rippling water. Behind me, a sharp flank of the hillside rises. A brisk twenty-minute scramble takes me up and over to Topknot. Yellow broom have taken root by the river and sway like sentries in the breeze. Rosemary and thyme pepper the slopes. A boulder weighs heavily on the earth beneath a cliff where an overhanging rock leans daringly into the empty space. I am certain that the section split off from the summit, a colossus crashing into the earth's crust below.

I look down on this place, the end of our land – the Final Fence. Peaks of impenetrable vegetation surround me, where bracken, brambles, thistles and broom lock arms. It is a landscape lost in time, wild and free.

A giggle bursts out of a place deep within me, almost as an act of disbelief. There are no interruptions, only my own thoughts battling against each other, sparring in the silence. Some win, some lose, and then they settle. Is that happiness spilling out of me again? As soon as it appears, it vanishes. How can I contain it? How can I acquire the skill to bask just a little longer in that feeling?

Golden eagles spy on me from their dominion flights, but humans are nowhere to be seen. Peace accumulates within me. It's a strange feeling. Pain seems to dissipate. Does the river carry it downstream? No one sees. No one hears. I enter into a private pact between me and nature. There is no signing of contracts. Just like the Basques, it's a handshake and a nod of agreement in a sacred place, just as it has always been done.

Did Cayetano enter a similar pact? Did he long for this sense of solace too?

The Final Fence becomes my source of sanctity and my place of peace. I have no idea how much I will need to cling to it.

7

STRAIGHT JACKET

THIS SENSATION OF PEACE FEELS precarious. I'm worried about Maneo, the shepherd. He owns the field opposite but uses our land for his 163 sheep. Tito mentioned him in passing, but I can't help but think he pulled the wool over our eyes. Do I remember him telling me that Maneo had access to the outbuildings and the goat farm? He assures me he did, but I can't remember.

'He'll be able to help you a great deal. He's a strong guy and he knows all the workings of the house and irrigation,' Tito assures me.

Maneo is a towering bulk of fleshy muscle and shiny skin. He has an earnest face with little eyes that stare out from beneath unruly hair. We start on a polite footing but there is something unconvincing about our exchanges.

He finds out we are a same-sex couple and I receive a text

message: *Is it true what they are saying? Are you two in a homosexual relationship?*

My reply is brief. 'Yes.'

'Then I must have nothing more to do with you. My religion will not allow it.'

Jack says, 'Aw, bye then!'

As we're trying to keep warm by the open fire later, Jack has an idea. 'Maybe we should go and have a big snog right in front of him. It might turn him on and he'll convert to the dark side.'

'Yeah! Gay rights now!' shouts Reubs and starts marching around the living room re-enacting his new favourite film, *Harvey Milk*.

'We don't need the likes of people like him in our lives, do we, Frodo Baggins?' Jack says.

'No, we don't, Samwise Gamgee. He needs go, he does. Leave hobbits in peace.'

It seems our technique of ignoring him works and Maneo soon clears the farm of his animals. He arrives with a friend and lifts the sheep one by one with his bare hands, bundling them into the back of a lorry. His friend looks like a German prince – charming face, crystal-clear complexion and piercing blue eyes. I later hear rumours of Maneo's involvement in a Catholic cult near Seville called 'Vatican II', and wonder whether the blond man might be a priest to take him back into the fold. They drive away, leaving Maneo's dogs: two Spanish Mastiffs and a little scruffy mutt.

Without the sheep, the barn looks enormously empty. The floor is about one foot deep in sheep poo.

'Great for compost,' remarks the ever-positive Jack. I love how he flips energy.

Every second Sunday, when Jack is here, we venture out for Sunday lunch. We begin to discover a whole host of culinary delights right here in the valley. A firm favourite is Arte de Cozina in neighbouring Antequera, where Charo, the chef, recovers old recipes from Spain's rich gastronomic heritage.

We have a favourite table by the fire and Charo shovels live coals into a *brasero*, sprinkles them with lavender seeds and places it in a stand under our table. We wrap ourselves in the thick, floor-length tablecloth.

'Luffly,' Reubs says. 'I love that, I do.'

He always chooses the most unusual dish on the menu: trotter, tongue, tripe. He is gradually working his way through the anatomy of the Iberian pig. As we leave the restaurant, Reubs gently reaches for my arm and says, 'Love that lunch, bruvr.'

Driving home we always say hello to Old Man Mountain.

'We should go up there one day,' I say to Jack, remembering its official name, Lover's Rock. 'Apparently, there's a metal postbox at the top where people post their love notes.'

'Off you go,' Jack replies.

'My boys,' Reubs says and places a little, chubby hand on each of our shoulders.

It's no wonder that this belly button of Andalusia has capti-
vated humans for over 5,000 years. The three dolmens of
Antequera are megalithic answers to the questions thrown up
by this mythical landscape, this valley where soils, irrigated
by rivers and springs, are so fertile that almost anything grows,
and this limestone crag, unmistakably human, rises above the
plains, quietly surveying all from its sleeping repose. Menga,
the largest and most impressive of the three dolmens, caused
an academic ruckus when it was rediscovered in 1903. Of the
many megalithic stone tombs (or dolmens) to be found in the
Iberian Peninsula, the vast majority are orientated to the southeast, but Menga is different. Its entrance aligns perfectly with
the silhouette of Old Man Mountain, framing its form with
megalithic stones. This tumulus is an attempt to answer
human's most enduring question: Why are we here? It was
constructed almost 5,000 years ago.

It seems I am not alone in my reverence of this mountain,
an upward thrust of limestone like a giant question mark on
the horizon. Has humankind always raised the same questions?
Here, the natural world conceals the answers in the folded and
creased landscape. My faith used to fill the gap, but now I am
free to dwell in the empty spaces.

As I tuck Reubs into bed, I pull his strong little body towards
me to embrace it. *Here is a man who doesn't let the outside
world affect him*, I think. 'If only we could all be a little bit
more like you, Reubs,' I tell him.

'Like me, bruvr? Why?'

'Because you don't let things get to you, do you?'

'Uh-uh!' he says, shaking his head.

Both my hobbits leave for England – Samwise to work and Frodo for a holiday to see Mum and Dad – and so I am alone in The Corner for the first time. It's a strange sensation. Not a bad one, just different. I'm not used to being alone in an old house made of stone, surrounded by olive trees, in the middle of nowhere. This is it. This is what I was craving, this feeling of being uninterruptible, unreachable, absolutely and utterly alone.

I rattle around and find myself pacing parts of the house I'm not familiar with yet, noticing the play of light and shadows at different times of the day. I see its internal arches, elegant and strong, as if for the first time. Why is an arch such an endearing form? The stark, empty spaces fill with my imagination. Late in the afternoon, a slanted column of light appears in the hay barn, shining through a gaping hole in the semi-collapsed roof. It casts a panel of light onto the earthen floor. It is a scene that should be painted.

It's true that this might not always be our home as we could lose it or we could move. As Jack always reminds me, 'Never get emotionally attached to bricks and mortar.' But this house is helping me shape my own home, within myself. It's the first place I have truly felt a sense of belonging, with nothing to deter it. I have often felt this in other buildings, beautiful places that have allowed me to slip into peace, but they have always been other people's homes.

But this house is our home, I remind myself. I can walk its hallways, stairs and corridors in the dark now, as I know them so well. I am moulding into the shapes around me. And just as I hope we have got here in time to repair the damage, I hope I got to my own wounds in time. I did try to heal them, as swiftly as I knew how. I hope that emotional restructuring does not buckle.

Strangely, I don't feel lonely when I'm here by myself. The days seem deeper and longer and my awareness of every hour more acute. I feel a sense of accountability to the house already and my days begin before sunrise. The light sets the pace for the day. Living here returns us to our most basic existence. There are no creature comforts. There is no heat without a fire. There is often no water. What it lacks in luxury, it makes up in nature. It is like living on the doorstep of the wilds. Once darkness falls, it feels like permission to stop.

Today I have been tour-guiding, showing an American family around the twin towns of Archidona and neighbouring Antequera, and I arrive after dark. I am surprised not to find two eager faces pushed against the metal trellises of the gate. They hear the car crossing the river and chase it all the way to the front gate from within the fence. Normally, it is a celebration of jumps and barks, energetic licks and cuddles, but tonight they are nowhere to be seen. My heart ceases to beat for a one count, two count, thinking the worst. I take a deep breath to gather myself as I begin to call their names into the darkness.

I quickly unlock the main door and turn all the lights on.

I hear a whimper. My eyes focus on something in the corner by the back wall of the garden and then I realise it is Beau.

He is covered in blood – mauled by the angry pack. Maneo's dogs must have jumped the outer fence. I bundle him into my arms and run inside to begin cleaning his wounds.

He is shaking but his wounds turn out to be only flesh-deep.

'You must have put up quite a fight, Beau-Beau. What a hero,' I tell him. I am like a pendulum swinging between relief and fear as there is still no sign of BB. With Beau now safe, I run around outside with a head torch, banging a dog bowl with a wooden spoon and screaming her name. I tune in to the distant barking of the enemy pack, menacing and gnarled.

I pick up a stick to clear the overgrown bushes down in the ditches and along the riverbanks, half-expecting to find her body there. I even get in the car and drive up and down the land, flashing the lights, honking the horn and hollering her name at the top of my voice. Nothing. I go home to sit on the floor with Beau. The hours pass. I do feel lonely now.

'BB is so clever. She will have run away in time and will come back when she knows it's safe,' Jack reassures me down the phone.

I hug Beau tighter and wait until almost three o'clock in the morning and then sure enough, out of the stillness of the night, I hear paws on gravel outside, then silence as she leaps the steps and appears in the living room. On seeing me, she rounds the sofa and lurches into my lap, covering me in earth and grass. Sure enough, she escaped and buried herself, probably somewhere up on the hill, until she knew she could return to safety.

I break a golden rule and the three of us sleep on our bed. I wake up with their little bodies pushed into the shape of my back.

It's disquieting; this disturbance of peace. Maneo's dogs begin to circle the house like hounds circling a city block. They are ever-present. Maneo reappears and takes to sleeping in his field. He takes to drinking and late one night, hearing a commotion outside, I peer out of the window to see him careering down the lane in his pick-up, leaning on the horn and screeching up a dust storm. I feel surrounded and trapped.

It appears Maneo has begun to lose his mind. It is his own mother who raises the alarm. One afternoon, I look on, as four Civil Guards drive onto the land and wrestle him into a straitjacket. He puts up quite a fight as they manhandle him into the back of a patrol car.

Silence; the absence of noise; silence that I can recall even years later.

Without their owner, the dogs begin to step up their reign of terror. I call the local police and they collect them to use as guard dogs. One of the policemen, Isco, loves dogs and assures me they will be fine. I take his number, just in case. The little Stig of the Dump is left to survive all by himself. Once Jack and Reuben return, we begin taking food up to Maneo's field to feed him through the fence. Who knows where he sleeps? He is a stoic survivor, that's for sure, and we develop a soft spot for him.

One chilly afternoon, we come back from a walk and in our absence he has played a card so brave, I have to applaud him. We find him in the living room, sitting on the sofa by the fire.

'He's got balls of steel!' Jack says. 'He's just made the smartest move of his life!'

'What are we going to do with him?' I ask.

Much to Beau and BB's disgust, we adopt him and name him King Arxi. With time, Beau, BB and Arxi make a solid trio of four-legged friends who walk daily in convoy and share extraordinary adventures on Topknot, the Pinnacle and beyond. Arxi has taken them under his wing and is teaching them to live by the beat of his wily drum. He is showing them how to master the wilds.

Very occasionally, a memory comes back to haunt Beau and he snarls Arxi into a corner. Arxi was part of the enemy pack. Beau is a little like me – he can forgive but he can never forget.

The land behind the house beckons. The gorge sucks me into its depths each morning. I thought I'd done my healing, but there is something about this place that forces me into a corner where only truth can set me free. Falsehood has kept me silent for years. The walks to the Final Fence are my mantra, each hike a return to the centre of me. Just like a labyrinth, there is one path in and then the same path out. It's not like a maze. I cannot get lost.

Just above the Cove, there is a wreck of logs, thrown together by violent floodwaters. They all settled in a stable clump. It's a natural climbing frame, an assault course made by the force of nature. I follow the line of logs and balance my way from one end of the mass of wood to the other. Beau sits and watches. BB follows me. Arxi stands guard. I connect to the Karate Kid in me and stand on one leg, my arms raised, poised.

The Corner, with its back turned gently on civilisation, is a place where I find my own truth. The waters of the River of the Silent Ones are urging me to be honest. I feel safe here. Nature hands me gifts. I notice every new wild flower. In the mornings, I hear the scurry of badgers down by the river under Badger's Drop. In the early evenings, I watch as eagles soar along the ridge line, dominating thermals with ease. I feel a connection to this place, on a depth I have seldom felt. Something in me is settling. I feel as if I am able to face myself. It will take months for me to understand what will happen, but as I walk twice daily to the Final Fence, something in me begins to unravel. It's the repetitive movement, the step sequences I take over the trickier terrain – right foot forward, left hand down. I feel as if I want to learn this walk by heart. There is a new flex in my emotions.

We cannot plan seismic emotional moments. We do not know when the fault line might appear and the lava flow. I have a sense of emotional activity just below the surface. An eruption is imminent. I have had the truth buried in me by fear; fear of what people might say, how they might react; fear of judgement, of wagging tongues and pointing fingers. I can hear someone ask, 'Why the need all these years later?' The need is mine alone.

Even though my relationship with Jack spells truth, there are things I haven't told him yet. A born worrier, finally I have nothing to worry about. The lack of secrets and the absence of lies is freeing. I am waiting for the right time to tell him, to share with him these things that happened a long time ago. They are my cracks, my fault lines, the holes in my roof, my imperfections. My damaged self. My Boy Richard.

When I do find the right moment, a moment too perfect not to choose it, we will cry together. We will cry a lot. The silence that falls around our embrace becomes a mesh that binds us. The space between us morphs and merges. It is not just that I know I can trust him never to use this information against me, it's that I know he is strong enough to hold and contain it. His emotional constitution is like a bank vault. I know he can lock the pain away from me and guard the key. There is a deep love between us, deep enough to reach the younger version of me. Before the pain. Jack can find me there and rescue me.

As I walk by the river, memories come back to bite me. I barely remember being a child. Perhaps I have blocked those years. Little by little I feel something in me rising. It was the untruth that pinned it down. Like rocks in my pockets, the lies have kept it submerged.

In our emotional landscape, how deep do we have to dig to excavate all the pain? Are we ever free of it? I remember reading the words of Ruth Foster, a Holocaust survivor who described her trauma as a rock cast into a lake. She waited years for the ripples to disappear.

> The ripples get smaller and smaller still, then the surface is calm, but the stone is still on the bottom. I appear like an ordinary human being, but the stone of my experience is still lying in my heart.

Trauma affects every part of us and to release it, process it, share it, talk about, dare I even say write about it, is akin to hauling that rock up from the depths. It could disrupt just as much on its way up as it did on its way down. We have to be gentle.

8

RAFA

We have said that the duende likes the edge of things, the wound, and that it is drawn to where forms fuse themselves in a longing greater than their visible expressions.

Federico García Lorca, *Theory and Function of the Duende*

AFTER A LENGTHY PERIOD OF abandon, The Corner needs attention, its former glory a distant memory. Count Cayetano would surely roll in his grave if he could see it now.

Many years ago, two brothers inherited the house and divided it into two parts, severing it down the middle. Patios have been split, entrances bricked up, an entrance hall was converted into a kitchen, a panoramic view onto the river is now a brick wall. A new staircase was built to access a dummy entrance, together with a new pool and terrace area. But the construction work is shoddy. Unlike the house, all the new additions were not built to last.

This is what we have bought– a damaged whole. The original beauty of the place has been tampered with, disrespected. Dare I say *abused*? The shape of the house has been twisted and bent into another form of itself. Before we begin to restore, I feel we need to understand the house in every season. We cannot rush the process. Locals might help us piece together the house's history so we can carefully and lovingly bring her back to life. There are broken windows, gaping holes in the roof, leaks, fallen fences, archways to reinforce, irrigation channels to clean and flush through, windows that don't close, doors that don't open, plaster peeling off walls and ceilings that are caving in.

If it is a part of so many local families' histories, then how has it been allowed to go to rack and ruin? Perhaps it's due to the fact it has been divided and altered to be almost unrecognisable. That and the flood. It's hard to imagine what happened that day in 2012 when the waters raged and took down everything in their path: trees, boulders and even the old stone bridge.

The previous owners of Riverside, as we call it now, were out-of-towners. Their only vested interest was money. They probably needed to tuck an influx of cash away, and where better than an old house in the country with land to boot? I know how little they cared because when I asked for a back statement of electricity consumption from the last ten years, the graph was a flat line, bar two peaks of use. They had visited twice in a decade, flicked a light on and left: once to check it was still standing after the flood; and once to remove anything of interest before selling it to us.

There is also the Spanish people's relationship with what is deemed old or rustic. Spain has seen much suffering in its not-too-distant past; the Civil War and the tricky years of austerity that followed. There were five families living in the cortijo during those difficult years, struggling through a subsistence lifestyle, hidden away from the world. In a downstairs barn, a tiny fireplace was added to help to keep a family warm through the long winters. Its chimney stack sits awkwardly on the side of the house, another improvised edition that spoils the building's symmetry.

Often, therefore, old is associated with poverty. There hasn't been a higher value placed on heritage features in property as there has been in other parts of Europe. I can cite dozens of examples of Spanish friends lowering old ceilings, bricking up old fireplaces and pulling out old windows and doors, making way for practical PVC, plasterboard and electrical fan heaters. Old is complicated and it's not practical. Much better to modernise than restore.

And we must not forget the *duende* – the mystery and the soul of art. Art, for me, is the greatest expression of understanding. It fills the gap where logic fails. The artist's paint fills empty spaces, the writer's words pour into the void. Duende is the undefinable spirit that lurks in artistic expression. It is impossible to prescribe where or how it appears. You cannot pinpoint where it comes from or how it occurs. It is a fleeting moment. Duende creeps up on you silently, and you can only recognise it if you are open to its approach.

The Spanish playwright and poet Federico García Lorca was famed for conjuring up the mysterious emotion of art that stirs the soul of the reader, the listener, the observer – the witness. He called it 'duende', and his avid followers, hungry for emotion within art, loved him for it. He gave his lecture, 'Theory and play of Duende', extensively in New York and throughout the Americas before his murder in 1936. I suspect he unleashed duende on the American literati. They began to understand the soul of Spain and have been obsessed with it ever since.

This house has duende. I am sure of it. I have felt it several times. The play of light and shadow that dances throughout the day like bull and matador. The wild that encroaches on the tame. Are we civilised or are we barbaric? Are we freer in a forest of tall trees or in a city of skyscrapers?

Lorca wrote, 'All that has dark sounds, has duende.' This house balances light and dark sounds, like any of the greatest symphonies. I hear the low vibrations. I accept its flaws. Perhaps this is why I treasure this house so deeply. It has been ravaged by storms, battered by floods, pelted with extreme heat and drenched by incessant winter rains. Still it stands, defiant and proud, sharing its scars and flaunting its broken parts. They cannot be ignored but they do not bother us. As we spend more time here, they become less apparent. Intimacy and familiarity normalise them and remove them from our consciousness.

But have we arrived in time to salvage this house? I call a structural engineer to take a look.

'There's no denying that the flood must have been colossal as there is movement in some floors and outer walls, but they were propped up well and in good time. This house is as strong as a fort. You've no worries here.'

The bones of this house are solid – supporting walls and a series of pillars that support the whole. I crack a smile.

Our plan is to restore the house to its original state. We want to tear walls down that weren't there originally, bulldoze all the outbuildings, remove the bad renovations and let the house breathe again. All it will take is patience, imagination, time and heaps and heaps of euros. Of the first three we are in plentiful supply. The last part is where we falter, so for now, we must accept the imperfections and learn to live with them. There will come a time when, if we work hard enough and save enough money, we will be able to press the button of the restoration project and bring the house back to life, not only for us but also for the community which was at risk of losing a reference point in its local heritage.

Traditional Andalusian cortijos are built with stone and mortar, the latter being mainly mud and sand. The process of ruin starts on the roof. Once one tile is missing, the whole structure begins its decline. Water begins to trickle, creep and crawl like hyphae into the wooden timbers and walls. With one tile cracked or missing, wind finds its way under exposed edges and more tiles topple. When friends ask us why we bought a ruin, I find it difficult to articulate an answer. Jack is a visionary who revels in a project. I think he can already visualise the house once restored, but he's not in a hurry to finish it. I love it as it is. We're similar in that we love the challenge the house poses. Being custodians of this house (as that is how I see it) brings responsibility. I feel we are here to prevent further decline. We have moved in and want to stop the process of deterioration, but there is so much to do.

'Nos viene grande,' I explain to my new friend, Luis, who owns the hotel up the road. A handy phrase in Spanish that means 'we're struggling'.

'Don't you worry, amigo. I've got just the man. He's been working with me for years. He's an all-rounder and looks after many homes in the area. You there tomorrow? I'll send him down.'

Rafa arrives promptly at 8 a.m. the following morning. He parks his white utility van at the gate and waits patiently until his presence stirs the dogs from their slumber. They can sound menacing, but with Rafa, it is love at first sniff.

'Buenos días, Manni,' he says.

'Morning, Rafa. Good to see you. Cold this morning!' I say.

'Clears the mind!' he replies.

His first handshake is very distant. He plants his body and stretches his hand forward, while leaning back. His hand clasps mine like a vice as if he is trying to prove his manhood. Jet-black hair like sculptured tar frames his angular face. His deep-set eyes burn with the intensity of Andalusian pride. The skin stretched over his jugular notch, above the gape in his workman's shirt, is red and hardened by the sun.

He wouldn't look out of place on one of Christopher Columbus's vessels, his muscular forearms hoisting the sails. Equally, he would look the part dressed in fine silk fabrics, strolling the patios and halls of the Alhambra Palace in Granada. He is innately Andalusian and, in that sense, quite timeless.

Beau catches a whiff of something edible in his backpack and doesn't leave his side, becoming his shadow until he breaks to enjoy his elevenses under the vines. He shares his ham and cheese *bocadillo* with three expectant snouts.

As we chat and introduce ourselves, I realise that we have found our guy. We walk around the house and garden and Rafa's skilled eye scans the scene. Seeing the place afresh through his eyes is daunting.

'Aquí hay faena,' he states with a glint in his eye. The term 'faena' describes the third and last section of the traditional bullfight, the moment when everyone retreats, leaving just the torero and the toro to stare at each other through the veil of death. The term has been borrowed and used in more colloquial Spanish to various ends. It can be used both positively and negatively. Here, Rafa is using it in its positive tone. 'There is much to do here!' Thank goodness he is up for the challenge.

Rafa's family name is Rincón. No wonder he feels at home here. Every Wednesday, at eight o'clock sharp, the dogs await his arrival.

'This place is like therapy for me. Imagine! It's my name! Rafa Rincón at your service! Getting out of the town and coming into nature. It's this' – he points to the hillside – 'that gives me energy. It's like a tonic.' He pauses, looks at me, is about to say something, then changes his mind.

I have found my Don Segundo Sombra.*

Studying Latin American Literature at the University of Edinburgh, I discovered the mythical literary figures of Martín Fierro and Don Segundo Sombra, both gauchos from the Pampas of Argentina: two earthed characters, wired to nature with wild souls. While travelling in Argentina I began my exploration of the national psyche; the debate between *civilización y barbarie* (civilisation and barbarism), crudely summarised as Buenos Aires versus the Pampas, town versus country, Porteño (someone from Buenos Aires) versus the gaucho (cowboy). In the Pampas, I spent time with a gaucho called O Campo and I fell under the spell of his quiet command of nature, his noble and strong soul. Rafa has that same *campo* strength behind his eyes. He has spent much of his life in the no man's land between two worlds, tripped up by the vices of town. How glad I am that he has found solace in the country. I grow to love having him in my corner.

'Right,' Rafa says, bringing me round from my memories.. 'I'll crack on. I think I will attack the fig tree first. Some of the branches are too laden and it's leaning to one side.'

* Don Segundo Sombra is a literary fictional character created by Ricardo Güiraldes in 1926. He represents the soul of the Pampas, or flat plains, of Argentina.

He makes an impact immediately, attacking each task with vim and vigour. The fig tree is trimmed, the patios swept and hosed. The tool room is organised: all liquids, gases and fuels are on the right; irrigation material in the middle; electrical equipment on the left. Gloves are all in one place, as are face masks and protective glasses.

Rafa's energy is like a battery in our midweek clock. I learn things from him that I doubt I could have learned from anyone else. In the tool room, the plaster on the ceiling has fallen down, exposing rows and rows of canes tied together with strands of string. They're looking decidedly decrepit.

'These will all need to come down,' he tells me. 'Probably because they didn't pick them at the right time.' He has already left the room with a pair of secateurs by the time I have observed the rotting canes. I hurry after him like a child following his grandfather. I want to learn.

'Rafa, what do you mean they picked them at the wrong time?'

He looks at me and leans in to his knowledge, not with condescension but with utter joy.

'Gypsies have always used cañizos to make things – baskets, matting, and to separate living space like this,' he says pointing back to the reeds in the ceiling that look like the pipes of a hidden organ. 'But they always pick them when the moon is waning in April and September.'

His words charm me into a quiet smile. 'I suppose it has something to do with the sap being drawn out, like the tides of the sea?' I question.

'You're not as stupid as you look,' Rafa jokes and whacks me on the shoulder with a gloved hand.

As the imprint of his hand smarts below the skin, he leaves me staring up at the ceiling, imagining when these canes were cut from the river, and who dried and worked them into this rigid structure. Sustainability at its best.

Rafa always leaves The Corner more beautiful than when he finds it. Over time, we develop a rare bond of trust and mutual appreciation. I know that he will do anything for me. He has my back and is only a phone call away. He becomes my protector. He makes me feel safe and offers me a vital link to town.

He is one of five brothers. I can identify most of them in town without needing an introduction, so strong is the genetic resemblance. They are all strong and robustly masculine, thickset and of similar height. They carry the same measure of intensity and purpose.

We decide to host a lunch party. Our new friends are the lawyers, bank managers, notaries, hotel and restaurant owners.

Among them are Rafa and his wife with the alarmingly beautiful blue eyes. Their outfits mark their appreciation of the occasion. I hug Rafa and ruin the starch iron of his crisp summer shirt. He smells of shower gel and pine-fresh eau de toilette.

'Thank you so much for inviting us, Manni. We don't normally get invited to these kinds of events,' he tells me.

'Well, I am happy you're here. It's important for us.'

'Que maquina eres campeón. What a guy,' he tells me. Apparently, we are breaking down some local walls.

'Would it be alright if I show my wife around? She'd love to see the place.'

'Of course. Estás en tu casa, Rafa,' I tell him readily.

Archidona is a small town and village memory dies hard. Reputations are difficult to shake off. On the grapevine, we learn of Rafa's past. His tearaway years seem to follow him and taint his reputation. Addiction, time inside and a deep depression took nine years to leave behind.

One morning he confides in me, 'This is my addiction now. This gives me the high I need.' He looks around at this sacred place.

When he talks of those dark days when he was gripped in the jaws of heroin, his eyes, the colour of toasted almonds, flush with shame and regret. I tell him how proud I am of his recovery, and I cherish the fact that The Corner is part of his continued healing.

Few would have thought it possible, but our little town of 8,000 inhabitants, perched high on a hill in the heartlands of Andalusia, was a hothouse of drug abuse in the 1980s and 1990s. When Franco died in 1975, Spain moved through the most complicated of political transitions. How do you bring about a peaceful democracy after a bloody four-year civil war, swiftly followed by a thirty-five-year dictatorship? Unlike the American Civil War, which was predominantly a north and south division, the Civil War in Spain created enemies in every community and ripped through the entire country, destroying families, businesses and friendships. There was devastating human loss on both sides. It always amazes me that Spain is such a tolerant and accepting nation nowadays, when not long ago the country was as divided as any nation in Europe has ever been. I admire their stoic practicalities.

As a nation it may appear that they have been able to turn the page, folding over a new leaf and brushing their bitter hurt under the carpet. They are a people who like to look forward. Indeed, the Socialist Government of Zapatero brought about the Law of Memory and, for the first time since the war, folk were encouraged to look back. Many were granted the permission and the opportunity to look into the deaths of their loved ones who had disappeared during the fighting.

In our little village, friends once asked a perfectly innocent question about the Civil War and whether the town had suffered many casualties. They were hushed to silence and told quite emphatically to never mention the war again. Even to this day, there are families that do not talk to each other and boycott each other's businesses. They neither forgive nor forget.

So, when the lid on this suffering and repression was lifted, Spanish culture exploded with a new vigour and gusto. I describe it as a jack-in-the-box. When you repress something for so long with a downwards force, as soon as the lid opens, all that recoiled energy is released with an upwards force of expression, of freedom, joy and partying. In Madrid, it was known as 'La Movida' – a new wave of cultural expression that pervaded all art forms. A ringleader in the world of cinema is the torrentially talented Pedro Almodóvar who, together with his brother, formed a production company and brought a highly evocative representation of Spanish personality and humour to the global widescreen. I adore his films, even to the point of taking a Spanish film course at university to understand them more deeply. He seems to take stereotypes to their extremes, but we all know someone exactly like the characters in his scripts.

Spanish people are quite naturally eccentric. They move en masse and to stand out, they must shout louder and be more comical than the next person. To be in a herd and to be heard is the case for the vast majority of Spanish people, where differences are quite naturally celebrated. We call one of our local cafeterias 'The Henhouse', and please understand that this is not in a defamatory tone. The café fills to the brim and the terrace marquee is the preferred dwelling place for the numerous smokers who like to accompany their coffee and toast with one or two cigarettes. Never have I seen such a nation of smokers; part of that newfound freedom. Their chatter reaches new heights of decibel-breaking noise pollution. If there are eight people sitting around one table, eight voices can be heard. Their conversations swirl and canter around their shared experiences and common ground. For a foreigner, this scene is immediately appealing and at the same time quite isolating.

I remember when I first moved to Spain and saw these tight circles of giggling friends, I thought to myself, *How am I ever going to infiltrate one of these circles?* They look so tightly closed, but they will readily open for a new member. But the invitation has to come from the inside. You must have a reason for entering. Oddly, the loneliness I had felt in London, I left in London. Perhaps Seville was exotic enough that I was happy to observe and learn, assuming the role of an outsider. The fact that I felt more comfortable in a foreign environment worried me initially. I felt beaten by London and vowed to return one day to kill the ghost of Neasden and prove to myself that I could ride at the front of the upper deck of a London bus with pride.

In my experience, it took four months to build the right credentials to break into Sevillian society. One morning I nodded a greeting to Miguel Angel, the official photographer of La Plaza de España. It was a place I had visited several times. Its symmetry manoeuvred me into a place of peace. It felt like a personal epiphany. I had been so lost for so long and right there, as I aligned myself with the square's architectural symmetry, something in me clicked; something which had been adrift in me found a resting place.

Each time I visited I noticed Miguel Angel taking photos of visitors, but had never had reason to stop and chat. I needed an 'in' and that 'in' came in the shape of his own curiosity.

'Oye.' He beckoned to me one morning.

I approached him with the satisfying knowledge that I was about to have a face-to-face conversation. My sorrowful sojourn was over; my emotional hiatus complete. His kind, inviting face communicated that to me as a flash of the sunlight highlighted his tanned skin.

'Hola. Buenos días,' I said to him as I held out my hand.

'Hola Tio. Que tal? I've seen you here loads recently. Where do you live?'

'I live here now. I moved here about four months ago,' I replied.

'And who do you hang out with?'

'No one,' I replied sheepishly. 'I don't know anyone here so I've just been hanging out with myself for the past few months.'

'But you should have told me!' he repeated.

Miguel Angel's kindness was the invitation to join the fold of Sevillian culture. His reaction taught me of their unbounding goodness and willingness to share. I was in!

Before I knew it, I had thirty friends, was invited to a wedding and my Spanish social life took off – all because one kind man had an acute sense of smell. He smelled my loneliness floating on the breeze, alongside the orange blossom. To this day, he is one of my most treasured friends and I thank him for having given me a golden ticket into the realms of Spanish culture.

9

THE FIRST OLIVE HARVEST

I THOUGHT I WAS FLUENT IN Spanish but The Corner has unlocked a whole new world of vocabulary I had never come across before. Rafa is my teacher and my guide. I feel like a beginner again, reminded of when I would walk around the kitchen at the bible school I attended in Bolivia, asking and committing to memory the words for drawer, spoon, tap, dishcloth, map, draining board and rolling pin, with a notebook in one hand and an inane grin on my eighteen-year-old face.

Back in the tool shed at The Corner, I grab things and repeat after Rafa.

Monkey wrench.

Spirit level.

Allen key.

Saw.

Strimmer.

Shredder.

Scythe.

Crowbar.

Chainsaw.

Garden fork.

Rasp.

Dibble.

Drawshave.

Drill.

With over 130 years' worth of collectable clutter crammed into every room, store and barn, even after 7 skips of discarded scrap, there is still a plentiful supply of odds and ends. From these early searches comes a catchphrase that, 'The Corner provides exactly what we need'. It proves itself true time and time again. Doors that can be used as ramps; road barriers that can be used as dividers in the henhouse; troughs that can be planted with flowers; and roof tiles with seeds. The potential for upcycling is endless. But it's the land that will provide for me on a level I could never have imagined. The Corner is a mere portal to the treasures that lie beyond.

On the scrubland stretching up the hill behind the house, there are 150 floundering olive trees. They appear like spindly stick figures, frail and crooked, clinging to the rocky soil with their exposed roots, their branches elongated and bare. Who knew that olive tree envy was a thing? I stare longingly at Antonio and Esperanza's trees across the way – huge canopies of health and prosperity. Olive tree envy threatens to engulf me. They are quick to encourage us.

'Don't go down that route,' Antonio hastens. 'We bought this land fourteen years ago and our trees looked worse than yours do now. In fact, they are the same trees, planted at the same time. So, with a little bit of tender loving care and some reshaping, they'll bounce back. Mark my words.'

Antonio and Esperanza don't live here, but they have a little shack up on the hill where they keep their farming equipment. They live in the village and spend some weekends out here on the other side of the river.

There is an innate sense of community here that forges a pride for the place. As outsiders, a same-sex couple and a brother with Down syndrome, not once have we felt rejected. Even though foreigners in Spain are sometimes called 'güiris' (similar in meaning to the term 'gringo'), we haven't heard this being used to describe us. I have a sense that our valley accepts us. We're the guys mad enough to buy the house by the river.

We realise that The Corner inhabits a dear place in the hearts and memories of the entire valley. Neighbours appear bearing gifts of vegetables and fruit and invitations to local events. Back in its heyday, most of our community were employed by one of the three cortijos in the valley. With the original 400 hectares of cultivated farmland and 40 mules, close to 50 workers would have worked here. One neighbour seeks us out to share with us the story of his engagement.

'Right there on the steps by the river. That's where I asked her to marry me,' he grins. Anita tells me more anecdotes about the farm. The more I visit her, the more her gaze softens. She still refers to Jack as, 'Your . . .' drawing a blank as to what to call him.

There are so many links between the house and the locals, and we don't take that lightly. We recognise that neighbours have an invested interest in making sure the house doesn't fall into ruin. It is part of their collective memory.

'Please make sure it doesn't fall down.'

'What are you going to do with it?'

'Are you going to restore it?'

'Will you rebuild the gardens that were washed away in the floods?'

'Thank goodness you guys have bought it. We're so happy it's fallen into the hands of such buena gente.'

'Make sure the roof is good and solid.'

February brings blue skies and soft, defining light. Frost bites the mornings and freezes the water in the pipes. It seems to take an age for the sun's warmth to reach us.

By eleven o'clock the ice has thawed and water runs again. Each evening we have to fill buckets with water for the loos and bottles to use in the kitchen.

Black olives cling to the branches in the olive grove. We were thinking we'd missed the window for olive harvesting and then a call comes from Rafa.

'What are you going to do with your olives this year, familia?'

'I'm not sure. Is it even worth harvesting them?' I reply feebly.

'Of course, it is,' he beams. 'It's a tad late but they'll still be good for oil. All the farms around you are still harvesting, so you should be fine.'

We strike a deal which seems very fair to me. Rafa brings a friend and all the necessary equipment. Jack, Reubs and I work together with them and we share the oil fifty-fifty. What a learning curve. It's arduous work and not for the weak or weary.

We buy a bright red twenty-seven-year-old Nissan and call her 'Poppy'. When we put her into 4 × 4 traction, she is the closest I have ever come to driving a tank. She's slow and solid and nothing seems to break her forward movement. Driving her around the olive grove is pure pleasure.

Nets called 'fardos', measuring up to 15 × 8 metres, made from hard-wearing nylon, form a semi-rigid floor covering, so that the olives do not bruise on the ground. We drag the fardos into position under several trees, normally four trees at a time. We wrap strips of old fardos around the trunks to avoid any olives slipping through the gaps. It's a job that requires skill and precision and takes a while to grasp. Every part of the process has a name or a term that makes me smile. The old strips of fardos are called 'knickers'. The tricky-to-reach branches in the very centre of the tree are called 'the armpit'. It's a systematic process wrapped with Andalusian know-how and wit.

Rafa and Juan Antonio are encouraging as they holler commands at us. We all work as one. Once the fardos are in place, Rafa revs up the petrol-powered vibrating claw. He moves the rubber U-bend at the tip into position around key branches and as the claw vibrates, it rains olives. The rest of us, armed with baras – which I call 'pole-vault poles' – whack and flick the outer branches, encouraging those more stubborn olives to release their grip and fall into the nets. We rotate underneath the canopy of branches until every last olive has fallen. Rafa is incredibly diligent and refuses to shout 'Listo!' (done) until every branch is bare. I admire his sense of detail and economy.

'Every olive counts, Manni,' he admonishes. Who am I to argue?

Once those four trees are stripped of olives, two of us gather two corners of each net in unison, dragging the nets to meet their opposite corners, rather like folding a ginormous bed sheet in half. I feel like a fisherman, trawling the catch of the day. This folding motion gathers all the olives in one place, from where we can bundle them into floppy, plastic buckets with two handles called 'espuertas'. We carry them between two and tip them into the trailer. The olives start to release their bittersweet, potent fragrance. We can sense it on our lips (extra virgin olive oil is an astringent). It lingers in the air and on our clothes like bonfire smoke. It's unlike anything I've ever smelled before.

Reubs spends a lot of time pretending to sword fight with his bara.

'Don't love sword for sharp,' he mutters.

Jack finishes off his quote: 'Nor the arrow for its swiftness, nor the warrior for his glory. I love only that which they defend.'

Reubs' face widens with the brightest of smiles. 'That's the one, Samwise Gamgee. You're good you are!'

Reubs' job is to make sure the dogs stay off the nets, and after an hour or so he trundles off down the hill, back to the house to fetch water and bananas for the hungry crew.

We toil on, starting at the top of the olive grove and working down, so gravity is on our side. After six hours, we have a small trailer half-full and decide to call it a day. We hitch Poppy up to the trailer and drive over the ridge, north of Archidona, to a little town called Villanueva de Algaidas. There, in a neat fold of land is Ramón's organic olive mill or 'almazara'. There is a strict order of arrival and we watch while the gentleman in front of us unloads his olives into the drop zone. The process is precise: removal of larger twigs and branches by hand as the olives move up the conveyor belt, blown with air to remove the leaves and stalks, then the rinsing and finally the mushing of the olives to a pulp, stones and all. The oil is extracted through a cylinder that spins at an eye-watering 7,000 rpm. Minutes later, a rich, thick, green oil begins to travel down the tube into the final holding vessel, before being decanted into 25-litre tubs.

Once his olives are in the cylinder, our olives can be emptied into the start of the process. It takes me an age to reverse the trailer (much to the amusement of Ramón the owner).

'You should have practised that in the privacy of your own home!' he jokes.

The technique seems counter-intuitive. I turn the colour of Poppy but finally crack it. Always living and learning. I find the whole process biblical in its purity and vitality. It feels like this is the way we should always be living. We wait patiently until our very first olive oil begins to dribble into the final holding container. It has the colour and scent of freshly cut grass, spiced with tomato plants and black pepper.

We return home jubilant, loaded with 110 litres of the purest EVOO. We drive to Rafa's house to deliver his share. He opens one of the bottles, sticks a finger through the lid and pulls it out coated with thick green olive oil. He tastes it with knowing eyes.

'Ojú, que bueno! Ya lo sabía. Ese aceite está que te cagas.' This oil is so good, it makes you shit yourself! A rather crude phrase which sounds harmless in Spanish, but which makes for a dreadful translation. Suffice to say, he loves it.

Before I go, Rafa tells me, 'It would be good to spray the trees with copper in the coming days.'

'Copper?' I ask. 'Why copper?'

'To heal the wounds,' he replies.

10

THE CUCKOO

S OLITARY AND CUNNING, A PAIR of cuckoos exert themselves over a significant terrain, scouting locations, and then the female lays eggs in up to twelve foreign nests, pushing the host eggs to the ground. When the cuckoo chicks are born, if any remain, they destroy the resident eggs or kill the chicks. The poor host mother, without her own young, then rears the cuckoo chicks until they can fly. What a cruel trick and twist of nature. If I were a warbler or a European robin or a blue or yellow tit down by the river, I would build my nest in the most secret of hiding places and would dread the first cuckoo call of spring.

Nests at The Corner appear everywhere and in the strangest places: behind the wooden slat blinds, lodged in and buffered by the window panes; under the house in the mule stables; in the downstairs kitchen; in chimneys and in empty rooms. With a flurry of darting flights, a nest can appear in a matter of hours. All the other birds, within the cuckoo's call, find hiding places for their own young.

The unique and unmistakable call of the male cuckoo marks the onset of spring. There are several sayings in rural Spain that refer to the cuckoo's call: that it only arrives after the snow; that it marks a plentiful year; that its absence marks disaster in the fields; that it brings rain; that when it stops, the earth will dry and harden.

'Have you heard the cuckoo?' I call to Antonio and Esperanza as they toil together in one of their fields, hoes in hand, their sunny faces sporting broad smiles.

'Loud and clear!' they respond and then in unison. 'Si marzo se va y el cuco no viene, o se ha muerto el cuco o el fin del mundo viene.' If March passes without the cuckoo, either he has died or it's the end of the world.

'We get to live another year then! Oh joy!' I chirp. I am happy to be on the receiving end of these nuggets of rural wisdom.

It's difficult to answer when friends question, 'How can you live out there, in the middle of nowhere?' I get it. Some friends think we are bonkers. In their cities, there are vast windows of opportunity, cultural inspiration at every turn and a buzz that leads them to achieve, grow, and accumulate knowledge, experience and wealth.

In the countryside, cuckoos and the rustling of leaves encourage inner reflection. Country living is not for the faint-hearted. Fuelled by silence, an internal journey is inevitable. Personally, that inspires me more than opera, more deeply than summer cinemas in historical squares or jazz bands in parks. As I hear the cuckoo call, it marks the onset of my own primavera. From the Latin, 'prima' meaning first and 'ver' – the origin of 'verano', or summer – primavera is the first or early summer.

I feel less diluted out here, more able to concentrate on being the real me. The urge to write is greater than ever. My first serious attempt in the palace gardens of Seville was a novel that I have been trawling around from pillar to post in a plastic storage box. This time around, the urge is stronger. I can feel something forming. There are so many questions in my mind that I would love to find the answer to, and I know that writing my way to their resolution is the only way. If only life would slow down enough for me to be able to gather my thoughts.

In Spanish culture, spring is the transition from the hibernating effects of the bitter winter through to the arduous heat of summer. It is a season of solace between extremes and this first spring at The Corner surprises us with its unique magic.

'How bruv?' Reubs asks when I take him to the meadow where wild iris carpet the floor.

'Aslan is on the move, Reubs,' I whisper.

'Ah!' He gasps, his eyes sparkling and his mouth agape. 'That's why.'

Insects scratch and the trees bud. Wildflowers alter the

palette of muted winter hues and decorate a thick-pile green carpet with the percussive rhythm of colour. The floral design changes daily as giant fennel stretch up from the undergrowth, holding their burst of yellow flowers to the sky. Squill, snap dragons, blooms of rosemary and poppies create a design of life. The occasional orchid reveals its hiding place like a lonely whisper.

The meadow looks like a work of embroidery, flipped over to its reverse side, revealing all the end threads, tied off and exposed. There is only the sound of nature with the gentle flow of the river's water to complete the symphony. There is no crash of cymbals, no boom of a bass drum. From the reed section, the sound of geese rises on the wind and the ducks quack their response in syncopated unison. The bee drone of the string section works as one, their constant hum forming a foundation of sound to support the orchestra. The harsh barks of Beau and BB – Arxi doesn't bark – mark the quavers and semiquavered accents of the brass section, piercing the score. Blue tits, yellow tits, wagtails and hoopoes release their shrill descants to elevate the scene. As the whole symphony fades, the invisible conductor lays down his baton. Silence reigns once more. And then, in the distance, as if from the upper galleries of this most perfect auditorium, the cuckoo calls once more, obstinate, persistent and entirely beautiful.

When the cuckoo calls, rain will soak the earth.

There is a bustle of activity in the neighbouring farms as olive trees are pruned to encourage new growth for next year and to avoid them becoming too tall or misshapen. The ideal olive tree is shaped like an enormous umbrella, the canopy consisting of three main branches, with gaps in between where the light can get in. Ideally, every single olive needs to see the sun.

It takes a skilled eye to know which branches to cut and which to leave. Rafa explains to me that one year, you trim, and the following year, you cut back more aggressively. I am delighted to learn that nothing is wasted. The larger branches are chopped for firewood and the finer branches and foliage are mulched by a big shredder that a tractor pulls between the lines of trees, leaving a fine sawdust on the surface of the soil to act as fertiliser to nourish the soil. I can hear the crunch and the metallic clang and grate of the plough as it works its way through the groves.

In an early April downpour, Rafa quotes one of his favourite refrains. 'Abril, aguas mil y todas caben un barril,' as he manoeuvres a barrel and takes the lid off to collect the spring rain. In April, there are a thousand waters and they all fit in a barrel. 'Let's see if it fills,' he wonders. 'On a good year it will fill right to the top.'

After the heavy rains, the river becomes unrecognisable. At the bend by Thyme Point, water crashes against the rockface, a washing machine effect ensues. Huge trunks, logs and other deadwood get trapped in the tumble, and occasionally, one piece is hurled upwards and finds a fragile new location balanced on a ledge or wedged between rock formations on the cliff. When the waters subside, the massive pieces of wood look oddly ill at ease as they teeter in the wind in their lofty locations.

The river bursts its course down by the weir and floods the access road. We are marooned. Normally barely perceptible, the sound of the day changes shape, backdropped by a constant cymbal roll of raging waters. Frodo, Samwise and I head down to the ford, and the force of the river keeps us alert and cautious. We call the dogs back from the edge, fearful that they could be sucked in.

Frodo leans on his Saracen staff looking worried.

'Don't worry, babes,' I reassure him. 'We have everything we need right here so we'll be fine. The river will die down in a day or two and we'll be able to leave.'

Knowing that we will be the only humans on this side of the river for days thrills me. The rising waters seal us in a confirmed privacy. There is nothing we can do. We simply bow to the power of nature.

A fire engine appears on the other side of the river, and Victor steps down and calls me on my mobile. I can barely hear him in the din.

'I'm passing the phone to one of the firemen. They want to speak to you.'

A burly man in uniform takes the phone and waves to us as he begins to explain. 'Good afternoon, gents. Are you all okay?' I raise my thumb. 'Is anyone else with you or is it just the three of you?'

'Just the three of us.'

'Okay. Please do not try to leave. It's too dangerous. You'll be stuck there for a few days at this rate. Do you have everything you need?'

When Victor takes the phone back, I pass on a message from Jack. 'The only thing we don't have is cigarettes.'

I see them all laugh as Victor explains.

Within the hour, Victor is back and he lassoes two packets of Marlboro Lights across the breadth of the river in a plastic bag weighted with a rock.

'I love this place,' Jack says as he recovers the bag from the oleander bushes that line the river.

Victor waves goodbye and we holler our thanks, but our cries are swallowed by the water before they reach him.

We settle into our temporary isolation. There is an increased sense of peace that forces me to look inwards. While Reuben sits cross-legged, straight-backed on his bed, Jack is happy pottering in his new allotment, planting out his broad beans, courgettes, beetroot and carrots. We are all in our happy worlds and I make use of the silence to scratch the surface of my memories. I feel strong enough now. I begin to fill a notebook with memories. There is no form to my scribblings but I know it is almost time to remember.

If there is nothing more, this is enough.

The gift of rain replenishes soils until the end of spring when summer brings its ardent heat. The upper crust of soil hardens, trapping the moisture under the baked surface. There it remains all summer long, and the trees use their underground root networks, rather like a London Tube map, to ensure that no tree is alone in its search for water.

The cuckoo stops calling. Perhaps there will be no more rain. Maybe the onset of summer, 'verano tempus', will happen earlier than usual. Or perhaps the cuckoo has gone to survey the terrain, to search for unsuspecting nests to parasite, in her quest to find a safe dwelling place for her fragile young.

11

PLANT A TREE

A S THE SUN STRETCHES OVER the eastern hills, tingling the cool air with the day's first strokes of warmth, birdsong coaxes us into bliss. The chatter and darting of house martins, swallows and sparrows accompany our sleepy stirrings. We are on the cusp of May. Low clouds hang in the valley, the azure blue of the morning sky draping the scene in a vault of timelessness.

It's a perfect day for planting trees so we stroll the land to find forever homes for two plum trees, a Californian walnut and sixty-six cypress trees. We bought them at a garden centre in the town of Lucena, just thirty minutes north towards Córdoba. Lucena is one of those towns that draws us in. It was once called the Pearl of Sefarad, a Jewish town, settled after the expulsion of the Jews and Muslims from Córdoba in 1236. We find a restaurant called Tres Culturas that blends cuisine from three gastronomic heritages – Christian, Jewish and Muslim. The result is a restaurant teeming with nostalgia for a society and culture lost centuries ago. Lope, the owner, greets us not as strangers but as if we were family, and we sit there grinning and savouring each and every morsel.

Back at The Corner the earth is still moist and malleable from the rains, dark and rich and fertile. Jack knows that walnut trees need nitrogen, so we mix soil with turf to refill the hole. The rotting grass will give the walnut part of its nutrients. Its spot by the river will afford it full sun. We wish it well as we stamp it home.

'We'll remember planting this in our old age,' Jack says to me.

Plant a tree, write a book, beget a child.

Two out of three is not bad.

Out of nowhere I say, 'However many years we have here together will never be enough.'

'Oh, will you just get on with the digging. Shut up with your nonsense and enjoy whatever time we have left,' Jack quips.

Sometimes I get scared by how little time Jack and I will have together. He is eleven years older than I am so at best, what do we have? Thirty years? It seems like such a short time. I often wish we'd found each other years ago, but then, I might not have been ready.

I spend the rest of the afternoon planting cypress trees. They are in little seed pots and stand about 15 cm tall. They appear fragile and weak as I press them into the tiny holes I dig with a trowel. I have always loved cypress trees. They mark land and gardens with strikes of vertical green and elevate the eye. Spanish people are superstitious and don't use them in home gardens. They associate them with cemeteries. Found always on the outskirts of towns and villages, Spanish cemeteries hark back to the Jewish and Muslim traditions of burying the dead outside the city walls. Cypress trees symbolically held the souls aloft, reaching towards the heavens. Another practical reason cypress trees were used in cemeteries is due to the fact that their roots grow vertically down, mirroring the shape of the tree above ground. In that way, they do not disturb the graves.

But here I plant them to accent the land. I plant two rows of ten out behind the alberca, a traditional water-storage structure used for irrigation and dug out from the ground, lined with brick and mortar. I plant one cluster of five cypresses in the orchard, another cluster of three by the henhouse and the rest in a long line to the left of the driveway. I hope they grow tall and strong. I heard once that cypress trees grow a metre a year.

We can see Manolo, the beekeeper, in his dazzling white bee suit, complete with hat and veil, waving at us from the hives. It's a considerable climb up the hill behind the house, to the south-facing parcel of land that he has chosen for his hives.

'I have a real problem this year,' he tells us. 'The females are friskier than normal and instead of worrying about honey production, they just seem intent on procreation!'

We all giggle at the idea of frisky bees.

'Primavera, la sangre altera,' I quote back to him; a Spanish saying capturing the rise of libido in spring.

'I have a colleague in Granada who doesn't seem to have the same problem,' he tells us with a glint in his eye. 'Apparently, it's something to do with the climate in Málaga that makes all our Malagueñan bees horny as hell.'

'Well, you know what they say about the Granadinos,' I joke.

I explain to Jack that the Granadinos are known for not getting enough sex or being bad lovers, and that's why they're always moody – malafollá (literally, 'badly fucked'). Do you know anyone from Granada who lives up to their reputation? I do.

I walk back into the house, opening shutters and windows, letting the sunlight spill into the shadowy spaces. It has a purifying effect on the faint dankness in the rooms that lingers from the months of closure against the harsh winter. Arxi and Beau, close but never too close, are sprawled under the fig tree. BB has bonded with Jack, much to my dismay. I found her, I bought her, I collected her, I chipped her and carried her for two months before her vaccinations . . . but she has decided that Jack is her master.

'I swear you did that on purpose. You've created a co-dependence in her. I will never forgive you,' I tell him, only half-joking.

'Er duh?' Jack smiles, pointing up and down his body. 'Irresistible! All the ladies love me,' he pronounces.

I have to concede that he's right. The ladies do love Jack, but the fact that BB has become his dog is infuriating.

'What's yours is mine, my darling,' he adds, adding fuel to the fire.

Reuben is sitting under the fig tree drawing a picture of Arxi. I hear him mutter, 'Uh-oh. Family flewd.'

Sunday lunch is rabbit stew, so I clear the breakfast table to make way for chopping boards, ingredients, pestle and mortar and knives. Spain used to be a land of rabbits. In fact, 'Spain' derives from 'Hispania' and the roots of this word, although disputed, lean towards the Hebrew 'í sháfán' meaning Island of the Hyrax, or the European rabbit. Other arguments cite the Phoenician term 'span' meaning 'hidden' to identify this far and distant land. I crush garlic and dried ñora, a red pepper from Murcia, bay leaves, sea salt and black pepper into extra virgin olive oil to form the base paste for the recipe. Many Spanish stews are best prepared in a wide-based cazuela, or casserole pan, with slightly slanting sides and handles. I grab one that we found in the kitchen.

The paste goes into the cazuela. I add sweet paprika and turmeric and place it on the stove until the mix begins to simmer gently. The rabbit, cut into eight parts, seals brown in the delicious paste and then I add the following in order: tomatoes, golden thistles, potatoes and vegetable stock. I turn the heat right down and go for a walk.

Reubs sets the table and then goes to get his Samwise, who is having a rummage in the tool room to see what gardening tools he can find, BB by his side. We sit down to enjoy the rabbit stew with a glass of Matarromera and some hot, crusty bread.

'Salud,' I say.

'And cheers,' Reubs adds.

'Whatever Booba. You live in Spain so you might as well get used to it,' I tell him.

'Nah,' he says, shaking his head. 'Living in Spain with British roots, me.'

'Alright my boys, let's enjoy our meal,' Jack says emphatically.

'Yeah. Family,' Reubs mutters as the first bit of rabbit reaches his mouth.

After Sunday afternoon siestas we decide to go for a walk to the Top of the Olives. It's a slow ascent. Reubs is walking with his Saruman staff. Jack and he spent an afternoon in the sunshine painting it black and then searched down by the ford until they found a white river stone to act as the orb. Frodo believes it holds magic powers and protects him. Later, much later, I will look for it and not be able to find it anywhere. One of the volunteers will use it or move it and, on the night of the storm, it will not be by Reuben's side. It will not be there to protect him.

'How far?' Frodo asks every 20 metres or so.

'Just to the Top of the Olives, Frodo,' I reply. 'You've been there before. You've been even further, remember? With Tamara on New Year's Eve.'

Reubs stops and points his staff to the exact spot where he and Tamara sat waiting for us to come down from Topknot. He has precise spatial memory.

'Everything the light hits is yours, Simba,' I quote to him as we reach the top of the hill and nestle in under an olive tree that teeters over the edge of a ridge.

'Shut up, bruvr. I'm Frodo Baggins not Simba.'

'Can't you be both?'

He looks at Samwise and asks, 'Do I?'

'You can be as many things as you want to be, Frodo Baggins. Whatever your heart desires,' Jack replies.

Reubs pats his chest where his heart beats and smiles.

On our way down, we spy something white by the back gate.

'Look,' I say. 'Is that a football?'

As we get closer the white shape moves to face us.

'Puppy!' Reubs exclaims. 'Look. Bless!'

Reubs bends down to stroke her as Jack and I look at each other, thrown by this apparition of fluffy, white beauty.

'We're not keeping her,' Jack says. 'We need another dog like a hole in the head.'

Under the Phoenicians, our village of Archidona, was called Arxiduna. We already have Arxi so we name her Duna. She turns out to be a cross of Spanish mastiff and Labrador. Someone must have pushed her through the fence and wished her well, fancying her chances with the family down by the river. There is no way her tiny legs could have carried her from the village alone. Was there?

Duna takes her role in the household seriously and parades the perimeters of the house and garden, barking at any distant movement to communicate that she is chief guardian. It's a task that comes naturally to her and I feel she does it half out of genetic breeding and half out of gratitude that she found us. She is noble, hardworking, forever loyal and mythically beautiful.

Her legs sprout quickly but she grapples to keep up with the others on the daily walks. She resembles a crane, her long spindly limbs barely coping with the brunt of her body weight as she negotiates the rocky, narrow paths through the under-growth like a cuddly toy on stilts. She edges her way into the pack with real cunning. Three dogs soon become four. Arxi now has an ally and grows in confidence if not in stature. He keeps close to Duna, his overbite teeth sticking out in a grin. They are four when they need to be but they happily break into two and two. Beau and BB firmly lay their stakes on our doorstep and edge Duna and Arxi out. They will eventually get the message and move next door.

12

REBUILD

'THIS RESTORATION CANNOT AND SHOULD not be rushed,' advises Jack. 'Stop making work for yourself. We have to learn to enjoy the house just the way it is.'

'All I'm saying is that there are certain things that need to be done right away,' I reply.

'Like what?'

'The archway out the back by the old sheep pen needs propping up otherwise we'll lose it.'

We begin to make a list, dividing the work into two groups: needs to be done now and can be done later. Both lists are equally daunting. The most pressing job is to erect fences to secure the garden and land. Jack is eyeing the chicken shed, the culmination of a childhood dream within reach. But hens will need roosting perches and boxes to lay their eggs. One thing is certain – Archidona is a small village but it has everything we need. People's willingness to help speaks volumes for the community.

I order ten hens and a cockerel from the pet shop, and when I drive into the village to collect them, there are also four ducklings sitting in a box on the floor.

'Take them,' beams Bea, the shop owner. 'Whoever ordered them doesn't want them anymore.'

'Jenny!' Jack pronounces when I arrive home. He thinks I've inherited my mum's shopping habits. 'Buy one, get one worse! You just can't help yourself, can you! Ducks need water,' he reminds me.

'Have ducks, build pond,' I reply.

I call Pepillo Maquina, who arrives with his bright yellow JCB digger and digs us a giant hole in the front orchard for 28 euros an hour. Rafa helps him avoid all our young fruit trees and, randomly, the hole ends up in the shape of a heart.

'Don't tell me that romance is dead!' I say to Jack as I show him the fruits of our labour. 'We have a heart-shaped duck pond.'

'How lovely,' he replies.

Rafa helps me line the hole with thick rubber sheeting that I order from Germany and within days, our four little ducklings are flapping around in their very own water playground.

He also helps us to tear the walls down between the two sides of the house. It feels great to reunite what had been divided. As soon as the walls tumble down, there appears to be a shift in the energy of the place, or maybe it's just me reading too much into it. In any case, I take great delight in removing the barriers. Reubs has a crack at the wall in the lemon-tree patio. Asking him to smash a wall down goes against his gentle nature, but he does his best, tapping bricks with a sledgehammer.

It's obvious that we are going to need help. David and Mark, our friends from the village, tell us about a volunteering scheme they use for extra help in their boutique hotel. It seems like a win-win situation so we sign up.

In this particular organisation, volunteers can register on the website for a few euros and access a world of opportunities to work away from home. The idea is that they contribute to an ongoing project by volunteering, in return for board and lodging. There is no remuneration involved. There are rules and regulations, but we don't read the small print. Volunteers can stay for days, weeks or months. Many use it to travel the world. Many use it to simply get away. A few use it to run away.

It is still chilly when Chloe, our first volunteer, arrives. She is tall and gentle and impresses us with her sunny demeanour. Her 'can-do' attitude and quiet know-how is inspiring. She dedicates time to Reuben, reading to him on the sofa by the fire. As next door is still punctured with neglect and filled with birds' nests, her job is to dismantle the nests, scrub the floors and walls, and paint the place from top to bottom. It seems like a mammoth task but she cracks on and finishes within a fortnight. She ensures every minute of every hour counts.

'I work at double speed to keep warm,' she grins.

She prepares the way for a stream of volunteers. We hope they are all as tenacious as Chloe.

I take her into town with me to get groceries. She is so much taller than the locals. In the supermarket queue a lady asks me, 'What do you feed her?'

'Lots of Iberian ham!' I reply.

Chloe has chosen ingredients to make her rabbit stew, spiced with garlic, tomato, rosemary and sage.

'Oh, the pressure's on,' taunts Jack.

My previous effort pails into insignificance.

'Stick to the day job, my darling,' Jack taunts.

'Yeah,' agrees Reubs. 'On your left you see Spain. On your right you see Spain,' mimicking a tour-rep sketch from *Little Britain*. We nearly fall off our chairs laughing.

Chloe gives us faith in this volunteering concept. I hug her tightly at Antequera bus station as she heads to Seville for new adventures. I thank her for all she has done.

When I drive back over the river, something clicks. It's the same sensation I get when I am walking on the Camino de Santiago. All of a sudden I am not a walker but a pilgrim. I know I am on the ancient route where hundreds of thousands of souls have trod before me.

My soul shifts in a similar way when I reach the other side of the river. I know I am home. I can shut the world out and be at peace, the river a barrier between here and there. It's here, in the confines of our little corner of Andalusia, that I can change frequency.

We are just beginning to peel off a layer or two of woollen jumpers, the spring sunshine thawing the chill that the house has been held in for months, when Hans arrives. He is a young, solid frame of positive Dutch energy. There is a broad, toothy smile lurking behind every word he utters in his perfect English. His handsome face harbours adventurous eyes and is crowned with a nest of unruly blond hair.

Hans' main task is to clear The Corner of the years of rubbish and accumulated junk that sits about the place. I do the rounds with him, pointing out everything that can be thrown into the brand-new empty skip that has been delivered and sits alongside the house.

'Don't throw anything out that could be useful or that looks old. If you have any doubts just ask me,' I tell him.

He does a great job filling the skip with old pipes, cracked tiles, sheets of bent and twisted corrugated iron and broken bricks. One day, when I am driving back from work, I spy a couple of things by the skip that look like they shouldn't be there: an old iron boot rack and a horse-riding saddle stand that is probably as old as the house. I love it. It has a beautiful patina worn by years of wear and use. I imagine we'll use it as a towel rack in one of the bathrooms when we restore the house, or at the base of one of the old beds as a clothes rack.

I must remember to rescue those two, I think to myself. Hans' idea of old and useful are very different to mine.

Through absolutely no fault of his own, Hans becomes the reason we know we have to fast-track the renovation next door so that volunteers can have their independence. We source a fridge, washing machine and a gas cooker to equip a separate kitchen in the scullery.

Jack and I are both introverts at heart. We need time alone and silent walks to recharge. Hans is clearly blissfully unaware. When Frodo, Jack and I are out and about, Hans spends long stretches of time at The Corner with only the animals for company. When we return home, he needs human contact. He crowds us with words and stories and jokes and tales of his adventures. It confirms our need for privacy at home. There are no hard feelings, though, and Hans leaves as happy as he arrived, heading off to continue his travels around the world.

'Next stop New Zealand,' he tells us. 'Off to shear sheep for a few months.'

June arrives with decisive heat. The saying – 'No te quites el sayo hasta el cuarenta de mayo.' Don't put your raincoat away until 40 May. – rings true this year. Once 9 June has been and gone, there is statistically no rain until after the summer, and the dial on the heat begins to turn. Thin sheets replace duck-down duvets, trousers disappear until September, socks become a thing of the past and the idea of putting our feet in a closed shoe seems inconceivable. From months of trying to keep warm, we pass to months of attempting to stay cool.

The searing temperatures accentuate the stillness of the air. Every living being seems to have disappeared, retreated to find shade in the crevices of the land. Only the insects hum.

Hannah and Sam arrive in a blast of June heat in their unair-conditioned car.

'Welcome to The Corner,' I tell them as we hug like old friends. 'You look like you've been microwaved!' I add.

'We feel like we have. Wow. Driving through Córdoba, we thought the car might melt,' Hannah says.

They embody the true spirit of volunteering. They come for all the right reasons, have access to their own means and quickly fit into the workings of the house. They understand our vision and spend their first days equipping the house next door. Together, we unearth treasures lurking in the barns and outbuildings of The Corner and upcycle them to a new purpose. Little by little, it begins to look like a home. Art finds its way onto the walls and rooms begin to take on a resemblance of comfort and cosiness.

Hannah and Sam flourish in the natural beauty of The Corner. In our profile, we specify that people should be nature lovers and at ease in their own company, comfortable in their own silence.

They are stargazers and they bask in the clarity of the night sky, away from the light pollution. Sam identifies planets and constellations and one still night when we are all lying on our backs pushing our gazes through the night-time abyss, we tune into his very clear instructions. He tells us to look to the bottom left of our field of vision, to find a slow-moving light mass crossing on a diagonal at a constant rate, until it leaves the panorama top right. He is showing us the International Space Station.

'Can't see it, bruvr,' Reubs says. 'Where?'

'It's gone now, Booba,' I tell him. We were all so wrapped up in our own wonder that we forgot to help Reubs find his. Nine seconds was barely enough time.

'Oh well. Next time,' Reuben adds philosophically.

Part of the volunteers' job description is to look after Reubs. I am acutely aware that living in the countryside has an impact on Reuben's autonomy and ability to create his own community. It is our dream and I hope with all my might that it becomes his too. Much to my delight, he soon finds the contact with *next door* a lifeline to his own wellbeing. He is striving for independence. Hannah and Sam skilfully and naturally invent tasks, ticklists and activities to structure Reuben's day. He becomes part of their lives and they become an essential and enhancing part of his. He even eats his meals with 'my people next door'.

'We're dumped!' Jack says. 'Manni who?'

It was a tough decision to bring Reuben to live in Spain. When Mum and Dad left Newbury to retire to Norwich, Reubs had not wanted to go with them. He moved into a Mencap care home. On paper it looked like a secure option. I only saw Reubs maybe twice a year and therefore his gradual decline was more apparent to me. He started to gain weight and developed a tendency to hoard.

Mum discovered that someone had been stealing from Reubs, using his bank card to make purchases over the internet. No one at the care home could explain it, so we called the police to investigate. There was a transaction for the purchase of an enormous flat-screen plasma television. The price? – £800.

117

'Do you know anything about this, Reubs?' my parents quizzed him.

'It's a secret,' he replied.

One of the staff members must have passed details of Reuben's card to a friend or crime colleague and they'd been clever enough to use a public computer, so it was impossible for the police to trace. Really? What about the delivery address? CCTV cameras? There were so many possible lines of investigation, but the case fell through due to lack of evidence. Reuben, as a vulnerable adult, had been the victim of a scam. Enough said.

Soon after this incident, Reuben was due to come to Spain to stay with me. He was travelling as an unaccompanied minor. He appeared at Arrivals in Gibraltar, twice his ideal weight, with dirty hair and nails, a spotty face, dressed in his pyjamas. It transpired that the staff in the care home hadn't allowed time for him to get dressed, so they sent him to the airport in his pyjamas. I hugged his colossal frame close. At that precise moment I made a crucial decision – he was not going back. My brother didn't need to live like that. He deserved so much better. He's been with me in Spain for seven years now.

Reuben receives allowances from the UK Government, which is why he thinks he works for them. He has a brown briefcase onto which he sellotaped a piece of paper where he wrote 'MI6'. He calls himself Bond, Reuben Bond. Readily, the UK Government agreed the move and Reuben was granted allowances that were payable in Spain under the shared EU scheme. A removal team picked up his belongings in Newbury.

His needs were simple and clear to him: *Card shop. DVD shop. English café. Supermarket. Nice people. English people. Little Britain*, he wrote on the piece of paper.

I found the perfect flat in Marbella but it was far too big and fancy for two. Our dear friend, Debs, suggested the three of us live together and, in that way, she could help me look after Reuben. It was the perfect solution. We moved into our 'San Pedro Palace'. Our first task was to show Reuben around his new neighbourhood. We accompanied him on walks to all the local services until we felt he knew the area well enough to venture out alone.

On the first few solo errands, we followed him like private detectives. We giggled as he paused at crossroads, talking to himself and trying to remember which way to go. After a few dress rehearsals, he was ready to branch out on his own and San Pedro de Alcántara became his new home. He was so happy. I was less so.

Expat Spain has never been my scene. I love the more traditional values of inland Spain and longed to get back to them. However, Reuben was my priority and I was happy to ride that wave for a while, to make sure Reubs settled into his new life in Spain. I had a great time into the bargain, finding haunts in Marbella and its surrounding area. But deep down, I knew that the call of the mountains would come. I am part mountain goat. You know how the Spanish proverb goes? La cabra siempre tira para el monte. The goat always returns to the mountains. I simply had to bide my time.

13

COUNT OF SAN FÉLIX

THE LONGER WE ARE HERE, the more unanswered questions arise. I decide to do some more digging. I remember the framed photograph of a painting of the house in the main room upstairs. History is my portal as I consider the crown – Cayetano de Alvear, Count of San Félix. This much I know.

I plunge into the infinite ocean that is Google by typing his name into the search bar. As I scroll through the results, little appears until I widen the search by adding 'Conde de San Félix'. More references appear and I learn his full name; Cayetano de Alvear y Ramírez de Arrellano. He was born in 1850 in Pamplona and died in 1931. Okay, we're getting somewhere. He is buried in Madrid, in the cemetery of Almudena. Pieces of the puzzle begin to fit together.

When I contact the local library, Soledad's enthusiasm is encouraging. There is a tender truth in her name, which means 'solitude', as she sits all alone in a building of books. I have the impression there is nowhere she would rather be. A historian herself, she puts me in contact with local researchers who help me on my quest.

At just fifteen years old, Cayetano joined the Spanish army as a second lieutenant. He climbed through the ranks; becoming Captain, then Commander and finally General in 1916. He was third Count of San Félix by royal succession. The title was first granted, by Queen Isabel II, in 1855 to Doña Felicia de Alvear y Fernández de Lara. The doña's two marriages were childless, and when she died in 1878 in Madrid, no heir claimed the title. Twenty-seven years later, in 1895, the title was declared caducado, or expired. But, in 1902, a gentleman by the name of Don Manuel Alvear y Ramírez de Arrellano applied to rehabilitate the title, claiming to be the great-grandson of Doña Felicia's parents. His claim was successful, and he became the Count of San Félix, and died childless in 1922, which is when his brother Cayetano picked up the title.

The words rise from the screen. Vast expanses of doubt and questions fill my mind. I long to know how he came to be in The Corner, and this information sets me on the path of discovery. I now have a solid framework to start from. Why Archidona? Why the lauburu? Why build a Basque caserío where there should have been an Andalusian cortijo? The frame of the jigsaw is complete, but there are so many missing pieces.

I decide to head into Archidona to see what other information lurks in the town's archives. By asking a local señora on her way to the municipal market, pulling her purple gingham trolley behind her, I locate the office of Registry of Property and Deeds. I politely greet a thin slip of a señora with a long, angular face and lifeless eyes, who reluctantly leaves her desk to attend to me at the enquiries window.

She looks me up and down, unconvinced by my muddy attire or dishevelled appearance, or both, when I tell her I co-own a cortijo and request the deeds to the property. She explains that there is a fee and I duly hand over three 50 euro notes, which she disinfects with a spray.

A week later, I collect a thick folder. I want to meet the count and I am getting closer. I can smell it. As I drive home, the folder on the co-pilot seat, I sing my way through the olive groves with the windows down and the sunroof open, swerving to miss all the potholes and bouncing up and down the humps and bumps of the country lane that leads from the village down into our valley. When I get home, I sit under the fig tree, with a cup of tea and a sharpened pencil, before I turn over the dust cover. I can't remember the last time I was this excited about anything.

Cayetano first became acquainted with The Corner through his wife. Her name was Doña María del Carmen Gumuncio y Cardenas. What a wonderful name. Doña María's mother, Doña Isabel de Cardenas y Grana, died in the house on 11 July 1891. Her last-minute will, written that same day in the presence of the notary Don José Rosal Benitez, stipulated the following:

She left her servant, Josefa Morales, 1,000 reales.

She left her servant, Antonio Cabello Sanchez Lafuente, 80 pesetas.

She left her other servants 25 pesetas each.

She left her niece 7,500 pesetas in cash and various pieces of furniture, which would be handed over to her on her twenty-sixth birthday, still the average age of independence in Spain.

She left her daughter, Cayetano's wife, 6,250 pesetas, repaying with interest a loan of 3,500 pesetas that Doña Maria del Carmen had made years earlier.

There were no other debts. Doña Isabel's tidy exit from this world stipulated that the entire estate was to be divided into two equal parts: one part going to her daughter Doña Maria del Carmen, and the other to her son Don Ricardo Gumuncio. Who got which half was to be decided by the tossing of a coin. Fortune fell to Doña María del Carmen as her half contained the house. She paid her brother the difference in value of 10,192.35 pesetas and, in this way, became sole proprietor of a vast estate and a beautiful farmhouse, located on a gentle straight section of the River of the Silent Ones. I am not a believer in luck, but this is one exception when I might just have to bend my hard and fast rule.

The deeds describe the estate as 'a gem of land for cereal crops' (una suerte de tierra calma). She was thirty-eight. Her husband, Cayetano, was forty-two. The couple enjoyed The Corner for almost two decades, extending the gardens, building a grand entrance and a new wing of more formal accommodation. I find a poem in a drawer of a mid-century cabinet in the living room, written by an illustrious guest, describing a grand party that they hosted in the house, with friends, family and colleagues travelling by horse and carriage to this corner of Andalusia.

Look around you. Such light! Such flowers!
The songs of birds by the river at all hours.
What sunshine, brilliant colours we see.
Where else would we rather be?
Don Cayetano with just the right amount of fame.
In this delicious corner of Andalusia we are not the same.

Written 7 August 1898

Praised by his military leaders for his 'intelligent and essential contribution' to the army, something must have happened because he returned to The Corner for a three-year sabbatical, from 1899 until 1902. I imagine the deep rest he must have enjoyed during those quiet years here. He had served all over Spain, from Almería to Madrid, from Barcelona to Córdoba, from Zaragoza to Toledo. What a delight it must have been to finally stop and to spend his days in deep insouciance. There is no better place to recover and rest the soul.

Sadly, Doña Maria del Carmen passed away in Córdoba on New Year's Eve 1908. She had left no will and, under Spanish law, the house and all its land fell to the children of her first marriage. Don Cayetano renounced all rights to any inheritance that might have befallen him. He simply walked away.

I can't imagine losing this place.

Doña María's children put the house and land up for sale in 1910 and it was purchased for 85,000 pesetas by The Most Excellent Don Manuel de Alvear y Ramírez de Avellano, Count of San Félix – none other than Cayetano's brother. It appears that the family enjoyed the finca – the estate – for a decade before his death on 12 January 1920. With no legitimate heirs, he left two-thirds to his wife and a third to his widowed, childless brother. Our dear Cayetano stepped into his royal title, purchased two-thirds from his late brother's widow and on 9 February 1921, signed the deeds and became sole owner of his beloved Rincón. The count finally had his cortijo.

I imagine our count returning here, a widower with no children, far from his birthplace, far from his professional base in Madrid, alone in this house. The army recognised his title by royal decree and placed him into second reserves. For the last decade of his life, he lived the cortijo's most splendid epoch. For home is never a physical place. Home is a sense we carry within us.

14

WATER

O VER 3,000 SPANISH WORDS ARE derived from Arabic. Any word with 'al' in it, is part of that group. 'Al' is the definite article in Arabic, hence Guadalquivir, the big river. 'Al-birka' is the Arabic for pools of running water and from there, popular tradition calls them 'albercas'. 'Birka' has the same root as the b–r–k sound in Arabic, which gives us 'baraka' for blessing. Curiously in our village, many people call albercas 'ambercas', giving the word the inflection of local dialect.

We are delighted to discover an alberca behind the house on a high pitch of land just below the olive grove. All around the top edges, oleanders, broom and hawthorn obscure its form and, as we peer through the borders, we realise that Maneo must have used it as a landfill. Broken pieces of machinery, old chairs, barbed wire, posts and pipes are strewn across the bottom, discarded and forgotten. It's time for another skip. I call Toledo and ask him to replace the full one with an empty one.

As we clear the rubble, the structure of the alberca reveals itself. Weathered stone steps lead down to the bulging forms of the original brick walls, straining with the effort of holding water for many centuries. Could it be Arabic? Could it even be Roman?

Water is sacred in Spain and we are blessed with three of our own water sources at The Corner: town water, cave water and spring water.

Town water is expensive and problematic as our stop tap is under a manhole opposite Victor's house. It all sounded enchanting when Tito showed us the system.

Two dogs guard the tap, so every time I turn it on or off, I experience a minor heart attack. The brown-and-white hunting dog lunges at me like a rabid monster and it's only his chain that breaks his charge in mid-air. From that tap, our plastic tube runs under the road, down a steep riverbank, under another neighbour's field, across the river, under a different neighbour's field, through an olive grove, over a hill, through another olive grove, under the fence, across the track and finally into the house through a crude opening in the 1.20 m-thick outer wall. The system is rudimentary at best.

I ask for a meeting with the water company in town. They know me by name now. When I suggest to the office clerk that the stop tap should be at our property, that water is a right and not a luxury, that's surely why we have to pay so many taxes to the municipal coffer, my argument is emphatically pushed back.

'If I were you,' explains the clerk between gum chews, ' I would zip it. If you asked for water today, you wouldn't even get it. Your house lies outside of the urban network. It's only because the house asked for water in the 1970s that you get any water at all.'

The system springs a leak and trying to fix it almost breaks me. It's all because we are the last house on the mains system. Any work or maintenance fills the pipes with air and the pressure keeps rupturing our tubes.

I love Spain, but I am the first to admit that the tenacity required to negotiate its bureaucracy is Goliath in its proportions. I have seen many a keen new arrival return home, crushed by the system. It separates the meek from the persistent.

The cave-water system is even more complicated. On the hillside on the opposite side of the river, on the high flanks of the mountain side, is the entrance to a cave. The narrow mouth leads into a system of underground rivers, lakes and tributaries measuring several kilometres in length. In all seasons, there is a constant stream of the purest, coldest water leaving the cave that has been tapped and guided into a system of pipes and water tanks. We have no idea when the system was originally constructed. We find remnants of old cement pipes that are from the early twentieth century. The water gathers so much pressure on its downward tumble from the mountain top that, at certain times of the year, the pressure measures up to 8 bars, almost as powerful as a fireman's hose.

All the farms in the valley share the water in established timetables that are written into the deeds of our properties. Our weekly slots are on Wednesdays from 3 p.m. to 7 p.m. and on Sunday mornings from 8 a.m. until 1 p.m. We drew the short straw there. Who wants to get out of bed on a Sunday morning to connect the water? During those allocated hours, we have free rein on the water supply and control the pressure by using no fewer than nine taps to establish just the right balance for irrigation.

In the winter and spring months we don't really need it but, come May, those nine hours a week provide blessed respite from the scorching temperatures — for us and for the bone-dry shrubs, fruit trees and all our flower beds around the house. We can unleash the sweet supply of chilled water and the vegetation laps it up with relish. That sensation of cool water helps to calm the body and mind as the cave water brings the temperature of the ground down by a notch or two, just enough to prevent us seeing red. On the hottest days, we direct a hose on each other or on the dogs, who are pleading for a sense of coolness, listless in their attempts to escape the heat.

The third water source is the spring, by the fruitless fig tree just past Badger's Drop. A water source trickling out of the rock face forms a pool and then continues down the steep cliffs into the river below. One day we wake with a decisive energy to face the challenge and head out there armed with shears and a machete. As we begin to cut back the thistles and tangled weeds, a rusty water container appears among the brambles. Shaped rather like a canoa, an implement used for decanting from one barrel into another, in the original system of 'solera and criadera' in the sherry industry, it looks like the front of a canoe. Its pointed part bears a hole from where the water flows and its long, flat, back edge is rammed into the cliff face to gather as many of the falling trickles as possible.

I find sections of a tiny aqueduct that must have fed water though to the alberca at the back of the house. It is raised on mounds and built organically into the terrain, with a neat edged border made of upturned red bricks. I wonder how long ago this system was built. Could it be Arabic? I know that bricks were introduced into Spain through the cultures of Al-Andalus. Before that, the Romans built mainly with stone, but the arrival of the Moorish culture brought widespread use of bricks and ceramics into the Iberian Peninsula.

Rafa has taught me to look with creative, practical eyes. If there's a problem, find a solution. I must admit that my solution is quite often simply Rafa. Even though his hours are from 8 a.m. to 1 p.m. each Wednesday, we see him several times a week as he drops off this and that, or brings his grandson down to play with the ducks in the pond.

When he sees me now, he wraps his arms around me and hoists me into the air. We enjoy a closeness that is unusual for both of us. Rafa always says, 'We search for a solution within the walls of The Corner and if all else fails, then – and only then – we head to the hardware store.'

Ferretería Linde in Antequera is a world unto itself. I think it's the coolest shop I know. I wonder how long it will be able to survive? In a town of 33,000 residents, it's hanging on as the major 'go to' for DIY and home-improvement supplies, keeping the larger wholesalers at bay. If it were ever to close its doors, it would be a sad day indeed.

Capability is Rafa's middle name and so we sit down to find a solution. Harking back to my old guiding days when I used to accompany busloads of American students around Spain's historical sites, I dredge up from the recesses of my mind, my knowledge of Roman aqueducts and water engineering. I remember those swims in the crystal waters under the Pont du Gard in southern France and the suckling pig that we used to chow down on, while gazing out of the window onto the aqueduct of Segovia, the two most pristine examples to my knowledge. Applying the same theories, water can travel along cisterns to reach a final destination, provided that there are no uphills and that the final exit point is lower than the original source. It is simple GCSE Physics.

'Correcto,' states Rafa. I am not teaching him anything he doesn't know. 'All we need is 400 metres of tubing más o menos (more or less), a few link joints, a 1,000-litre holding tank, a filter, a tap and some good old Andalusian cheer.'

The first task is to carry – yes, *carry* – the water tank 500 metres out to the source. I look at it on the driveway and laugh. It is the size of a small car.

'I have a bad back. Two herniated discs,' I tell Rafa. He waits for the punchline. 'A riding accident on a mule called Amigo.'

When he has controlled his laughter he asks, 'Well, what else do you suggest ?' He is right of course. There is no other way.

His company energises me and I garner strength for the task. We find two old metal fence posts, rusted with the lacquer of time and use them as carrying poles. Threading them through the metal framework on the tank, we set off like two Egyptians carrying a Pharaoh. There is no question of 'if' we can make it. Rafa cuts his path through the undergrowth and along paths barely wide enough to take a human, let alone two humans balancing a water tank between them.

At Badger's Drop, I feel my centre of gravity toppling and scream to a halt. Rafa is thoroughly enjoying himself at my expense. A sharp intake of air, and several heave-hos later, we arrive at the spring and shove the tank into position as close to the metal container as possible. Rafa creates a support platform by wedging the gate posts into place between rocks and trees and manoeuvring the front of the tank to rest on them. An empty tank is one thing but, once filled with water, it will weigh more than a tonne.

We lay a final section of tube to lead the water from the collector into the top of the tank, keeping it in place by creating a slink looped over a higher branch. Hey presto, the tank starts to fill with water. I get excited thinking we have finished the job. How wrong I am. The next task is to lay 500 metres of plastic tubing from the source, down the riverbank, along the river, back towards the house, up the slope to the alberca and in. It requires a concerted effort of coordinated heaving and dragging the pipes into place and then fastening one to the next with a link joint. As the morning draws to an end, we have the alberca within sights. All we have to do is cut the last section accurately, so the end of the pipe extends over the edge of the structure.

'Hecho!' Rafa beams. 'That wasn't too bad, was it?'

'Bloody hell. You're a machine,' I reply and throw myself onto the grass.

'It'll take a while for the pressure to build up but I figure that once the tank is full, 1,000 litres, together with the initial drop, will create enough pressure to push the water through. Well . . . I hope so.' He cracks up at his own comment. I am not amused.

We collect tools and sit by the alberca, waiting patiently to see if our little mission has been successful. We have all the time in the world. A good twenty minutes pass while we chew on the end of grass stalks and rest. Rafa brings the end of the tube to his ear.

'Can you hear anything?' I ask him.

'Only you and your dumb questions,' he replies. 'No, I can't hear anything actually. Strange that.' He shoots me a quizzical look. I choose to ignore it. The alternative just doesn't bear thinking about. He begins to speak to himself as if I'm not there. 'That's so odd. I was convinced that with a 1,000-litre tank, it would have been enough. Then again, I haven't measured the height of the source from the river. Maybe the alberca is higher after all. Oh god, maybe I should have used a bigger tank.' He brings the tube to his ear again. 'Nothing. Absolutely nothing.'

'Give it here!' I boom and snatch the tube from him to see if I can hear anything. His timing is genius. As I bring the pipe towards my ear, a huge torrent of spring water splutters and bursts out of the tube, drenching me in the coolest of fragrant spring waters. It takes me a while to react to the shock and by then I am drenched. Rafa moves away, beyond reach and howls with laughter.

I place the tube over the edge of the alberca and watch as a glorious flow of fresh, spring water tumbles to the bottom and begins to dance as it forms a puddle, then a pool, until the entire bottom is covered with water and the level begins to rise. I could sit here for hours, simply watching it fill.

'That is amazing,' I beam as I give Rafa a wet hug. 'Thank you, compañero. I'll never forget that. This has been one of the best mornings of my life. It's a total game-changer.'

'You've just struck gold,' he says with the genuine sentiment of a human being who rejoices in other people's good fortune.

In the alberca, throatwort, a beautiful plant with a hideous name, clings to the cracks in the mortar and pronounces its presence in upright splashes of lilac. Toads share their water park with fish we introduce that go forth and multiply. As the sun dips towards Old Man Mountain in the west, swallows, house martins and warblers skim the surface to drink before bed. As soon as the level rises above waist height, I slip into that natural habitat and as I let myself sink, my skin chills in the cool depths. I lose myself for a few blissful minutes.

If we thought June was hot, July is in another league of heat. Nothing can prepare us for the intense heat of an Andalusian summer.

There is no cool part of the day. The mornings are simply not quite as hot. We are listless and sticky. Our side of the house is hotter than the volunteers' section as it receives the full pelt of the afternoon sun. Sleeping is a struggle as we have no fans. One day the temperatures reach 46° C and it seems almost dangerous to be here. I feel as if my body melts into the air around me. Water does nothing to quench our thirst. The dogs search for the coolest places in the house and doze the day away. BB's preferred spot is inside the corner cupboard of next-door's kitchen and that is where she spends her days.

But we have the alberca – the life-giving, cool-giving, dream-giving, relief-giving alberca. The only way to cool off is to sink into its delicious, perpetually cold water. We spend more time in it than out of it, even walking up there at night to slip into the dark waters and rest until our body temperatures drop and we can approach the idea of sleep.

15

RAGE AGAINST THE MOUNTAIN

THE LAND AND ALL THAT live in it and on it ache for water. Every living tree and plant has stretched its roots under the baked earth's crust since 9 June, sharing any scant nutrients they can suck into their secret sinewy defence system. They have done well and shown stoic fortitude, heads bowed through the intense summer highs, an African sky beating down domes of stifling heat. They have been waiting patiently but they look as if they can't hold on for much longer.

When will the rains come?

As Jack and I are falling asleep one evening, covering ourselves with only a thin cotton sheet, Jack says, 'You've left a light on.'

I look into the patio and it's true. Stark, white light floods the walls. The leaves on the lemon tree are luminous.

'Bugger,' I mutter. 'I was just falling asleep. You stay right there, Your Highness. Don't mind me,' I say as I clamber out of bed. As I walk around the house checking every room, there are no lights on.

I tiptoe back to our bedroom and open both French doors onto the lemon-tree patio. A light so pure that it feels almost celestial spills into the room.

'Jack,' I say in wonder as I shake his foot. 'Look! It's the moon!'

Jack sits bolt upright in bed, his mouth aghast.

'Look!'

We both play with our arms and legs, showing each other the light striking our bodies as if we were in a club pointing out the effects of UV lighting on white clothes.

'That is amazing,' I gasp. 'Let's go to the Final Fence.'

That part of Jack that keeps him from telling me to stop being so stupid and causes him to put on his trainers, shorts and T-shirt is just one of the reasons why I love him.

'Now, dogs. You can only come if you're quiet, you hear me!' Jack urges them in his sternest dog voice. They all understand and fall into line, as quiet as mice.

We walk as if we're treading on recently fallen snow. As the moon rises, it unleashes its power of plenitude. Everything glows in its still and silver shine: each branch, each bow, each burly trunk a sculpture of light.

Jack doesn't say anything but he does grab my hand. We can see everything so clearly, the idea of a torch would be futile.

The scene looks wintry even though we're reaching the end of summer, and all around us, concentric circles of silence. There is an odd criss-cross of my perception and my mind's interpretation of the scene. It is night, but I see day. Everything appears wet and glistening but it is all bone-dry. Is this what synesthesia feels like? I want to dance. I want to run screaming through the meadow and do cartwheels all the way to Thyme Point. I feel giddy with white light and tiny in the presence of the fullest moon I have ever seen.

When we reach Thyme Point, we perch on our favourite spot and each of the dogs takes up their place to view the spectacle. We are in a royal box watching the greatest light show on earth. It's a private show. If there are other living beings out here watching this with us, they are as hushed as we are by the beauty. I look at everything as if I am never going to see it again.

I am only aware of myself when Jack gently touches my hand and says, 'Come on, darling. Let's go back to bed.'

We walk back in silence, hushed by this miracle of light. As I slip under the white sheet, I feel different to the person I was an hour ago. Drenched in a silver sheen, I paradiddle myself to sleep, tapping my toes in sequence.

When the first rains release their moisture onto the crisp, dry landscape, the olive trees stretch out their branches, opening their leaves to catch the glory of water. Now at last they can drink. Now they can clap and dance in the wind, their olives dangling like tiny green baubles on a Christmas tree. Summer is no more.

Jack heads back to London and Reubs and I lay low for a few weeks, hemmed in by water. The river grinds into action, almost as if it had forgotten how to flow quickly. Water slides off the hills and makes gulleys in the lane as it tries to reach the valley floor. Except for two walks a day with the dogs, there is little else we can do. Reubs draws. I work away on my laptop, tapping keys with fingertips. The days slip slowly by.

It's Sunday today, always my most difficult day. As a child, Sundays had always been about church and Sunday roasts and family time. At thirteen, we were given the choice to go to church or not. Until that age, there wasn't a choice. Little Goody Two-Shoes here continued to go.

I was devoted to the church. I used to love it: those hymns with rousing melodies, those prayers of heightened humanity. But when my devotion caved in, Sundays became spare and odd and filled with a blend of loss and pain and melancholy and secrets. When Jack, Reubs and I are together, Sundays are great, but today we are only two-thirds of our trilogy and the hours stretch before me like a straight road through a desert.

As my coffee is percolating (Reubs and I treated ourselves last week and went to the big Carrefour in Antequera. He bought elderflower cordial and I bought Illy coffee), I sit in the kitchen watching the dawn crawl over the eastern hill. First light brings the flies. Where do they come from? They flourish in the moisture of September and the cooler temperatures bring them indoors.

As I am sitting there idly, I have a flashback to the skip at the side of the house. The iron boot rack! The saddle stand! Shit! Like a fool I go around to the side of the house to confirm what I already know. They are nowhere to be seen. Shit! Why didn't I remember to rescue them? They'll be long gone now. That saddle stand was so beautiful.

I sit there idly as an email pings into my inbox. It's from Kate, my sister-in-law in the USA. She's up late. I'm up early. She has forwarded me a blog post. The title catches my eye: 'Picasso and the Pilgrimage'. I start to read about Jillian as she writes of her journey through sorrow. She had met the love of her life. They planned to marry. I connect with her words and fall into her story.

'I love how you are with my mum. It's great to see you both together. That makes me happy. You make me happy,' her fiancé told her as their heads hit the pillows. They fell asleep and then he died. He died in her arms. Sudden Adult Death Syndrome. She spent the next two years, numbed by pain, confused by therapy, wracked with anxiety, reeling in the grips of acute grief. Writing about it helped her. As her writing was so honest and human, she began to help others.

She made a decision to travel for the first time since his death. Finally, she felt strong enough and this was a pilgrimage in his honour. He had always dreamed of coming to Spain, mainly to see Picasso's *Guernica* painting. He had a healthy obsession with it and Jillian decided to come to Spain to find out why. Her blogpost ended with this sentence: 'I'm going to Spain. I'll start in Madrid, to see Picasso's masterpiece and after that I'm not sure. I'll see where the wind takes me'.

There was no doubt in my mind. She was coming to The Corner. I wrote her a very direct email, introducing myself. Three weeks later I collect her from a hotel in Málaga city.

We share interests, passions, concerns. The conversation and laughter is fresh and real.

The following day blusters with dramatic cloud formations, shifting quickly over the mountain ridges.

Jillian wants to go for a walk. 'The river is a natural border to the south and southeast and all the rest of the land has a perimeter fence, so you can't go wrong.' I hug her. 'Have a good time.'

'I will,' she replies.

We both know why she is going. I admire her strength, the grit that carries her through her torment. She neither pretends nor wallows. Her mind is crystal-clear. There is no way we should tackle this life alone. We are tribal and need to be connected to like-minded people. We are not wired to live alone.

Hours pass before she comes home. Hours and hours.

The weather closes in. Horizontal rain batters the hillside. I light the fires. I am not worried. Jillian comes home drenched and shivering with cold.

I throw her a towel. "Did you have a good time?" I ask her as I look into her eyes.

'I had an amazing time," she replies. "Amazing in every way.'

'Good. I think that's why I invited you,' I say. 'For whatever just happened. Come and sit by the fire.'

We never talk about it. It's not the right time to process it. Sometimes it's better to leave thoughts where they are, better to maintain the silence. I eventually read about that afternoon in her blog. It is an entry called 'The Corner' and I devour it line by line, each word a gift.

When Jillian came to Spain, she was raging. She'd been raging for months, stuck firmly in the angry part of the bereavement process. Her blood-curdling anger gripped her. It was preventing her from moving forward. Spain had been an initiative to create inertia and hopefully dislodge the rage. Serendipity played all her cards, as one domino fell into the next: the blogpost, Kate reading it, thinking of me, me reading it, inviting her, her accepting, her arriving and then, the very day she needed to get lost in the embrace of the raw elements, the weather turned and began to pelt her with every element known to Mother Nature. It rained vertically, horizontally and diagonally that day. Every angle of her being was exposed to water. The wind ravaged the tall grasses and the trees bore the brunt of the gusts by leaning into them. Jillian felt exposed and battered by the wind, but never beaten.

She found herself in one of those rare moments, when the natural world around us drowns out any noise. Scream and our scream is silenced. Holler and our holler disappears. Cry and our cry cannot be heard. Nature is greater than the force of our pain.

Jillian screamed at the world but the world didn't scream back. She hollered the question 'Why?' until the very question meant nothing. She cried until her tears were whipped from her face by the pulsing winds and diluted by the torrential rain. Slowly, very slowly, little by little, the rage left her. She raged against the mountain until her strength weakened. Only then did she consent to bend her knee to a greater force. She surrendered and her rage left her.

16

ANITA

We wonder at the River of the Silent Ones that flows so
gently, we know not if it is river or sea.

Ibn Zamrak, fourteenth century

THE RIVER OF THE SILENT Ones lives up to its namesake
through the summer months, barely audible as it ambles
past the house, low and slinky.

September's rains transform the river into a tempestuous
beast. It bursts its banks again down by the ford and cuts us
off from the outside world for almost two weeks. Jack can't
get home. Reubs and I can't leave. I love cancelling all plans
with one of the most original excuses I have ever had to relay.

'I have to cancel our tour to Granada, I'm afraid, as I live
in the country and we're marooned.'

'Reubs and I are really sorry, but we can't come for lunch
on Sunday as we can't get out!'

Thank goodness we have a larder stocked with all the essentials and a freezer full of supplies.

Reubs had been enjoying a routine of crossing the dry ford and walking as far as the tarmac in the relative cool of the mornings. Unbeknown to us, he had a secret guide. We only find out much later when Victor tells us that Reubs always appeared at his house to wave hello and then spun (slowly) on his heels to head home, Arxi always by his side. Little Arxi, wily and wise.

'Every single day, Arxi was with him,' Victor will tell me later during one of our many conversations. When I stop to talk with Victor, I can feel a friendship blossoming. I hope he feels it too. Friendships happen organically here as we fold into each other's existence. Time is our common denominator. It surely took Victor a while to realise we are not fair-weather neighbours and that we are here for the long term.

But now, there is no walk to Victor's house. No crossing of the river. I take Reubs down to the ford to explain why he can't leave.

'There's no way we can cross at the moment. It's too dangerous, Reubs,' I explain.

'How long?' he asks, his face oddly expectant, his eyes unusually questioning, as his right hand grips Saruman's staff.

'Not long now, Booba. Until then, we'll have to go to the Final Fence.'

'Uh, no bruvr.'

'Or Top of the Olives?' I suggest.

'Well, yeah. Olives. With my Samwise I do.'

When Jack makes it back, driving slowly through the river in a heavy 4 × 4, Frodo and Samwise take a walk up to the Top of the Olives each evening. Samwise takes a can of beer, Frodo takes a can of shandy and they sit there with the dogs chewing the cud and chatting 'man to man'.

'What do you talk about?' I ask one evening.

'Don't tell him, Frodo Baggins,' Jack urges.

'Secret, bruvr,' Frodo says, smiling. He loves getting one over on me and I love letting him. His need for clever social interaction is as great as yours or mine.

'You leave the White Wizard to me!' booms Samwise.

Reubs explodes with happiness. Incapable of containing his joy, he gets up to share it with Jack.

'I love you, my Samwise Sam,' he tells him as he leans in for a hug.

'I love you too, Frodo Baggins. Now sit down and finish your dinner.'

I love nothing more than to watch these two interact. They give something to each other that no one else can.

October brings a redefining light with skies the colour of Moroccan añil (blue). Nature has been hiding from the suffocating heat of summer and the relentless rains. Trees bowed to their greater powers, animals surrendered, imprisoned by their captors – the Andalusian sun and the September rains. Nothing could escape nature's reign.

But October unlocks prison doors and the world can dance again. Animals cry and shriek with joy. The earth breathes. The dogs play once more. There are many wonderful months in inland Andalusia, but October is perhaps the most beautiful of all, when pure delight returns. October brings the return of days when the sun is only a monarch and not a dictator.

After the rains, the earth's baked crust can be broken again. The wild boar are on the rampage. They are trying to get all the way to the house. I need to remind Rafa to reinforce the fencing at the back to keep them out. As I walk to the Final Fence, I see that they have been through the meadow and churned the top soil over like a plough. The path no longer exists and rocks are strewn everywhere. They've made it ugly, but then it's their land. If the wild belongs to them and we are merely the keepers, then who am I to complain? But still it grates. They churn up the beauty. The wild invading our civilisation. It's a battle and I never wanted it to be a battle. Finding the harmony is complicated.

We buy Reubs a Fitbit. He loves saying the word.

'Fit–bit,' he says with a punchy pronunciation. It makes him giggle.

We initiate him into the idea of walking 10,000 steps every weekday.

'Ufff. That's a lot,' he protests, his face screwing up like a chamois leather. 'How far? Victor's house?'

'No, a bit further. All the way to Anita's house. But when it's done, it's done, Reubs. Shall we walk the first 10,000 steps together?'

'Good idea, bruv. Just you and me. Bruvrs.'

We paddle across the river in wellington boots, hiding them in a bush on the other side and change into our trainers.

'Four hundred, bruv,' Reubs says looking at his wrist. 'That nearly 10,000?' he asks.

'Nearly,' I reply.

The walk to Anita's house, third on the left once we reach the tarmac, takes us along a ribbon of gentle rises and falls and a series of sweeping bends to rival any racetrack. We are flanked by olive trees left and right, which appear to stand to attention as we pass. A hoopoe flies by so close I can make out the white dots on its plumage. Reubs is walking well. To take his mind off the walk, I grab his hand, his squidgy little palm in mine, and sing a silly song we made up when we walked the pilgrimage route in the north of Spain.

It's a long way to Santiago.
It's a long way to go.
It's a long way to Santiago.
And I'm walking with my bro.

'Shut up, bruv.' Reubs laughs. 'We not in Santiago. We here. Archidona.'

'You're right, Reubs. We're here. We're home,' I say and then add. 'Does it feel like home to you, Reubs?'

'Well, bit home.'

'Do you miss anything?'

'Well, people I miss. Just a bit. I got you and Samwise. That's why.'

He is right. When the three of us are together, we want for nothing.

Anita's tidy house is sporting its annual coat of *cal*, the quicklime paste that covers homes all over Spain. It's one of the many traditions introduced into this part of the world through the cultures of North Africa. So much of what we do here was introduced through the kingdom of Al-Andalus. Two shores, one culture.

The house looks like a Lego house of white perfection. A metal trellis fence surrounds her tiny triangular garden plot, where her bloomers and petticoats waft in the wind on a washing line tied between a loquat tree and a forty-year-old olive tree.

Ever since her husband Pepe died, thirty-two years ago, she locks herself in using a hefty brass padlock on the inside of her dark green gate.

I shout 'Casaaaaa' and clap my hands wildly.

'Bruvr!' Reubs jests. 'What you like. Spanish!'

'You try it,' I say. 'Clap your hands and shout "casa". That's Anita's doorbell.'

Anita appears in the doorway, rubbing her eighty-two-year-old hands on her purple pinafore. From the ground up she is wearing slippers, thick beige stockings, chequered woollen skirt, cardigan, blouse and a silk scarf tied in a simple knot around her neck. Her short hair frames her agile little face like polished silver.

'Now, what do we have here? Let's see. Let's see. Oh goodie. My new favourite people. Come in. Come in. Get off the street and come and sit by the fire.'

Taking a key out of her pinafore pocket, she unlocks the padlock and slides open the bolt. I step down into her patio that brims with potted plants and hanging baskets, so perfect in their appearance that I touch one to make sure they're not plastic. Reubs stands behind me, clapping his hands and saying 'Caaassssaaaa' with a wide grin on his face.

'Oh come here, dear boy, and give me two kisses. Give me some of that goodness you have in your bones and make me twenty years younger. People like you make the world a better place.'

'What she say?' Reubs asks.

'That you're adorable, Booba.'

'I am,' he smiles.

Anita looks at me and asks, 'Where is your . . . ?' She doesn't know what to call him.

'He's in London,' I tell her.

'You guys travel more than I have hot dinners. You think nothing of it, catching planes like buses. Now come and sit down with me inside.'

Anita has lived here for almost forty years and used to work in The Corner with her late husband. Her memory is as sharp as the thorn of a prickly pear and she loves to recount the workings of the farm in vivid detail. I will invite her to The

Corner one day in the not-too-distant future and she will wear her best knitted twinset and her string of pearls. She will arrive and see the round wooden table under the fig tree set for tea and proclaim, 'But who do you have coming for tea? The Royal Family?' I will tell her the table is set for her and her eyes will glisten. She will enjoy perhaps a glass too many of sweet orange wine that I bought on a recent visit to the wonderful hilltop town of Vejer de la Frontera in the province of Cádiz, and her emotions will heighten. I will show her the goat farm, the buildings where she used to work with Pepe, and she will cry, struck by the stark memories of those happy years of love and toil.

'Oh, how we worked here!' she will tell me.

She will cry and we will hold her while the tears drop and dry.

As she chatters, she squeezes fresh orange juice and gives us both a full glass. It's cold and delicious. It tastes like a mocktail of sunshine and rain. There is a fly on the table and Anita is nimble with her pink plastic swatter.

'Por San Simón, cada mosca vale un doblón,' she quotes with a lively smile.

'Reubs, we've already had the day of Saint Simon. So one fly is worth two points!'

'¿Que dices?' Anita asks.

'I'm just translating, Anita. Explaining that the flies are on their way out,' I reply, thinking that I could never call her 'Ana'. Anita is a diminutive of Ana, but she is so cute and lovely that Anita suits her like a mitten. To call her Ana would take away from her personality.

Reubs rolls his eyes, tuts and says, 'Spanish,' with such good humour that I hope will never wane.

I translate as much as I can for Reubs, but it's like trying to keep up with a galloping horse. There is so much life packed into Anita's tiny frame that her expression is as dense as espresso coffee – rich and potent and filled with energy. Her tales, told in lyrical, lilting phrases are straight out of a Federico García Lorca play. She is, for me, the embodiment of the Andalusia I love so much. I develop quite a soft spot for her and stop off each time I go into the village, for a natter and a nibble of whatever she puts on the table for me to eat.

When I can squeeze a word in, I explain that Reubs is going to walk to her house every weekday.

'He won't stay long, Anita. But he might have a little rest here with you.'

I explain to Reubs and he does the Makaton sign for orange juice, pretending to squeeze an invisible orange with his fingers. It strikes me as odd because I haven't seen Reuben use Makaton for years. He needed it when he was little but I would never have imagined that he would need it again.

I look around Anita's garage which is where she spends most of her time. A fireplace hugs the corner by the road, a makeshift kitchen snug on the opposite wall and a small rectangular table in the middle. The table is dressed with a tablecloth of spring colours, topped with a transparent plastic cover, making it look like a dried-flower arrangement under glass.

There is nothing surplus to necessity, except perhaps the little line of trinkets and keepsakes along the narrow mantelpiece over the fireplace. On the wall, a calendar from 1988 hangs, opened at May, showing a faded photograph of one of Córdoba's famous patios in bloom.

'I will look forward to this every day of my life,' Anita says as she waves us off. 'Thank you for coming. Thank you for coming. Wait. Wait.' She scurries back into her garage and reappears to press two apples into our palms. 'Go with God. Go with God. And say hello to your . . .'

'Say hello to who?' I urge her.

'To your . . . companion,' she replies. A look passes between us that bridges a generation.

I hug her gently before we head home.

'You see, Reubs?'

'What, bruvr?'

'You can make a real difference to people here. She is lonely and seeing you every day will make her happy,' I tell him.

'Will I?' he asks me as he stops in the middle of the road.

'Yes, brother. You will. Now, get a move on. What does your Fitbit say?'

'Four something.'

'Well, it will say nine something when we get back and you'll have to walk up and down the drive until it hits ten.'

When we reach The Corner, Reubs is about 500 steps off the mark so he frogmarches around the car singing 'When all the saints, come marching in' until his Fitbit vibrates on his wrist. I watch as his face lights up with pride.

As he's laying the table for dinner, I hear him say, 'This is the life, bruvr.'

I hope with all my might that it is.

Over dinner I feel the urge to share something with him, tell him something I haven't told very many people. Here I am, as a grown man, an older brother, taking strength from a brother ten years younger. I wonder whether he will understand, then decide against sharing with him. Some things are on a need-to-know basis. And he certainly doesn't need to know that. Not now and perhaps not ever.

Maybe I am underestimating him. In the eyes of most he is disabled – *labelled* disabled. I see him as one of the most able human beings I have ever met: his ability for grace, his ability for compassion, his ability to trust, his ability for patience, his ability for joy. I see more ability than disability and I hope it is the same for him. My aim, as his big brother, has always been to create a space for him where he can live his life to the best of his ability, not a life that reminds him of his disability *every single day*.

An hour before dark, Maneo appears at the gate, hat in hand, with an earnest smile. I learn later that he is fresh from the psychiatric hospital in Antequera.

'Hola. Buenos tardes. How are you?' he asks me. 'I want to say I'm sorry for the way I treated you and your friend. That was wrong of me and I'm sorry,' he continues. His eyes are fixed on the middle distance and he is sweating profusely.

'That's good of you to say so, Maneo,' I reassure him. 'Thank you for coming. It means a lot. Are you feeling better?'

'Yes, I'm feeling better now. More myself. I am selling my field if you'd like to buy it, for 48,000 euros.'

'Forty-eight thousand euros. That seems like a lot of money, but I'll have a chat with Jack and let you know. You look after yourself now.'

We shake hands and he drives slowly down to the river, through the water and over to the other side, disappearing back into town. His truck barely makes a noise.

In the morning, he appears at the gate again. 'I just wanted to say sorry for the way I treated you. You and your friend,' he tells me.

I look at him carefully and pity him for his complexities. He is struggling to move on. I reassure him that we harbour no ill will and that all is forgiven. His eyes plead with me for reassurance. I search the hard drive of my Bible study days for a phrase that might help release him from his cage of confusion.

'Estamos en paz, Maneo,' comes out of nowhere. 'We are at peace. You don't have anything to worry about.'

There is a flicker of happiness in his dormant gaze as he takes to the wheel and drives towards town. He never comes back, not even when he sells his land. Fortunately for us, our lovely neighbours, Antonio and Esperanza, from further up the hill, buy it. They appear one morning with a wheelbarrow of potatoes and a bag of peppers. We're even closer neighbours now. Surely, peace is assured.

17

LIQUID GOLD

I AM STRUCK WITH A SENSE of timelessness. Time has no place here.

Is it 1889? Can I see Count Cayetano greeting his neighbours who are enjoying their paseo down by the river? Should I tilt my hat? So little has changed here since the house was built that I have these moments of suspended time, like a reverse déjà vu, a tunnelled memory pull. I feel displaced and located in equal measures.

The sun has not altered its path through the sky. On this same day a hundred years ago, the sun appeared at exactly the same spot, just to the left of that craggy outcrop, the slant of its light on its own precise angle. We are merely passing on this perpetual stage, Cayetano and me both, our unpredictable movements set against the constant cycles of nature.

A breeze tickles the yellowing leaves, easing them off the trees. They spiral-dance their way down, finding a space on the ground's new autumnal carpet. This is it. This house. This light. This breeze. This sunlight. This warmth. This silence. This long, quiet day with nothing to do but saunter through its gentle hours. I am at one with the house, this hushed bulk of stone, witness to the birdsong and the slurp of the river as it slips by.

As temperatures begin to plummet, we prepare for what we now know will be a long and bitterly cold winter. We install two wood burners, stockpile two tonnes of logs (a mix of holm oak and olive), buy hot-water bottles, electric oil radiators for all the bedrooms and reinforce our thermal underwear departments. During a stay in London, I visit an outdoor adventure store in Covent Garden and invest in some merino-wool base layers and a polar buff for my neck and head. The cashier looks baffled when, on asking me where I was headed, I reply, 'Spain'.

The olives are ready and so are we. We have all the gear and some idea. Ramón from the village has kitted us out with everything we need: big floppy buckets with handles, poles, nets and a vibrating claw. We have even invested in a shiny new trailer. I ordered it from a company on the outskirts of Seville that makes trailers and horse carriages to supply the Sevillians with the carriages they love to ride in their April Fair. Each time I drive from Málaga to Seville, I feel like I'm driving back in time.

Rafa arrives just before eight o'clock with his son Rafa, Juan Antonio from the village and another guy we end up calling 'Cheesecake' due to his obsession with said dessert. In the presence of these three men, Rafa wraps his arms around me, squeezing all the air out of my lungs and lifts me off the ground.

'You've come a long way in a year,' he says and plants a kiss on my cheek. I grin with deep satisfaction as if my headmaster had just awarded me with a prize for effort.

'Buenos días.'

'Buen día.'

'Buen día.'

'Encantado.'

'Placer.'

'Buenos días.'

We all shake hands and introduce ourselves. There is a formal process to the beginning of any olive harvest. Roles are assigned, responsibility shared.

'Vamos a la faena,' Rafa shouts, commanding the ranks.

It is mid-November and the olives drape from the branches like traffic lights of green, purple and black. A black olive is simply a green olive that has ripened on the tree.

'As they begin to turn from green to purple is the optimum moment for an early harvest of extra virgin olive oil,' Rafa insists. 'If last year's oil was good, this year's is going to be fuera de serie.'

Rafa is a chip off his father's block and works with similar intent. Juan Antonio appears less well humoured, sour-faced, as if he has just smelled something unpleasant.

'Are you going to join us?' I ask Reubs as we head up to the olive grove.

'I will, bruvr. I will,' he replies.

The ground surface is still crisp from the morning's chill. We're a motley crew, trying to find ease with each other as we climb to the very top of the grove. I help lay out the fardos and then stand to attention like a sprinter on the starting line waiting for the gun.

'Vamos a la faena!' I chant as I nod at Juan Antonio. His face cracks into the warmest of smiles and his eyes fill with kindness. As the day progresses, he proves to be a proper comic, cracking jokes every time Rafa stops the machine.

'Doctor, I'd like to have a vasectomy.'

'It's an important decision. Have you spoken it over with your wife and children?.'

'Yes, doctor: seventeen votes in favour, two opposed.'

At eleven o'clock we pause for breakfast. Rafa has an extra bocadillo for the dogs. The valley bowl is warming up now and we can shed coats, hats and scarves. Each person finds their own spot to switch off for ten minutes. I lean against one of the olive trees. Rafa leans back on his elbows. Juan Antonio remains standing, facing the sun. I feel like I am sitting in a painting by Sorolla, each person a few strokes of the impressionist artist's brush. Contentment rises in me like a hot-air balloon. It is fleeting but I feel it, a strange elation.

When we've had just enough rest, Rafa claps his hands and says, 'Señores, these olives are not going to pick themselves. We need to fill the trailer before two o'clock and head off to the mill.'

As we are packing away our picnics and gathering our tools, a figure appears at the bottom of the olive grove, gingerly making their way to greet us. It is none other than Frodo Baggins, carrying a bunch of bananas and a bottle of water, blinking into the morning sunlight.

If last year we were slightly lost, we are now beginning to find ourselves. Home is this, this connection. The fibres of home are neighbours' smiles and offers of help. An invitation to lunch or a handshake on the lane, friends' hugs when they arrive and their tears when they leave. Home happens when those that love you most know you've found it. They don't heap questions of doubt at your door, rather encourage you down that rocky path. When, all of a sudden, you know where you're going. Home is happening, right here.

'Well done, Booba,' I holler. 'Nearly there.'

I hear him say, 'Nnya' as a smile as wide as the valley sweeps across his face.

Part II

18

HOUSESITTERS

WE HAVE COMPLETED ONE FULL cycle.
One lauburu facing left.
One lauburu facing right.

We have lived one year in all its glory. Nature abides by its own invisible rhythms. We apply time and days and months and years in an attempt to understand it. We are but custodians here and when we leave, others will come. We will not affect the constancy of nature. But while we are here, we can learn from its wonders.

This December sunshine warms the skin but not the core. A morning mist clings to the valley floor just long enough to glimpse the sun. The patterns of winter are the same as last year, but they feel different because we are different. There is less an element of surprise and more a feeling of belonging. Anticipating those warmer days that we know will come helps us to endure the cold more easily. From an hour before dawn, all is birdsong.

'Just imagine, Booba,' I tell Reubs over breakfast in the kitchen. Both of us have heavy dressing gowns on and are wearing slippers, the gas heater behind us pumping out fierce heat to keep us warm. 'Not long now and we'll be able to wear just shorts and T-shirts.'

'Well, bit hot I like,' Reubs replies. 'Not very hot.'

'We've got fans now, Reubs. So we can stay cool even in the summer.'

Reubs' favourite job – in fact, I think it's everyone's favourite job – is collecting the eggs every afternoon.

'Three today, bruv,' he said yesterday when he brought them up to the kitchen. 'Not bad.'

We love our eggs fried on a low heat in a glug of our early harvest extra virgin olive oil, served with a toasted mollete and crushed avocado. A mollete is a type of bread baked in Archidona. It's round and dense and floury. One of the bakeries has a delivery service and we recently found out that Roberto, the van driver, is willing to drive all the way out here to sell us fresh molletes every week. As far as I'm concerned, it's a game-changer – the post office won't deliver letters out here, so I have to rent a PO Box at the village post office. On a recent visit to check our PO Box, as I'm leaving, I bump into José Vicente. It's good to see him and we hug warmly. I decide to ask him how he convinced the owners of the riverside part of The Corner to sell to us. His face breaks into a grin he cannot control.

'I told you – you'd have to get me really drunk if you wanted to know,' he reminds me.

'And are you?' I ask.

'Not in the slightest, but do you really want to know?' he dares me.

'Sure,' I reply.

He looks away, swallows and says, 'I told them you're a couple of raving homosexuals and barking mad. And loud. And that you have a guy with Down syndrome who lives with you. And that you have yappy dogs. And that you throw huge parties for weird friends.'

There is a pause before I laugh. For a split second he thinks he's offended me. I see it in his eyes.

We are waiting for the return of the house martins. We know what shade of pink the blossom on the American redbud tree will be. We know that when the clocks go forward in late March it will feel like we're meddling with the underlayer of nature's time, swivelling and rotating our own structure in an attempt to control something that is indomitable.

Just after the frenetic nest-making of the sparrows and house martins, we'll hear the first call of the cuckoo. The Barbary nut iris will be limp by the time the king's spears raise their white spearheads into the air. On the slope leading up to the Pinnacle, they will look like an army formation standing to attention.

We know we'll be able to pack the winter duvets away towards the end of March, after airing them in the morning sunshine that pours into the lemon-tree patio. The young fruit trees will need 10 litres of water a week, at least until the April rains come. We know the chickens will start to lay more eggs than we can eat and Reuben can start to take a few a week to Anita. She will try to give him something in return, anything, sometimes a muffin, sometimes an apple, sometimes a pear. She is used to the old system of trueque (exchange), when neighbours in the countryside exchanged a surplus batch of fruit or vegetables for something different. Old habits die hard.

As my busy guiding season looms, the perennial question: Can we find trustworthy volunteers who are able to help us look after Reubs and The Corner? I trawl the volunteering website looking for suitable candidates and line up a steady stream of people for the year. It's far from ideal, but what am I supposed to do?

We find diamonds in the rough, it's true; but they are rare. I seem to draw a series of short straws and the line-up of our volunteers looks like something out of the film, *The Usual Suspects.*

A young man from Austria arrives, wracked by guilt because he is refusing to step into the family business. He comes here running away from his parents' expectations. He's on anti-depressants and breaks the driver's door handle off Poppy in a moment of rage. We are never able to replace it as she is so old. Long after he has gone, I remember him each time I drive Poppy.

An army veteran from France arrives who suffers from PTSD after serving two tours in Iraq. He spends a lot of time up by the alberca doing push-ups and squats. He is kind and strong and tortured.

A guy from Liverpool arrives who is sweet-natured but has to leave because he can't sleep. He says it's too quiet here.

'You sure can pick 'em,' jests Jack.

And all the time, Reuben latches onto these people, hoping they will be his friends.

A lady from Germany arrives, fresh from the pilgrimage route of the Way of Saint James. Unwittingly, she brings bedbugs with her and we spend a terrible few weeks trying to get rid of them. I still itch and scratch at the thought of it. We have to call a specialist from Málaga and burn all the fabric divans. Plagued by perfectionist obsessions, the lady refuses to take responsibility, and complains that there are no hand towels in her bathroom and leaves.

A lass from North Yorkshire arrives, escaping an abusive relationship, and we hear her being bullied on the telephone at all hours of the day and night. She has a kind of breakdown and sits by the log burner rocking in a chair. I drop her off at Málaga airport and she returns to a friend's house to try and unpick herself from the guy's abuse.

A Croatian didgeridoo player arrives who cannot talk. He can only shout. He is blind in one eye from being bottled at a Full Moon party in Thailand where he got off with some other guy's girlfriend. He eats standing up and follows his food to his mouth with his good eye. None of the other volunteers can bear to share a house with him so I have to pay him to leave. He spends the money on cocaine and goes on a two-day binge in the village. He calls me. I find him destitute in a doorway and he asks for more money. I consider giving him another 200 Euros just to get him on his feet but know that I have to be cruel to be kind and simply walk away.

I feel exhausted by other people's problems that they bring across the river. And all the time, I'm guiding five days a week, returning to The Corner, hoping to find house and home and Reuben intact. He seems to be bearing up well. Tick sheets give an order to his day and I try to make sure whoever is next door is including him as much as possible in their meals and routines.

A family from Finland arrives with two unschooled children. The father explains, 'We don't teach them anything unless they ask. So it is an education fuelled by interest and curiosity.' One day I find the two boys playing with knives in the barn and, when I go looking for their parents, I find the mother sitting behind an olive tree, high as a kite, staring into an abyss that exists only in her mind. I drop them off at the local bus station.

I am exhausted. I prepare an uninspired picoteo (selection of nibbles) of olives, breadsticks, jamón ibérico, cheese and pâté. The table under the fig tree is filthy with bird poop and fallen leaves.

'Hang on, Reubs. Don't put anything down yet. I'll run in and get a cloth.'

When I return from the kitchen, he is standing there with nothing but patience. I badly want to talk to him about everything but can't seem to find the words.

'You alright, bruv?' he asks me after several minutes of silence.

'Not really no,' I reply.

He immediately stops what he's doing and rounds the table to give me a hug. 'Come here, bruvr.'

His gentle caress is everything I need and more. It sets me on a different mental path and helps me to swing my mood.

'It's hard, Booba.' I tell him. 'I've had enough of takers. We're having a bad run.'

'I'm fine,' he says as he nibbles on an olive. 'I got you. That's why.'

I could eat him. 'Sorry I can't be here more. I have to work, Booba. Samwise will be back at the weekend and then we'll all be together again for a few weeks.'

'My boys,' he smiles. 'Miss my Samwise Sam, I do.'

Life seems so simple when I'm nibbling olives with Reubs under a fig tree as the sun sets over Topknot. There's something so unwavering about Reubs that calms me down.

But once he's in bed and I've kissed him goodnight, sleep stays far away. I meander in my mind, looking for solutions. Have we bitten off more than we can chew? Is this dream attainable? Sustainable? There are moments of delicious alignment to be sure. But do the benefits outweigh the problems? Accomplishing dreams is about staving off doubt, but doubt is knocking heavily on my door this evening. How the hell did we end up with a sprawling farmhouse that is falling down around our ears, with hectares and hectares of wild land that refuses to be tamed? Has it all been a form of twisted trickery?

We don't have the resources. We don't have the money. We don't have the time. What were we thinking?

Most days I remain on top of the challenges as I deal with only the most critical of problems: leaks, broken windows, snapped taps, fences pushed down by wild boar, dead chickens in the coop, lost dogs, rats in the kitchen, birds in the chimneys. Tonight, the to-do list swirls in my head and I can't make it stop.

I hear Jack's words: 'Stop making work for yourself.'

A door is banging. It is probably the side entrance to the barn. We have to wedge it shut with a big metal drum and someone must have moved it. I should find a torch and wander down to close it but I'll disturb the dogs. They'll bark and wake Reubs up. And so I stay, the weight of worry pushing my head into the pillow.

I know from experience that sleep, if it does not come quickly, will evade me for several hours now, so I get up to make a cup of tea. I poke my head around Reuben's bedroom door to watch him sleeping for a few moments. There he is; at peace, surrounded by his posters of Whoopi Goldberg, his James Bond memorabilia, his signed photo of John Partridge propped up on his bedside table. He demands so little and yet I want to give him more than I have ever wanted to give anyone. His innocence demands that. I only want to give him what he deserves. What of his dreams? Have I cut him off too much from a world he can relate to? I sigh as quietly as I am able before I tiptoe to the kitchen to boil the kettle.

What is it about this kitchen that screams Spain? Is it the spice rack filled to brimming with tiny tins emblazoned with

1970s font styles in primary colours? Perhaps it is the paella pans and cast-iron pots hanging haphazardly from the hooks on the wall. The exposed gas water heater in the corner communicates function over form and the tiny wooden chairs upholstered in a thick-weave red-and-yellow cloth look as if they've been pinched from the local flamenco tablao (live flamenco venue). Could it be the metal draining cupboard hung centrally over the tiny stainless-steel sink? Surely, the 5-litre bottle of olive oil in the corner kind of gives it away. I could be in no other country than Spain.

I do love it here, in this land of vast landscapes with its complex past. It still makes me tick, this country of light and laughter. It saddens me that I seem to be losing both. I try not to brood as the tea brews, but how am I supposed to deny that I feel cut off from my dream while being in the middle of it? It's all around me but I cannot reach it.

I am travelling with clients and Samwise Gamgee is in London. Spring is unseasonably busy and Frodo is at The Corner by himself. Well, not by himself. He is with Jordi and Leti, volunteers from Salamanca, who arrived a few days ago. I assume he is fine. I hope he is. I barely have time to worry as I guide people around Spain, all with their own needs and challenges. It's funny how guiding requires so much psychology. I have a tricky season guiding feuding families and couples that don't seem to want to talk to each other. There are so many people who appear to be happy, but I suspect that their repeated exclamations of 'We're so lucky' are piled high on unhappiness. Perhaps this trip to Andalusia is their own escape from a miserable life back home.

But I don't want to be morose. I have a laugh when I'm guiding. I act the clown and fool around. I am light-hearted and personal. I figure if I tell them titbits of personal information, they will eventually open up. I call my nine-seater van the 'Grand Confessional' and attempt to get people to talk. Their banter eats the kilometres up on the long drives between Seville, Córdoba, Ronda and Málaga. You'd be surprised what people tell me while speaking to the back of my head, as I drive them through the olive groves of my beloved Andalusia.

They often ask me if I am married.

'I have a partner but we're not married.'

'Oh and what does she do?'

'He . . . has a communications agency in London.'

That always precludes a moment of quiet from the back seat. By the length of the silence, I can gauge how well we are going to get along . . . or not.

An awful feeling invades me when I get a phone call from Debs. She is on her way to The Corner. Reuben has sent her a message: I. lonely. can. you. come. get. Me.

Reuben never asks for anything. At least he rarely has until now. By the time I get home, I am already angry.

Jordi and Leti cry when I challenge them. Crocodile tears. They were 'yes, yes, yes!' to my face, but now I find out that they are lazy 'no' people hiding behind convincing smiles. I sense that we have begun to lose Reuben, this shift being so unlike him. I know him. He wouldn't cry for help unless he was desperate.

I want them out of the house. I don't want their apologies or their promises to make up for it. The damage is done. Debs says Reuben is really quiet, as if he's retreated into himself.

'But don't you worry,' she tells me convincingly. 'I'll soon get him whipped into shape. We're going out for a bit of dinner and a little trolley around the bars. He'll like that.'

'Thank you, Debs. Maybe keep Reubs with you for a few days to get him plugged back in.'

The sense of betrayal stings, but then so does my sense of guilt. When I ask them to leave, Jordi pushes back and starts laying claim to the house through old established tenancy laws. He even says the farm vehicle, Poppy, is theirs.

'This is our home. We live here now and by the same means, Poppy is our car.' He starts quoting Spanish law. I see red. I can feel the outer skin on my body swell up with heat and panic. We have been duped. I feel unprotected and a dereliction of duty stares me in the face, but I have no recourse. My belief in the volunteering scheme finally shatters. Standing before me are two stowaways, catching a passage on a foreign vessel for a few months and now staging a mutiny. I find it hard to contain my rage. I tell them they need to pack their belongings and leave.

'We can't. We have nowhere to go. And we don't have any money to get there anyway.'

'Not my problem. You need to go and *now*!'

I hate getting this angry. I can feel the very tissue of me curdle and crystalise with pulses of ire. This is not a feeling I am comfortable with. I know it will take me a long time to undo these knots.

We hedged a bet with these two. We risked exposing the sanctuary of our home to characters that should never come under our wing of trust.

I rent them a friend's apartment in the village until they can find a way to get back to their home city. They trash the apartment and I have to pay double cleaning bills. I pay happily as I am simply glad to see them leave. I will write furious emails to the management of the volunteering scheme and they will all remain ignored or never even acknowledged.

When Debs drops Reuben home, I rush to the real heart of the matter and hug him as tightly as he lets me.

'My dear darling brother. You alright? Were you lonely, babes?'

He looks up at me and his tongue curls around his lips as he formulates the words, 'Just a bit, bruvr. That's all. I'm here now anyway.'

I'm hoping Debs got to him in time, before he began to cave in. He's a brave brother but there is only so much loneliness one can bear.

After dinner I find Reubs on his bed, colouring in a big red heart.

'What you doing, Reubs?'

'Hello, bruvr. Colouring heart for you.'

'Reubs, did anything happen when I was away?'

He looks at me with those soft hazel eyes. 'No, brother. Not much.'

'No, I mean before. With the guys next door. Were they horrible to you?'

He looks at his stone lion that sits on his windowsill and says, 'No.'

'Look at me, brother. It's fine if they were. You're not going to get into any kind of trouble. I just need to know. Did they do anything horrible to you?'

Keeping my gaze, he emphatically replies, 'No, bruvr.'

'Did they ignore you?'

'Well, a bit yeah. They talk that Spanish thing.'

'Did they chat with you at meals and things?'

'Well . . . .'

'What, Reubs?' I urge him.

'Well. Meals here,' he says, pointing to the bed.

'What? You ate here? By yourself?' I try to keep my voice calm for him, even though the rage is sweeping back.

'Well. Yeah, bruvr. Here.'

The truth will out. They brought Reuben's meals around to him on a tray. Meals on wheels. No chit-chat, no support, no friendship, no entertainment, no structure, no communion – all aspects of the volunteering profile description that they had accepted and promised to abide by. Surely, we can find better humans than that?

When Joe, a new volunteer, arrived I was convinced we'd found one. His smile was a breath of fresh air.

19

THE STORM

A STORM ANNOUNCES ITS APPROACH WITH a menacing, ever-darkening sky. Light barely filters through the dense leaden clouds. The birds stop singing. Each tiny sparrow, finch, house martin and warbler urges its wings to take it to a place of safety. I've often wondered where they go. Do they hide in a tree, a cave, inside a chimney or perhaps in one of the back barns? I wonder whether they observe the storm just like we do, with the same wonder and trepidation. The air pressure rises outside at the precise hour that the weather forecast had predicted. The storm is here, brewing above the house.

Frodo looks through the windowpane, wishing his brother was here, waiting for the first flash of lightning.

'Not yet. Not yet,' he says to himself softly. 'Where's my Samwise Gamgee? Where's my bruvr? Am fine. Am brave. Can't find my Saruman staff.'

Don't look away. There he is. Zeus unleashes a sheet of

lightning so vivid and vast that the entire sky lights up like a strobe. While the effect is still blinding the backs of Reuben's eyes with clusters of bright, white spots, thunder shakes the house. Everything trembles, from the foundations, up the walls and through the roof in a single thud of fury. It's as if Zeus has picked up the entire building with one hand and thrown it to the heavens, so close is his power, so ominous his strength. Reuben becomes part of the tremble, part of the storm.

There is a flash-strike of sound, so loud, unlike anything Reuben has ever heard before, that it almost shatters the insides of him.

He stands motionless awaiting a second hit. It comes but with far less intensity, so does a third with even less, and then there is a void where the storm moves on upriver. A mountain giant crashing his way to the Final Fence and beyond, waving a gigantic torch in his hand, piercing the night with its powerful beam before he takes his next tremendous leap.

The storm has passed but the storm inside Reuben rages on. He cannot sleep. He cannot stop the quake. He calls Mum, but Mum is fast asleep next to Dad in their small double bed, in their small bedroom, in their small bungalow, out by the airport on the outskirts of the city of Norwich. Samwise Gamgee is in London. Gandalf the Grey is in Seville. The new volunteers are over on the other side of the house, sound asleep. Of all days to be alone.

20

THE BREAKDOWN

Reubs gradually retreats into a sense of solitude, spending more time in his room and less time with people. Being social has always been second nature to him, but now he struggles to mingle.

He develops traits of obsessive behaviour, always looking to the sky and wondering about the weather, checking both the time and the temperature on his phone. Eating had always been a cause for celebration in his life, but now he is afflicted with stress and worry.

'Will this make me good sleep, bruvr? This good for me? Can I eat this?'

We begin to detect the signs of an eating disorder. He develops gout but doesn't know how to communicate the pain, so it lies undetected for weeks. One day I look down and notice his big toe nail as black as tar.

'Oh, Booba. My darling, why didn't you tell me?'

'I know, bruvr. Odd,' he replies.

'Is it painful?'

'So painful, bruvr,' he replies and makes the noise of pain. 'Uufff.'

Reuben had been so capable and independent that maybe I had relaxed too much. Something in him has changed and when I am home, I scramble around to make sure he has structure for the days ahead. We start making to-do lists with boxes to tick once he has completed a task. I try to give his days shape so he doesn't lose the shape of himself.

There are weekends of brotherly hugs, dinners and watching DVDs, but when I leave for another trip, Reuben remains alone on our side of the house with support from next door. It's not ideal. I know it's not ideal, but for the meantime it's the best we can do. I am in the middle of my busiest tourism season ever and work takes me all over the country guiding groups and families through 'the Spain they never knew'. Reubs is sliding into a depression but we don't realise it until it's too late. He stares it in the face with bravery and courage, willing himself through every day, until finally he caves in.

It is an extremely hot day and we are taking a walk in the sun. He overheats. His heart starts to beat faster than normal. He is on the brink of an existential crisis, this boy, my brother with Down syndrome, trying to make sense of his world. It is coming and he can no longer fend it off. He looks at me and says, 'Brother, I don't want to die' and then physically collapses in a heap. We hold him as he cries. We wipe his tears, but the damage is done. He is broken – a part of him has just caved in. The storm brought a new fear.

To be floored by depression is to be caught in a sticky cobweb with so many layers of despair. Understanding how you got there is intrinsic to recovery. Logic plays a huge role, as does discipline, routine, love, patience and will power. Reuben has an incredibly deep emotional intelligence, but it is instinctive rather than academic. His grasp on life is limited and unwittingly, we have always perpetuated that, extenuating his existence in the no man's land of reality and fantasy. This is different. He has no handholds in this new place of darkness.

We all return to the UK to celebrate Mum and Dad's 50th wedding anniversary. Reubs has an act to perform. He has been practising for weeks, reciting a poem from *The Lion, the Witch and the Wardrobe* about Aslan being on the move and the arrival of spring. There is no performance. Reubs refuses to take to the stage and seems to fall further away from us. It is a hard decision to make but we agree he should not return to Spain with us and, as a temporary measure, he stays with Mum and Dad in Norwich. When he feels better, we'll bring him back to The Corner. Hopefully, it won't be long.

The house begs to have Reubs back. His room screams silence every time I walk past. The shape of him now an empty space. I tousle with my feelings of guilt. I left Reubs for long periods of time to fend for himself, assuming he was strong and self-assured enough. I didn't realise how fragile he was – none of us did.

The Corner echoes with his absence. I try to separate the individual layers of silence to hear the memory of his voice, of his giggle. But there is nothing. I had no idea silence could be so loud.

Where there was abundant life, now the house feels quiet. He has become one of the Silent Ones. Fear has come to nest inside him and we will need to dismantle its resting place, twig by tiny twig, to ease it from him.

His room is emptied of his spirit. I hear the echo of his sweet words, his rounded pronunciation which makes every spoken word so *Reuben*. I can hear his furry slippers slide along the tiles in the corridor, the peaceful flow of his movements, his t'ai-chi lifestyle. It is not just him I miss, but the way he makes me feel. I realise that I am not me without him – or at least, less the person I want to be.

21

A WILD NIGHT

M Y OLD TWO-MAN TENT WHICH I bought when I went Interrailing is still in immaculate condition. I find a sleeping mat and an inflatable camping pillow and begin to pack my rucksack. I feel like I am seventeen again, walking out of the house with everything I need for the next twenty-four hours, on my back a colossal rucksack, on my face a wide smile.

'Have a wild night, my darling,' Jack says as he hugs me tightly. ' I will miss you.'

As I walk to the river to head upstream, I imagine Frodo and Samwise high-fiving each other and celebrating the fact that they can have a Hobbit Night, without the wizard. If only Reubs was still here.

The only dog that accompanies me the whole way is Duna, the diligent guardian, committed to keeping us safe. The ascent up to Topknot is more arduous than normal as I am weighed down by camera, telescope, tripod, notebook, food and water. Not just for me, also for the dogs, in case they decide to visit me. The June sun is still high in the sky and beats down on me with a perpetual glare. There is no shade to rest under, only tall grasses that spike through my hiking shoes and socks, finding flesh to dig into with their twisty needle-like stalks. Duna follows me at a distance, joining me on the summit for a celebratory cuddle.

The last view of the house tucked into the corner of the valley floor falls away from view. I sigh as I turn around and head into the wild. I walk the crest of the hill and stare in wonder at the valley beyond. My dad calls it 'The closest I've ever been to the Garden of Eden.' A hobbit might call it Middle Earth. My mother calls it 'Never again!'. It was tough but by guiding, holding, helping and encouraging, with several rests, I did once make it out here with Mum. I needed her to see it – my thin place.

I stand in awe as a rare sense of satisfaction seeps through my veins. Just as swiftly, that negative pull creeps up on me again, catching me unaware. I stand still, catching my breath.

I brush against a sense of peace but as soon as it embraces me, there is a tug on it, from a deeper place, and I am left in the balance of a battle of good and bad. Dread meets dreams. My future meets my past. And me, I am here, held in a vacuum, in a void, in a state of zero emotional gravity, only vaguely present, as a quiet panic begins to fill me from the inside out. I can feel the level rising and I react quickly to snap myself out of my drowning subconscious.

As I move away from the luring of the mysterious darkness that calls my name, there it is, a tangible sensation of vertigo. It's like reaching the end of an emotional bungee jump as the power of the taut elasticated rope retrieves me from colliding with the hard ground and pulls me back to safety. I take in air quickly and expel it to shun the feeling.

When I was younger, this feeling used to grip me for longer periods of time. I remember feeling terrified, in that green wallpapered bedroom, under the eaves of our red-brick terraced house of my childhood. At night, I would push fingertip depressions down into the softness of the polystyrene underroll. I grappled in the dark with an invisible enemy that sought to tip me off kilter. I never gave it a name. It was only a vague dusty cloud. It just came back to me. I haven't heard it for years. The voice of my little ruins. A ghost-like, ill-timed whisper that lasts longer than it sounds, like a branch of leaves dragged through cooling ash, hushed and terrifying. There. I can hear it, a faint memory slithered through a vortex of fear. It pulls me into that place, where my childhood faced my future.

Nowadays, it rarely visits me and when it does, I square up to the threat and ask it to leave. I will never let it in. I will never let it rob me of moments of happiness. I stand there, defiant, like that little boy back in the attic, but this time, my attic is a mountain top with no walls to hem me in and nothing that can keep me from the force of exhilaration. It leaves me and my soul settles back into its cradle.

I know I've looked for happiness in all the wrong places: in dark clubs, rather than around dinner tables; in acts of anonymous pleasure rather than a coffee with a friend. Dark for light. The unknown for the known. The pitfalls of searching for happiness where it is seldom found. Now, in my life, I try to let light lead me. Light from the sun, light from a candle, light from the moon. I shun the darkness. It has gripped me several times and I now know how to read the signs and attempt to cancel out its pull on my soul. I recognise when I need nature's healing and today is one of those days.

I hike over to the flat patch of land that I had in mind for my overnight camp and begin to pitch my tent. I am sheltered from the setting sun to my west by an acebuche – a wild olive tree – and buffered from the wind by an outcrop of rocks behind it. The land welcomes me into its contours. I am enjoying my own company.

It has been at least ten years since I last pitched my tent. As its contents spill from the bag, memories of Andorra, Aix-en-Provence, Barcelona, Toledo, Austria, Glastonbury come flooding back and before I know it, working through the memories, she is up in all her North Face glory. Some pegs are missing and others are bent beyond usefulness, but I pin her down as best as I am able and then stand to admire the scene. I look around for Duna, but she has left me. Hugely intuitive that dog, as if she knew that I needed to be completely alone. I sit and stare southwards as the last rays of sun wane from the valley floor.

I write. I think. I stare. I bask in the sun until it dips out of sight. Nature is charging me and I happily store what it is willing to offer.

I hear her before I see her. A slight splice of the air above my head, featherlight, and a fleeting shadow at my feet. I look up and see her glide, impossibly close, majestic in her wing-spanned wonder. I am drawn into her dominion and hold as still as I can, contracting breath and muscle. She, a golden eagle, finds lift over the Pinnacle, dips down towards the river and then swoops up and over the ridge and disappears behind Midday Peak. I can no longer see her but she is still here. I cannot blink. I cannot breathe. I am struck down by beauty and the only thing I can do is giggle. There is no other reaction, no words, no one to share this with as I blow up my inflatable pillow and lay out my sleeping bag before darkness sets in.

The moon begins to heave itself over the eastern ridge. I bask in its shine for a while. Just as I think this place has expelled all of its magic, the eagle glides in front of its white light. The image imprints on some deep part of me.

In the morning, I sit and watch the colours change as the sun rises. From dull greys and blacks, through to purples and blues and finally to the blaze of yellow and green. My hunger is the only reason I want to leave. I need to linger here. How can this place be so right for us, but so wrong for Reubs? It seems that all our steps here were guided. Every decision had been so natural and we made them with unforced judgement. In the beginning, there was so little doubt.

How can everything feel so wrong when everything felt so right mere months ago? Samwise and Gandalf the Grey miss their Frodo. Jack has lost his hobbit. I have lost my brother. I am the same. Jack is the same. The Corner is the same. It is only Frodo that has changed, an internal landslide altering his landscape and ours. Only now is it beginning to sink in how much of a trilogy we are. For each of us, there are two other reference points. Jack and I have each other, but who will be Reuben's reference point now? I miss him, my little Boobalish.

Showing Reuben a way out of his web of sadness proves to be the most difficult process any of us have ever experienced.

Mum and Dad are now sole carers for him, but nothing they try seems to have any effect. When I take a trip back to Norwich to see him, I try tough love but that doesn't work either. He takes two whole hours to get from his bed to the breakfast table. He is regressing in his speech and his movement as if he is forgetting himself. At times he uses a wheelchair, unable or unwilling to walk, hiding from the world behind a large, brimmed cap and a thick scarf and an inflated travel pillow wrapped around his neck. We are running the gauntlet of medical tests to see if there is any physical problem. Surely we can get to the bottom of it.

Friends who haven't seen him for a while assume he is play-acting the role of a grandfather. But no, he is not acting.

This is very real. He begins to sink into emotional quicksand. Before our very eyes, he falls ever more silent and out of reach.

Jack steps into the gap. He is a man that has always put his money where his mouth is so he decides to take charge and moves Frodo Baggins down to London. The two of them fall into a routine that seems to work. Tuesdays, Wednesdays and Thursdays in London and then the long weekends in Jack's cottage in Dorset. Jack is finding creative ways to prop Reuben up and help him to regain his confidence. Private care handles his daily needs for two days a week but the quality of the care is poor and expensive.

On Wednesdays, Jack and Reubs go into the office together. Reubs has his own desk where he spends the day colouring in and making cards for people.

'All vital work, Frodo Baggins,' Jack tells him in a serious tone. 'Make sure you finish that drawing today as the success of the company depends on it.'

Reubs smiles and mouths something.

'Sorry. What was that, my Frodo?' Jack insists.

Reubs just manages a mutter. 'You like Wolf of Wall Street, Samwise Gamgee.'

Reubs takes a shine to a couple of the young guys in the office, and they take it in turns to take him out for lunch either at Pret or Leon around the corner. People are getting to know him and greet him on the stairs. Jack says his smile is beginning to return. It's such a huge relief and I am proud of Jack and so grateful for his sacrifice.

'Of course!' he replies when I thank him. 'I have to get him back. He's my Frodo!'

But we all know this situation is not sustainable, neither financially nor emotionally. Reubs is beginning to get better, but every day still requires a huge amount of effort and energy. He needs constant care and it's draining. I can see the strain beginning to show on Jack's face.

22

JOE

In the bark of a tree
My love scored her name.
The tree was so sensitive
That it died of pain.

Count Cayetano de Alvear, Cantares

TODAY WAS A BAD DAY. A bad, bad day.

I feel like I need one hundred years of solitude to process this. There is no breath in me. Jack is in London fighting a different battle that is not really his to fight. Reubs has taken a turn for the worse. Jack feels as if I have dropped the ball on Reuben's recovery and he is probably right. He's seldom wrong. But how can I split myself even further? I feel chasmed. My boys have to come first. I need to try and adjust my focus and concentrate on Jack and Reuben's needs. They need me.

But Joe's mum and dad arrived this afternoon with their two living children. They were the parents of three. Joe – one of our volunteers – had two brothers. Who needs me more today? Jack or them? Jack has reached the end of his emotional tether. I do not know what that feels like yet, but in time I will. In the future I will understand, but right here, right now, I do not know how he is feeling. I do not know how isolated he finds himself. I do not know the depths of his despair or the strength of his love for Reubs. He must add anger to his list of emotions because I cannot fathom what he needs from me.

Here I have a mother staring up at me from an abyss of agony, pleading with me to help her understand. I have a father numbed with disbelief. I have two beautiful brothers whose legs suddenly give way. They fall to the floor bellowing like wild deer. They stare into the empty space of their shock. We have all lost someone who was important to us.

What happened this morning has left me detached from myself. I have spent the day trying to remind myself who I am. I can only imagine how they feel. I can only make cups of tea and pass them tissues.

The Corner is giving us the very best and the very worst of life. The best lies within. The worst invades from outside. Are we always bound to be stretched to the extremes of life? Can we not find an even keel?

As much as it hurts me, I must let my boys go, just for a while and simply hope that one day they will understand and forgive me. My spirit is pierced.

191

Fernando, my friend from the coast, is here within an hour and he has taken control. I am so grateful for his clear head. He makes sense and can think logically when all I can do is cry and smoke and sigh and cry. Friends from the village have opened their hotel for the family. I would have scrambled to find a focus. Their goodness has kicked in and they are offering Joe's broken family a safe place to lay the horrors of today.

At a time when words are useless, we resort to gestures. The silence isn't uncomfortable. It is the only option. We may as well be inside a cathedral built with blocks of pain, the quietest of noises echoing down the empty nave of this family's suffering. We are all suspended in an emotional vacuum. I feel weightless. They must feel infinitely further away.

I knew him. They loved him.

He lived in our house. His mum gave birth to him.

I was his friend not his father.

He was not my brother.

We are all dust. We sit and hope that the particles of ourselves will eventually settle and we will know what to say or do. Fernando puts the kettle on for another round of tea. I thank him with my eyes for I cannot speak. I try my hardest not to picture the scene.

Joe had applied to work with us as a volunteer. The tone of his message was upbeat and detailed. He seemed honest and credible. He needed a change, having spent months looking after a grandfather who needed palliative care. This seemed admirable. On video I saw a smiling young man, heavily tattooed with green, blue and red ink defining his arms. He wore a white Lacoste polo shirt and I noticed that all three buttons were fastened. Joe answered his own questions and hardly needed a prompt to steer the conversation. He spoke in a jolly staccato and had a flip-top laugh.

Joe arrived early one February morning. The drive out to Antequera's bus station was picture-perfect with long-reaching views through the chilly mountain air into the agricultural plains and beyond to the winter blue horizons. Driving past Old Man Mountain at first light is always a mystical experience. The soft light holds him in delicate slumber but when all is quiet, I half-expect him to open his eyes and burst out of the earth's crust.

'You know about my tats, don't you?' he asked as he rolled up his sleeves to reveal intricate tattoo sleeves of bold colours, emblazoned with personal emblems and symbols.

His thin body had become his canvas for tattoo art. He talked about them as a soldier might his battle scars. There were two new ones on his neck, perhaps the boldest of all, multicoloured wings that reached up out of his polo shirt and up to his jaw line.

'These are quite daring. Kind of "no going back" kind of thing. I didn't have these when I spoke to you on the camera, like,' he said, pointing to his wings.

Using *like* at the end of his sentences betrayed the months he'd spent in Liverpool over the years, a city I have never been to. His attire was arranged carefully, buttons either done up or left loose but neither by accident. He was enormously proud of a brand-new pair of Adidas. I warned him that they weren't very farm-friendly and would get ruined by dog walks and brambles. I looked at his face. Handsome. Photogenic. I found his chatty nature refreshing, and his attitude to work and routine seemed honest. His northern accent charmed me back into my childhood memories in Yorkshire.

With each new volunteer, I know there is a revealing moment when we drive over the river to our private hideaway. Crossing the river is a physical and symbolic step into our sanctuary. When I drove Joe over that river divide, the routine feelings of doubt and concern invaded me. Would he understand us? Would he live and let live? Would he take stress away or add to it?

He took to the work with dedication and optimism. We gave him clear instructions and he took to each new task with fresh energy. His first job was to paint the brand-new back gate gun-metal grey. March was cold this year but he didn't complain. He worked in his Adidas tracksuit bottoms, wellies and layers of warm clothes that he had found about the house, white gardening gloves and a straw hat that he borrowed from the scarecrow each morning. His white earphones, connected to his phone in his hip pocket, were a constant feature. I regret never asking him what he was listening to.

'Morning, Joe,' I called, waving my hands.

He popped his earphones out. 'Morning, mate. Alright? Yeah, it's good. I'm good thanks. It's alright, innit? Am I doing an alright job? Arxi is helping me out.' Arxi remained by Joe's side throughout the day.

Joe decided to stop smoking. It seemed like a sensible decision and not uncommon at The Corner for volunteers to quit something or take up something new. It's the kind of place that inspires people to change direction. It's the river again, creating a physical barrier that isolates people from their pasts, gives them an opportunity to clarify their priorities and reboot before crossing back over into the world at large. Time stands still here: hours turn into days, weeks, seasons and years. All is marked by nature's pace as the seasons orchestrate symphonies of colour, heat, cold, rain, wind. Exposed to the elements, it's a sink-or-swim situation. Joe looked as if he was going to be one of the ones that swam.

We took a walk together and he confided in me. It was a clear attempt to bond. He confessed to having bouts of mental-health issues. Walking with someone is an easy way into the sphere of honesty as you are both moving, and the movement eases not only speech but understanding. Eye contact is optional.

'Thanks for telling me, Joe,' I reassured him. 'I appreciate that. We all have battles and they're better out than in.' As we walked, I remained silent to let him talk. Silence was uncomfortable for him, so he preferred to fill it with words or with music. He spoke of his family and how much he would love it if they could visit him at The Corner. I wondered how much of the truth he was telling me.

At The Corner, everyone gets two days off each week. For his first break, Joe took off to see a friend in a neighbouring town.

'It's alright though as he doesn't drink, so we'll just chill.' Joe filled in his own gaps.

The first time I truly understood the extent of his addiction was on an arrival day for more volunteers. These two arrived in matching BMWs, with the contents of each car organised into plastic crates and tidy suitcases. They were charming and embodied the true spirit of the volunteering scheme. We took them out for a welcome lunch. Joe began to drink beer and a smile appeared that I had never seen before. After the meal, he wanted to stay in town. Jack had already grasped the situation, but assumed that Joe was old enough to make his own decisions. Joe arrived back long after we'd all gone to bed.

'What happened, buddy?' I asked him the following morning as he made his late appearance.

He looked away. His voice was a whole octave deeper than usual. 'Oh, you know. Got a little happy. Stayed for a few rum and cokes. I can't believe how strong they make them here. It's mad.'

'How did you get home?' The village is 4 km away.

'No idea. I must have walked, I suppose.' He laughed. I did not.

Joe's first proper walkabout lasted three days. He went to visit the friend who didn't drink. His two days off turned into three. He arrived and scuttled up to his room to sleep off whatever he had imbibed. There was no apology, no explanation. We had words. He assured me it would not happen again.

'We just went a bit mad.' He laughed. I did not.

Joe's second walkabout lasted over four days. He went to Málaga and got himself into a four-day bender. I located him through the hostel he had been staying at, as I had recommended it.

'Joe, the Irish guy?' said the hostel receptionist. 'The one with all the tattoos? He was staying here but he's lost everything. Told us he got robbed. He's in a bad way.'

This time, we had to carry out a full rescue mission to get him back. Jack came back for a long weekend as Reubs was spending a few days with my parents. It was so good to have Jack back for a few days, a problem halved and all that.

'Why am I approaching this whole situation as if Joe were my son? Why am I losing sleep over someone I barely know?' I asked Jack.

'Because you care, Manni. Maybe too much. That's your problem. He is your problem now.' Home truths hurt.

As Joe stepped off the bus, his shoulders hung with shame. He was the prodigal son, but I was not his forgiving father. He needed a warm embrace.

'I think it's best if we get you home and we talk about this in the morning, don't you?' I chastised.

'I'm sorry, mate. I'm so sorry. I really am. I feel awful.'

I let him stew. I did not see the tears, but I saw the hand that wiped them. As we drove in the darkness, Old Man Mountain was witness to our every move, his ancient wisdom hiding in the peaks and troughs of his profile. He has witnessed centuries of humanity and remains unchanged. Eyes to the heavens, ears to the horizons, he hears every word. By the time we arrived home, I had softened and urged Joe to get some rest.

Jack does not suffer fools. We sat around the round wooden table the following morning underneath the fig tree. It felt fittingly formal. Joe fiddled with the cable of his earphones and fidgeted in his chair. Jack made eye contact.

'What happened, Joe?' Jack asked.

'I just lost it. It all got out of hand. I am sorry. I really am.'

My emotions sat like a boulder on the empty table.

Joe added, 'It won't happen again.'

'Too fucking right, it won't happen again.' Jack was angry now. I hate seeing him angry. 'Who do you think you are, treating us like that? You've been away for five days and Manni's been worried sick.'

'I know. It's a shocker. But please don't ask me to leave.'

Jack and I looked at each other. I could not call it. Jack took the slack.

'You can stay, Joe,' Jack told him. 'But this cannot happen again. You know that, don't you?'

'Yeah, I understand.' And with that he scratched off over the gravel, a scolded child.

'Oh god, I feel awful,' I said.

'You're too soft, Manni.' Jack told me. I have seen him do it to other people, but he rarely does it with me. I decided I would go and walk the dogs with Joe.

His mood seemed leaden. *How hollow he must feel*, I thought. *An empty tattooed shell*. The dogs scrambled through the tall grasses as we climbed through the olives. Beau stopped so I could remove a grass seed from between two of the pads of his back-left paw. Arxi caught the scent of a hare and hurtled off, nose low to the ground, his little legs barely touching the rocky ground, and BB and Duna joined the chase.

'Thanks for coming to get me, mate. And for the bus ticket. I'll pay you back.' I heard Jack's words in my head – 'Too fucking right you will!' – but said nothing. I had thought that Joe would talk as he usually did, but there was a heaviness in his stride as if he were pulling a weight up the hill. I gave him a nudge.

'It just all got a bit mad. That hostel is dangerous. There was a party the first night and we all got absolutely hammered. This weird thing happens when I get drunk. I get confident. I don't want it to stop. I bankrolled a party for a group of us. They thought I was some fucking rock star. Taxis. Bars. Clubs. We just went on a blind bender.'

'How much did you spend?'

'Everything I had. About 1,300 euros.'

'My god. They saw you coming. Why would a rock star stay at a youth hostel?'

He laughed and it felt good to hear. 'You got a point there. Shit!'

'Just booze or something else?'

'Just booze,' he replied as he snapped off the end of an olive branch. He gazed into the distance. 'And then I lost my phone. Someone stole my passport. I ended up sleeping on the streets. I had no way of contacting you, otherwise I would've. Good call calling the hostel. Dunno what I would've done.'

We opened the gate at the Top of the Olives and began the steep ascent to Topknot. There is no path so we each forged our own through the broom and hawthorn. Thistles scratched at my calf muscles so I pulled up my socks.

It was an unremarkable sunset but it strengthened as we scrambled to the summit. I noticed that Joe was sweating profusely.

'I am so out of shape, man. That's it. I'm gonna get fit.' He paused before continuing, 'It's amazing up here, man. This is your back garden, mate. It's bonkers.'

We sat to draw in deep breaths of the crisp air. Two northern guys enjoying a sunset. Both from loving families, both with brothers, both eager to please, both lovers of life, both caring souls, both with struggles, both with chequered pasts, both with a need to forgive, both with a need to ask for forgiveness, both with truths, doubts, fear, both with tattoos, both from England, both in Spain, both with pain. Our similarities far outweighed our differences.

'The light's really good now,' I noticed. 'Do you want me to take some shots of you up here?'

He stood up, rearranged himself, flattened the collars of his sky-blue polo shirt. The green dog lead hung around his neck and dangled over his mid-frame.

'Look this way,' I told him. 'Look down the lens.' Click. 'Now, look towards the house.' I spun around. Click. 'Try to look just a little happy.' His smile burst the frame. Click. That last shot is a uniquely beautiful photo of him – so beautiful his family decided to enlarge it and place it on the altar at his funeral.

'It's alright for you,' he quipped. 'You are happy.'

His words stopped me in my tracks. 'But I haven't always been happy, Joe. I have been terribly unhappy in my life. Happiness is not something that just happens. We have to make it happen. It's a long process, mate.'

The third and last time Joe went walkabout, he was missing for nine days. After the Málaga episode, he settled into a disciplined routine of work, exercise and healthy eating. He blossomed. He and the other volunteers struck up a genuine friendship and we could often hear their chatter and the sizzling of sausages coming from the other side of the house. I love to hear laughter. I love that The Corner feeds people's souls and makes them happy. There is great healing in laughter, and it can lead to deep relationships. Joe did not leave the house for six weeks.

His parents came to visit but, rather than coming to The Corner, they rented an apartment in Córdoba, as his mother had always wanted to see the Mezquita. He returned with a spring in his step and a new tattoo of an olive branch on his hand. It was a beautiful piece of tattoo art. The perfect tint of silvery green climbing up his fingers and over the back of his hand. The Corner had obviously marked him and he chose to decorate his body as a testimony. It was so well drawn that I wondered if he'd actually taken an olive branch up to Córdoba for the tattoo artist to trace.

After his parents' visit, he remained a further four weeks at The Corner without leaving. He stayed off the tobacco. It appeared all his urges were weakening and his will power was kicking in. It's as if The Corner was giving him the strength to be the person he wanted to be. But then one day he announced that he was going to see his friend – the one who didn't drink.

'I'll only be gone a couple of days,' he assured me.

Eight days later, he still had not returned. When four days ran into five, six and seven I searched his room for some clues for contacts of friends and family. I had never been into his room before. Some of his clothes were neatly folded, but most of his possessions were strewn around the floor with no sense of order. It was messy but not offensively so. In his bedside table I found a short list of handwritten names and numbers on a piece of card, wallet-sized and carefully cut out. Mum, Kevin, Dad, Bro, Alison, Jackie . . . I decided to call his father. He did not seem particularly concerned. Perhaps this had been happening for years? What did I know? There was little emotion in his reaction. We would be in touch if we heard anything.

The eighth day passed and nothing. On the ninth day, I had to go to work. During lunch with clients I read a text: Joe is back. He is in a bad way. If you need to speak to him, call my phone as he has lost his.

I excused myself from the lunch table and called the number of one of the other volunteers. They passed the phone to Joe. His voice was not his own, deep and distant. He launched into another apology but this time it was different. I was different. He was different.

'Look, Joe. Stop there. Save me the details, mate. You left us high and dry . . . again. I've had a real nightmare trying to find you. That's it. Done deal. You need to pack your things and the guys will take you to the bus station. I don't want you there when I get home,' I told him.

I returned to my clients in the restaurant, but could not put Joe out of my mind. Driving home, a text message pinged into my phone. It was from the other volunteers: Please reconsider. Please don't throw Joe out on the streets. He has nowhere to go. It could be bad.

I'd been up for thirteen hours already by this stage in the day and I was exhausted. Tiredness clouded my thoughts. My phone rang. It was Joe from a brand-new phone. He was at the bus station in town.

'Mate,' he cried, 'please don't throw me out. I swear I can sort this out. I love it at The Corner. I want to stay. I need to stay.'

I called Jack, now back in London, who suggested we discuss it with Joe in the morning. We had forgiven him once, twice – this would be the third time. I asked the guys to go back into town and collect him. I still had another hour to drive.

Twenty minutes from home and another call came through, 'Manni?'

'Yes, all okay?'

'Are you nearly home? You need to get back quickly. Joe is bad. Worse. It's getting ugly. He's just realised that you have deleted him from The Corner WhatsApp group.'

Of course I had deleted him from the group. I had deleted him days ago. He no longer deserved to be on it. He had blown it. He knew that. He knew we would insist that he leave. Tonight was a mere formality to be able to talk face to face. Apparently, when he saw that he had been deleted, he flipped into a whole other range of anger. Was that group his last link with reality, his last connection to humanity? Thankfully, I was not privy to his rage. Later, one of the other volunteers told me he had ripped paintings with his bare hands, tried to take doors off their hinges, smashed lamps and clawed walls as if he were attempting to scale them. And for the duration of his rampage he had screamed and wailed: 'It's alright for them. It's fucking all right for them. They have this place. They have each other. Manni has everything and now he's throwing me out! They're going to do this, aren't they! I don't want to go. I can't leave this place. I have *nowhere to go!*'

There were other words screamed. The guys almost told me when we were recollecting the events hours later. Their eyes met and there was a mutual agreement that it was better not to tell me. I have never asked.

'Try to calm him down and I'll be there as soon as I can,' I told them.

I stopped at the petrol station to buy a packet of crisps and a bottle of water. It felt wrong but I was hungry. Those crisps may well have saved my life.

It was dark and quiet when I got home. The dogs met me at the gate, the house quiet in the fading light. The other volunteers were all in the kitchen, clutching cups of coffee, their faces betraying a life shock.

'It was terrible, Manni. I've never seen anything like it. He was literally tearing the walls down.'

'Where is he now?' I asked

'He's gone. He left. He packed his things screaming, "They don't want me. They don't need me." It was hideous, and I'm sorry, but most of it was directed at you. He kept screaming your name and saying, "It's alright for him!"'

'Did he go into town?' I asked

They looked at each other. 'Well, we thought that's where he was heading, but we watched the front road from the upstairs window and he never appeared out the front. He must have gone towards the Final Fence. We followed him out there, but it was getting dark. We called his name from the spring but there was no answer.' They looked worried.

'Maybe I should go after him. Give me the headtorch,' I said.

The volunteer who had worked as a psychiatric nurse grabbed my wrist, gently but firmly enough for me to listen to him intently. 'I really don't think it's safe for you to go. It's dark now and he is really raging. He is out of control.'

Silence seeped between us and we sat with it for a while, considering our options.

'So, we let him calm down and I'll go and get him in the morning?' I asked.

'Sounds like a good idea,' he said and then added, 'Can you lock us in on your way out, please?'

In a house where most of the doors are never locked, this seemed extreme, but then I hadn't seen him. I hadn't witnessed his fury.

'Manni, you have no idea.'

I took the dogs into our bedroom and slept with one eye open, wishing the night hours away so I could find him and speak with him, hear him out. I couldn't fall asleep, wondering whether he was warm enough. Before first light, I got out of bed.

'Coffee,' I spoke aloud. 'Come on, dogs. Let's have a coffee, and then we'll go and find Joe.'

As soon as I was beyond the alberca, I called Jack. It was early in London, but he was already awake.

'The boys looked petrified when I got home and I'm sure they've seen some stuff in their lifetimes.'

'God, yeah. You be careful and let me know when you've got him. I've got to get Reuben up. Our train leaves in forty minutes.' Reuben. I hadn't thought of him in over twenty-four hours. My head was full of other problems. 'Love to you both. Give Reubs a hug from me. Wait. I think I've got him. I've found him.'

He was kneeling under a wild olive tree. 'Okay. Good. Let me know.'

Joe was facing away from me and he hadn't heard me approaching. I wondered if he had his earphones in. I called his name.

'Can he not hear you?' Jack asked.

I took a wide circle in front of the tree so as not to startle him from behind. I waved my arms in his field of vision. I would hear him out. Perhaps we could get through this and he could stay. He still hadn't seen me. The dogs approached to nuzzle him, but there was still no response. And it was then that I saw it. I interpreted the scene in cinematic precision. But I still couldn't understand why he wasn't responding. Why had he not seen me?

'God. No! Please, no.'

'What? What's happened?'

'I think he has killed himself.'

I knew that my life was about to change; that I would be different from this moment on.

'What do you mean he's killed himself?' Jack was talking from a warm kitchen in a warm house in London, while making his coffee. Here, frost clung to the tall grasses.

'Jack. I think he's dead. He's not moving.'

'Have you touched him? Are you sure?'

NO. PLEASE, NO. NO.
PLEASE, NO. PLEASE. PLEASE.

I have tried to remember what happened next, but fail every time. I do remember the cold touch of his skin and the shape of his mouth. I have no recollection of my flight through the meadow or whose legs carried me over the Rockies, over the spring, past Badger's Drop and along the Straight. Who opened the wooden gate by the alberca? Who opened the gun-metal grey gate that took me screaming onto the lane? There was only white silence in my mind. Then a wail filled me, something primal, brought into my body on a sharp intake of breath to steady myself. My steps faltered as I stumbled into the main house and through the lemon-tree patio. The guys were making coffee. I did not say the words. There was no need. I lunged at one of them, I do not remember which, and he took me into his arms. In the eyes of the other, I saw a world of hope fall away into the dark of his eyes.

'No!' he mouthed.

I grabbed him and the three of us shook together. What do you do? There is no suitable reaction. Only tears. They fell freefall from my eyes. They even came out of my mouth as I spluttered the words to make it feel real.

'He's gone. Joe is dead.'

It is the kind of weeping no one should ever have to experience. We were inside the scream, drowned in tears. There was nothing behind our eyes and no sound from our heart. I was a boy in a vicarage worried that something was wrong. I was a frightened man in a hospital waiting room. I was sitting in a doorway in the loneliest village in London crying into my coffee cup. I was filled to the brim with emptiness. I was emptied of fullness. I was eggshell, I was sunlight, I was rain. I remember only the searing heat.

Silence.

Joe has gone. He is no longer suffering. He has left his suffering here for us to deal with. Will I ever be the same again? I feel that something in the very fabric of me has shifted. How long will it be until I am allowed to smile?

His family pack his scant possessions into a rucksack and a holdall, removing all physical traces of him, but they can't take away the hurt he has left behind. How are they supposed to remove it? Is there a way? Is there something they can do? I think his mum would remove the pain for me, were she able. When we look at each other, I know she knows. She knows I know and yet, neither of us can find the words to begin to explain. There is only silence between us. Yesterday we were strangers. Today I am handing over her son's clothes and muddy trainers.

'Is there a note? Did he leave a note?' she pleads, refusing to believe he didn't.

This is when she breaks in two, when I tell her there is no letter. I hope I never have to see anything close to this awful ever again. To watch a mother implode and fall to the floor, a bag of bones and silent tears, her soul crushing within her. I kneel down to hold this complete stranger as she convulses. I wait until she lifts her gaze to look at me. We stare at each other across the barricade of impossibility that fills the space between us.

Before I ask the questions I need to ask, they are gone, back on a flight to Ireland with Joe's belongings in a bag. There isn't enough room on the plane for their pain.

Did he do it to spite me? If he envied my happiness, did he kill himself to damage my joy? I don't think so. I like to think he wasn't that type of person. He didn't have that kind of voice. His voice rang true and clear. I prefer to think that whatever he consumed during those nine days away put thoughts there that were not his own. Those thoughts weren't Joe's. His mind was hijacked, poisoned thoughts gaining passage through alcohol and drugs.

And what of his siblings' silence? Their lives had gone to plan. They looked like they had made the right decisions in life, that life has treated them well and fairly. One of his brothers tells me later: 'We know Joe was happy with you. He had never been happy anywhere, not for a long time. We thought about getting in contact with you, but we didn't know you. We didn't know what type of human being you were. So, we stayed silent, to give him a chance.'

I understand their logic, but this is where we need to remove the stigma of mental health. If Joe had been allergic to peanuts or if he was coeliac, that information would have trickled through. We still have a long way to go to remove the stigma. We must not remain silent.

I suppose it is inevitable that when tragedy strikes, our emotional vessel is so churned up that all the sediments settled at the very bottom, from years ago, become part of the mix. That is how I feel now. Opaque. I have lost my clarity. I feel unhinged and my feelings feel foreign to me. The hand that touched Joe's dead body still feels cold. I can't sleep. Sometimes I can't breathe. I can see pain behind my eyes. And there was me thinking that I had dealt with it all; with all my pain.

Jack has reached the end of his emotional tether and I do not know what that feels like yet. In time I will. In the future, I will touch rock bottom. But right here, right now, I do not understand. I try to adjust my focus onto Jack and Reuben's needs. I need them just as much as they need me. Joe was not family. My boys need to come first. But there is something immovable in my path and its name is pain.

I feel like I need to be alone for a long, long time.

When I told Joe I hadn't always been happy, I meant it. My life has been peppered with sadness. There were days when I wanted to give up and disappear, to turn off the pain. That is as close as I ever want to be.

'If only you had lived my life, you would understand,' Joe told me once.

My biggest regret is that if only Joe had not stayed silent, I would have understood. If only he'd trusted me with his secrets, I could have helped him set them free. If I could have told him my story, he would have listened.

All my hurt and pain has risen to the surface of me. And there was me, thinking I had dealt with it all. I don't often ask for help, but I know I need help to get through this one. But who can help me here? I can't process all this in Spanish, can I? Can I really touch on these deep issues in my second language? English friends vouch for a therapist called Jorge, who works on the coast, and I decide to call him. He can see me next week. Until then, I hunker down and move through each day like a shadow. I am unusually aware of every movement. Words feel heavy and odd. I am numb with pain.

Guilt won't let me sleep at night. All the things I could have said or should have done lie with me like bedfellows next to the dogs. I am sharing my headspace with unfamiliar forms and I don't like it one iota. I want them to leave me in peace. I want them to go.

Jack and I have hit our first proper hurdle. Our relationship has been plain sailing until this point but we have now reached an impasse. I do not understand him. He does not understand me.

23

THE SCREAM

JOE'S SUICIDE TAKES ME TO the brink of myself. I am on the edge of the dark. It's as if my very being opens like an old wound, a gorge through my soul. A soul incision. I am buckled. We have a lot in common, this house and me, with its onset of cracks and decay. Old hurts start to spill up. Pain bubbles over. I am taken back to my own childhood as I imagine his. Death can be a natural and peaceful occurrence, but if a life is ripped from us by tragedy, accident or acts of terror, it is nigh on impossible to find peace with it. There is no night and day. The dark hours are filled with nightmares. The light hours are filled with rising panic attacks. I have no power. All I can do is watch from outside myself as the memories summon me.

Darkness haunts me. The silence stretches my thoughts too far into the shadows. I can hear that voice again from my childhood. The non-whisper. My mind is all paradiddles and double paradiddles. An image plays over and over in my mind on repeat, despite my efforts to block it. Sometimes it's like a scene from a big-budget Hollywood movie; other times it's a blurry rendering, like a painting that's been left out in the rain.

I fear a panic attack could alter my emotional wiring. I have no control over it but once it comes, there is no stopping it. Like a milk pan boiling over, a surge of nervous energy rises from the deepest part of me and begins to froth and bubble.

I am driving home from a day's touring on the coast when it happens. I have just taken the right-hand fork on the motorway behind Málaga to make my way onto the toll road. Four carriageways split into two and two, and I feel something inside me tear. There is a point of subsidence deep within me, that specific spot that holds me together. My fulcrum crumbles. I am driving at 120 mph and I feel like I am travelling at the speed of light. I brake and pull over to the right but there is no hard shoulder, nowhere to stop. I put one hand on my heart and the other on the steering wheel and brace myself to drive through it. Now I know how Reuben felt when he said, 'I don't want to die, bruvr.' It's a fiery emotional blizzard and I have to drive though it just like I had to run through a stitch that came when I was racing the 1500 m for my school in Berkshire. Run through it. Don't give up. Keep your eyes on the road.

Hold Wheel Hold Hold
Wheel Hold Wheel Wheel

One night of these long dark nights of disquiet, ramblings in my mind, nights when sleep is far away and I am racked with anxiety, I lay in bed wide awake. Sleep is the last thing on my mind. I can't get that bloody saddle stand out of my head. It was gorgeous. A one-off. I'm so annoyed with myself. As I lie there trying to think about something else, I hear a sound that penetrates me, coming from outside.

The dogs start howling. They are not barks as such, but primal sounds from hounds in their baskets. Something very out of the ordinary is happening outside. I tug on my dressing gown, push my feet into the shapes of my slippers in the dark and peer out of one of the front windows. I hear two screams. I have never heard anything like it.

Leaving the dogs behind, scaling a wall, I turn on the torch on my phone and head up the track, in the direction of the screams. Silence. A quarter moon hangs in the sky, pinned by a thousand stars. I have to stop to gaze up as my breath pipes into the night sky. It is around 4° Celsius.

I pull the dressing gown tighter around my body. I hear a rummage and a faint snarl, the scamper of tiny steps. Are they paws or hooves? And then I hear a second round of the double scream. A howl that still haunts me like a high-pitched death groan. It's a terrifying sound. I retreat, too petrified to continue. I enter the safety of the house.

Another double scream. Always in pairs. The further I am from it, the more desperate it seems. I tell myself off for not being braver and decide to go back, but through the back of the house, through the goat farm, so that I can approach the scene from behind the safety of our metal fence. As my every step crunches, the noises crystalise and I can hear grunts, jaws locking and low growls. I am close now. Just 20 metres away. And then the third and penultimate double scream. It enters me and still hasn't left, filling me with the sound of suffering.

Could what I am imagining be as terrible as the reality? Only one oleander bush separates me from the scene, but I cannot take myself there, I cannot bear to look. Those two last screams and then only silence and the gnashing of teeth. I hope the soul of that poor, tormented animal finds peace immediately. Beasts of the night, retreat. Leave the poor animal alone. I know I will regret not taking myself all the way. Why come out here in the middle of the night if there was nothing I could do to save the poor animal? Why couldn't I have been quicker and braver? I muddle my way back through the outbuildings, chastising myself. Ninety-five per cent is never good enough.

I cannot not find sleep. I slip into the warm bed beside Jack, who reaches out to me from deep sleep and draws me to him. Wide-eyed, I try to find the tone of the scream in my head, attempting to replicate it. Midway between a bawl and a blatt, the screaming howl of the night still haunts me.

At first light, there is no fear and I walk up the lane to find the carcass of a beautiful roe deer, chewed, eaten, ear ripped off, staring at me as the first rays of sun catch a glint in her eye. Her chest bears the hole of a rifle's bullet. Surely she had tried to get away but was taken down in her weakness. If I had a hat, I would take it off and bring it to my chest. I hold a minute's silence for her and bless her passage. My neighbour tells me that I have to get used to occurrences such as these.

'We live in the wilds, Manni,' he says. 'Try not to think about it.'

Please don't say 'these things happen', I think, and then he does.

We live in a world of beauty and brutality and there, in the balance, am I.

24

A LISTENING EAR

If you see that I fall silent,
My thoughts have not flown.
I am never more occupied
Than when I am alone.

Count Cayetano de Alvear, *Cantares*

I have always tried to do things well. Maximum effort reaps its rewards. In the last few days though, I can feel myself slipping. It's as if I couldn't care. Is it depression? Is it PTSD? When I focus on an object, it flickers. Something is wrong with my vision. It feels like the internal, invisible parts of me are caving in.

Even the most banal tasks annoy me. Making a cup of tea. Ordinarily, I would relish in the ritual of waiting three minutes for the tea to steep, adding a sticky teaspoon of our own honey and a glug of milk. Right now, I can't be bothered. Even my tea tastes bad. I normally look for the 'Best Brother' mug Reubs gave me for Christmas a few years ago. Now, I grab any old mug. I couldn't care less.

There's an anger lurking just below the outer shell of me and I don't like it one bit. I feel irritable and anxious. The whisper in my head is back. It begins at dawn and I shun it throughout the day. I'm not okay. But at least I know I'm not okay. I know how to read the signs now. I need to go and see someone, talk this out, before it takes root.

It's bizarre how it creeps in, this wicked serpent of depression. It skulks and inches forward when I'm not watching. Before I know it, it's gripping me like a boa constrictor. Once it has me in its grip, the only way out is to dismantle its power. There is no wrong way to do that: therapy, exercise, diet, pills, laughter, walks in pine forests, swims in the sea. These are all antidotes to its power.

Jorge's office is spartan: painted chairs and bad photos of beaches framed in plastic gold. There are no certificates on the walls. His eyes tell me everything I need to know. Instinctively, I relax into his confidentiality. Here is a man who understands. It feels such a relief to begin. I take a deep breath and tell him everything about Joe. He understands. He really understands. He pauses before he shares a similar story with me.

We switch roles as I listen. Jorge is a broken version of himself, the version he becomes every time he recounts his own experience. Will I ever be less broken? Will I ever feel whole again?

Jorge is glad I stopped to buy that packet of crisps. He is the one that tells me that they probably saved my life. Had I arrived four minutes earlier, there would have been brighter light, making the decision to go and find Joe more probable. Had it not been for that strong hand on my wrist within the very last glows of the day, I might have gone to find him.

'You were the source of his pain,' Jorge reminds me.

'*Paradise Lost*,' I murmur.

Jorge is showing me the corners of my suffering, shining a light into the darkest shadows. I feel as if the very skin of me has been torn away, so exposed that even air might bruise me. Deftly, using words as footholds and silent pauses as places for me to place my thoughts, he leads me up and over my guilt. He is the greatest guide.

'The dead don't die,' he tells me. 'He will stay with you. Embrace the pain. Accept its weight. Don't fight the memory or the images. Let them in and learn to live with them. That's the only way to avoid dualism and conflict. In time, you will learn to forgive, and then you won't be able to walk around swinging a big bag of blame.'

When I leave his treatment room, I go into the local market for a café con leche. How can Jorge know me so well?

'Do you want something to eat, love?' I hear a kind Spanish voice but can't focus on her features.

'Not right now, thank you. Maybe later.'

I sit for what seems like hours. Something in me just shifted and I don't want to move until it has settled. I might never get back here. I feel therapy is like this. Good therapy unveils your own secrets and I might never be this close to them again, so I'm scared to move on until they've whispered every last truth in my ear.

There is a din around me of morning market banter, but I can only hear my thoughts. I hone in on my own silence and turn inward to face the very core of me. Jorge has started to guide me home. I can see the path. I am crying. I can see the labyrinth and need to follow the path to the centre. That's the thing about a labyrinth, I remind myself – you cannot get lost: one way in, one way out.

A stranger's hand lays its tender weight on my shoulder and hands me a tissue.

'You just let me know when you're ready for breakfast, my darling. I can't have you leaving here with an empty stomach.'

She talks as if she understands. Perhaps she does. I never see her face. She senses I don't want to talk and brings me toast and two cloves of garlic for me to scratch on my bread, extra virgin olive oil, sliced tomato and the most delicious Iberian ham, cut wafer thin and oozing with flavour. When I have finished, I leave 10 euros and walk silently to where I think I parked my car.

It has been raining and the waters of the river are high. I stop the car to check the flow and the water level against a marker we have plotted on a low wall that sits by the ford. If the waters don't reach the base of the wall, then it's safe to cross.

The dogs greet me with licks and kisses and wagging tails, but there is no one else here. I am totally alone. It's not very often that this happens. There has either been Samwise, or Frodo, or volunteers, or Rafa, or friends or visitors. Not today though. I am totally alone. Should I feel nervous?

Oddly, this is the least alone I have felt for weeks. I have been craving this: time to sit with myself and let my mind hover. I smile at the idea of it just being me in this vast house. Such a privilege. My echo is louder in this empty chamber and my confidence feels bolstered.

All I want is peace. All I need is peace of mind, for the storms in my head to die down. I crave the absence of sadness and guilt and shame and fear. I simply want to sit. Right here. Right now. Sit still and watch the flames of the fire until they are no more.

I have to let the power of silence break me. It is a skill I am still learning, to look away from the obsession of remembering. Here in the silence, alone but not lonely, I begin to get the hang of it.

25

NO SECRETS, NO LIES

EVERYTHING FEELS MUFFLED AND I walk around as if the edges of me have been redefined. I do not want this feeling to define me. I do not want these feelings to linger around The Corner. I set fire to wild rosemary, thyme and sage in a blackened brasero and march through the house making sure the smoke reaches every inside corner.

I head back to England to see my boys. I move through Málaga airport like a ghost. It feels like I succeed in trying to make myself disappear. I avoid eye contact for the entire journey. My soul is cast downward.

Jack is throwing Reuben a 'Back in the Room' party, not because Reuben is back in the room, but that Jack thinks it might be a way for him to claim the space he used to so easily inhabit. Reubs needs mechanisms to remember how he used to be, and Jack is a genius at inventing them. Reubs gives a speech. It is wonderful to see my Samwise Gamgee and Frodo

Baggins together, but I feel like I am looking at them through tinted glasses. There is a disconnect.

A new distance has appeared between Jack and me, as if the river has widened. We know that the only way back to each other is to build a bridge of truth and words. As Reuben sleeps, he tells me of his struggles and the endless need for badgering and encouragement; the energy it takes to create a healthy structure so that Reubs can regain his life skills and a positive mindset.

'It's relentless, Manni. You have no idea. And you have been more focused on a stranger's family than your own.' His words burn.

'And I haven't seen my friends for months,' he continues. 'You know I love my Frodo, but we need to work out a longer-term solution. I can carry on. You know me. But at some point, I need to get my life back.'

I have been unaware of his monumental sacrifice until this moment. I can see it on his face. Dark rings of worry beneath those steely eyes. I readily admit that I have been focused on the problems at The Corner.

'Well, you should not abandon us like that. It's not fair,' Jack says.

I agree with him. It's not fair. Life is not fair. I stand my ground and take a deep breath as I begin to explain the quagmire of emotions I find myself in. I pour us another glass of Matarromera. Jack knows me but he doesn't know all of me.

'No secrets, no lies, right?' I say to him.

'Oh Jesus. What have you got to tell me? Do I need my tissues?' he asks.

'Maybe,' I reply. 'Even you might cry.'

I tell him a lot but I don't tell him everything. Everything that is bubbling just below the surface. I can't find its form yet, not even for Jack. He knows me better than anyone and I want him to know more of me. I want him to know all of me, but no, I'm not ready to break my silence. Not yet. Once I begin, I won't be able to stop and I'm not quite ready.

'I need a fag,' Jack says as he lifts his hand off my knee.

'Don't go. Don't leave me,' I beg him.

'Hang on, my darling. I'm not going anywhere. I'm just getting a cigarette. Want one?' he asks.

'Yes please,' I reply in a stony tone, and then I begin. I monologue for almost an hour. It feels good to untangle all of my emotions.

After a pregnant pause, Jack says, 'Bloody hell. I didn't know all that,' between drags on a fresh cigarette.

He didn't know that I was questioned by the Guardía Civil to eliminate me as a suspect.

He didn't know that the first Guardía Civil that came to investigate couldn't get to the body. To access that spot in the furthest valley you have to walk an extremely narrow path alongside the gorge and he suffered an attack of vertigo.

He didn't know that the police found a criminal record in Joe's backpack.

He didn't know it had taken a Mountain Rescue Team to remove Joe's body.

He didn't know that Joe had ripped paintings with his bare hands, screaming my name.

He didn't know that Jorge says I made the right decision not to follow Joe when he ran into the night.

He didn't know that I haven't been able to go to the Final Fence since it happened.

He didn't know that there were only twelve people at his funeral.

He didn't know that Joe's eldest brother broke down when he saw The Corner, crying, 'Joe was happy here!'

He didn't know that Joe didn't leave a farewell letter.

He didn't know that I cried for days and haven't been able to sleep for weeks.

He didn't know that I had a panic attack on the motorway and had to swerve into the slow lane.

He didn't know that I want to write about Joe's suicide one day in the hope that it will prevent other young men taking their own lives.

He didn't know that when Fernando came to my rescue, he brought a packet of cigarettes with him and I chain-smoked the lot.

He didn't know that Rafa came to Joe's funeral and he cried, confiding in me afterwards that they had talked at length about addiction. Rafa thought that he'd helped him and that he couldn't believe he was dead.

He didn't know that on the night Joe died, I stopped to buy a packet of crisps on my way home.

We sleep in a tighter ball of limbs than we've ever slept. No secrets, no lies. My body and soul feels exhausted as I fall asleep, but I am so relieved I have told Jack.

There is something foundational in our conversation, as if a master builder is underpinning the structure of our relationship. Where there was emptiness, relief floods in. Where there was anger, there is understanding. There are words that need to be passed gently, secrets that need to be held as they are shared. Jack holds me, bracing me with his strength.

I feel like one of those historic buildings that I used to observe being demolished in Seville. Walls are torn down, leaving kitchen tiles and bathroom units exposed and incongruous. It was like seeing the private parts of other people's lives, things normally hidden from view, perched on high walls in plain sight. The history of the building was scraped away leaving nothing but an empty lot, but the facade stood proud, pinned up and protected on both sides by an intricate framework of scaffolding. Those precious facades, remnants of architectural styles that graced the Andalusian capital throughout its history, cannot fall. They cannot be lost.

That's how I feel. As if the facade of me, the part that people see, is teetering in the wind, propped up with brackets and ties, while the rest of me needs to be rebuilt. Thank goodness for my base – Jack – for without him I fear my entire structure might crumble. We are able to spend some time together, back in the UK, far away from The Corner, and we meet each other somewhere in the middle of our misunderstandings. I acknowledge his exhaustion and frustration with his Frodo. I still feel there are so many tears to cry.

Before I leave for Spain, there is one more thing I need to tell him.

'There is an offer on the table,' I say. 'José Maria from the hardware store in Antequera has a buyer for The Corner.'

'But we're not selling it,' Jack replies. 'Are we?'

We look at each other and there is only silence.

'With everything that has happened,' I continue, 'I don't know if I can do this anymore. You and Frodo here. Me there. It doesn't make any sense.'

'You have to call it,' he says as he wraps his strong arms around me.

26

MY CHURCH

I breathed deeply the breath of the sleeping fields. It was a serene darkness, enlivened by bright lights like sparks from a noisy fire. As I let that silence enter me, I felt stronger and bigger.

Ricardo Güiraldes, from *Don Segundo Sombra*

THE DOGS FOLLOW ME FROM inside the fence all the way to the gate when I get home. I hear Jack's words in my head: 'Never get emotionally attached to a house'. *Easy for him to say*, I think to myself. The Corner for me is much more than a house. It is my first home, the embodiment of years of yearning. It is daydreams manifested in bricks and mortar. How could I not get attached to this place, our home in the corner of this peaceful valley, still aching with beauty despite everything? The world keeps bringing problems over the river, but she stands defiantly in the dazzling midday sun.

The dogs rip my jumper and lick my ears, celebrating my homecoming more than me. I sit down to bring them close, four pairs of eyes, eager for an adventure.

'Shall we go for a walk?' I say. They run circles around the car, barking with excitement.

I look up at the lauburu, the one that goes backwards – the beginning. I walk around to the riverside of the house as if to check that the other lauburu, the one that goes forwards, is still there – the end. Everything between the two is our house, a life to live in all its fullness.

This decision is going to be complicated. I hear the words of Jorge calmly guiding me away from the pain: 'In through the nose, out through the mouth. One, two, three, four, five, six, seven.'

As I follow the river, my legs take me along a path so familiar I barely have to think where to tread, the shadows of the house retreating behind me as the silence draws me onwards. I tune my ear to the river below me, in the shadow of the mountain, and hear the faint burble of water as it skips over the rounded backs of stones and dances down towards the valley.

Ordinarily, I walk this path twice a day. It is a path I know so well and yet it all feels different now. This is the first time I've walked it since . . .

Name it.

Face it.

Don't reject the memories.

Already the grass has begun to grow beneath my absent feet. It doesn't take nature long to claw back into our spaces.

Webs that spiders have trellised between broom bushes brush my hands and face.

I try not to reject the storyboard that flashes through my mind as I step up onto Thyme Point to watch the river from above. I want to be hidden from sight, to retreat. I remember that it is possible to hide too well, to retreat too far. All four dogs join me on the rocks. Duna stands guard behind me. Arxi is in his own world, nose turned into the wind, hoping to catch a scent. Beau sits a metre away from me, facing the same way. And BB by my side, leaning into my thigh, lets her bulk fall into mine. Settled. Now all I can do is wait.

The question looms. Should we sell the dream? Have recent events made living here untenable? Is the world trying to tell us something? Sell this house that has already given us so much these past four years? To leave would make a mockery of the emotional investment we have poured into this place. There are no simple answers, but nature always has a habit of sending me signs.

On the opposite side of the river, a female ibex appears, her red coat standing out against the sandstone hues. I suspect we have interrupted her resting place and she makes to return to the wild. Her hoof-tips find the slightest of edges on the otherwise smooth, vertical cliff face. She follows a series of switchbacks and then settles on a ledge against a patch of chalky stone, almost disappearing. Precarious. Genius.

We watch each other and her gaze locks on mine. Don't worry, little one. We're not going to hurt you. The fact is, I want to do the same. To disappear. As I sit here, I want to empty my mind, toss all thoughts down the mountain, in an attempt to rockfall my worries. Inevitably, shards of thought puncture the stillness. Let them come. Don't resist. I close my eyes and hold my hands up to the heavens. A strange thing to do, reminding me of being in church as a teenager, but this time I reach out not to receive a blessing but to blend with my surroundings, to bring nature in.

Only the ibex, four dogs, the elements and me. I remain still as the tears roll in, each one taking a little of the pain with it. BB nuzzles even more firmly into my hip. All is quiet. This decision is too difficult to make, so I will sit here, in this place of peace, my new church, until the decision makes itself.

Duna's piercing bark makes me jump. Sixteen legs scurry towards the Final Fence to follow a scent Duna has picked up. I run after them and catch a glimpse of it just before it disappears around the flank of a slope and into the undergrowth – a silver fox with a grey tail that looks like a bristle brush dipped in white paint. I stop and smile. I am already imagining what quick remark Jack will come out with when I tell him I have seen a silver fox at the Final Fence.

I replay the scene over and over in my mind, how stealthily silent it was. The dogs caught its scent but didn't catch its movements. It outsmarted them and skulked away to safety. How many other treasures have I been missing? I had forgotten how wonderful it is out here. The house is the wardrobe that leads to this Narnia, this Garden of Eden that lies behind the gorge and into the hidden valley. So untouched, so pure, so wild.

27

GONE

Last week Rafa called me on the Friday, excited to tell me that he was going away for the weekend.

'I haven't been away for years and the opportunity came up, so I'm taking Sensi to the seaside.'

'Good for you,' I told him. 'Enjoy and take lots of pictures.'

He enjoyed a wonderful weekend, eating fresh seafood and walking in the sand with the love of his life. On the Sunday morning, he walked onto the terrace of their hotel room to enjoy the view of the sea, suffered a massive heart attack, and died. He was only fifty-nine.

I loved Rafa and I said goodbye to him along with what seemed like half the village. It was a crushing blow to his family, his father so infirm the brothers decided not to bring him to the funeral, his sister tinkering on the edge of broken-ness by the death of her son just months prior. She was propped up like a ragdoll and, had her family let go, she would have

233

fallen. Rafa had stood as a beacon for recovery, an image of grit and resolve, a man who had brought himself back from addiction to commitment. He had lived in town but was happiest in the hills. Everyone knew that he'd found his freedom in nature.

If you have never attended a Spanish burial, I want to paint for you the picture of humanity that occurs as a cherished Spanish soul leaves this earth. Those that have attended one will know this scene by heart. The tradition stems from over 700 years of Islamic and Jewish culture, where for mainly practical reasons, in the hotter climates, bodies were laid to rest within twenty-four hours. The community is called. News travels through the valley at the speed of light. It is Clara, the vet, who calls me.

'Have you heard?'

So soon after losing Joe, Rafa having been with me at every step, his sudden death has me reeling once more. Joe's ashes are barely cool and here we are saying goodbye to my Don Segundo Sombra, my link with town, my rock, my friend and protector. The force that made our vision seem tenable.

The municipal mortuary is a white, modern building on a street called The Chapel of the Virgin of Pain. It looks like a pleasant primary school from the outside and feels like a doctor's surgery once we step past the threshold. Thankfully Rafa was the only resident to have died that day, so there was no elbow-jostling for space or division of mourners. We were all there for him. Outside, groups of friends and family huddled in clusters to reminisce, having already given their *pésame* to the family who were keeping vigil by the door where Rafa's body lay.

'Pésame' translates literally as 'condolences', but it is far more involved than that, as if often the way with language. The word 'pesar' refers to weight and in an emotional context to pain: the sorrow expressed when someone dies.

The family had not slept for twenty-four hours. It felt like 800 people had come to drop off their heavy hearts at their feet. I was moved by a community upholding Rafa's name, accompanying his family in their grief. It was a feat of stoic endurance. Perhaps it's better to expel a large bulk of grief and sorrow in a concentrated purging of communal emotion.

It's so different to the way we do things in the United Kingdom, where every funeral seems orchestrated, controlled and limited by protocol. This was a wailing of the masses. It felt archaic, visceral, primal and entirely beautiful. No one was in a hurry to leave. Shops were closed. Cafés remained shut. I scanned the crowd and spotted the mayoress, neighbours, the florist, the ceramicist and the candle-stick-maker. How desperately sad that some people don't comprehend how vital they are to a community until they have left it.

Not sure of the protocol, I asked the pertinent question and friends confirmed my suspicions: 'Yes, you should go and give your heavy heart to the family.'

It was only when I hugged Rafa's son that I realised how much I was going to miss his father. There was desperation in our embrace as we fought for breath through the tears, as we lost control and gave way to unbridled grief.

How I miss Rafa. His wife loves to come now and she cries every time she sees the pond. She gazes at its heart shape and says he made it for her.

28

THE FINAL FENCE

I CAN'T QUITE PUT MY FINGER on it. The reason why I can't leave this place. It's this house and its permanence in an ever-shifting world. I sit in the living room, tuning into the world beyond. I can hear the rustle of leaves as the wind passes through branches: the suck and draw of opposing currents. I can hear the scratch of my pen on paper. I can hear the flame of my candle flickering on its wick. Bird calls. The drone of a bee. A distant banging of an open door slammed shut by a gusty breeze. And underneath all these sounds, like a base note that carries the melody, the slip, slip, slide of the gliding river.

It is moments like these that I cannot lose, for I dreamed of them all my life. I dreamed of being here, of being the man I am today, hoping one day he would feel whole and occupy a place far from fear, far from pain.

The world may come in and rip away this peace, but still we persevere. There is something here that never changes.

There is an ancient presence. I know the count felt it too, this inexplicable pull towards and into a place of reckoning.

Reubs is with Mum and Dad to give Jack a few days' respite. Jack has flown out to be at The Corner for the weekend. Having him with me completes me in a way I can only explain by writing a book. He crosses the front garden carrying a spade and a garden fork. I hear the scramble and pitter-patter of sixteen paws as the dogs follow their master to the back allotment. Rafa built raised beds from railway sleepers that we bought from a reclamation yard in the northern Spanish city of Ciudad Real. They were delivered on the back of a truck and craned onto the land, near the gate that Joe painted.

We hired Pepillo Maquina to scrape off the top layer of sheep poo, left behind by Maneo's flock and pile it up by the allotment.

'We'll have a bumper crop by February.' Jack beams.

Our daily walks to the Final Fence seem to take me deeper and deeper into myself. It's where I meet an outstretched version of myself. There appear to be fewer limits here. Jack and I sit on the boulders beyond the Cove. A clump of pampas grass flanking the riverbank looks like a crowd of people waving goodbye. I play Poohsticks in my mind as the water slips by, and I imagine Jack does too. Sometimes he goes very quiet and I know to leave him alone with his thoughts.

'It's so good to be back. I'm miserable in London,' he says.

'Are you, my darling?'

'Oh totally. I love my Frodo Baggins, but it's tough. We're quite isolated. I don't quite know what to do with myself anymore.' I am struck once more with how much of himself he has given to Reubs over these past months, a part of him that is difficult to claim back. I look down and notice that one of my shoelaces has come undone. While I am bending down to tie it, I hear Jack's tight whisper: 'Otter. Otter! Look!'

By the time I look up, if it was there, it's gone.

'Three of them!' Jack is delighted.

'I don't believe you.'

'I swear,' he giggles.

'Then why are you laughing?'

'Because it's hilarious,' he replies. 'You saw them, didn't you, my dogs?' he says in a celebratory tone as all four of them crowd him for attention.

I will return to Otter Pool countless times over the following weeks and I will never see them. Simply the possibility of seeing otters has me rooted to the spot for hours. Did Jack really see them?

As we are sitting there, the weather changes. I feel the air lighten around my ears and there is a drop in temperature. The cloud cover thickens and darkens over the gorge. The rain comes heavily all at once. There is no gentle start to rain here, no preamble. It begins in earnest, decisive and instant.

'Vamos!' Jack shouts as he launches himself from the boulder in the direction of home. The dogs begin to howl so we howl with them, hurdling rocks and vaulting fallen trees with the energy that the storm unleashes. I can hardly see Thyme Point as we approach, the rain now a curtain of grey. The storm intensifies: more rain, ever darker.

Jack grabs my arm and pulls me under a wild olive tree to shelter.

'Let's let the worst pass,' he spits, his hair flattened over the edges of his handsome face. I kiss him. I have to. This amazing man who never ceases to find the fun, even in the bleakest moments. It is a mindset he is teaching me. Melancholic Manni, he calls me.

We stand there dripping wet, giggling and patting the dogs reassuringly.

An olive tree can have so many uses. This one protects us and keeps us from harm.

'Right. Ready?' Jack cries. 'Let's go!'

We both scream like warriors hurling battle cries into the wind. We make it back to the house just as the rain stops, as abruptly as it started. The sun reaches through the damp air and we stand there steaming with big grins on our faces.

'That was so much fun,' I say. 'So much bloody fun. I needed that.'

We strip off and take it in turns to hop into the shower, hoping that the gas in the bombona (gas cylinder) doesn't run out before we are warm.

29

MUSIC

Hush, be still guitar,
So I can set my tune apart.
So I can count the beats
Of my suffering heart.

Count Cayetano de Alvear, *Cantares*

I NEED HELP. I AM RUNNING on empty. I need someone to
help me, someone that can give and not take anything else
away. Please.

Juan arrives with all the contagious energy of a traveller
who is living his dreams. His wanderlust led him to us. He is
a giver. I know, when I am away, The Corner will be in capable
hands, and I start to clamber back into a sense of wellbeing
and normality.

Juan is from Argentina and a talented musician, using his
free time to play, recite and write music. His melodies and

rhythms pulse through open windows, across the patios, up and away over the rooftops. He seems reluctant to play too loudly at first, so I strain to listen to the sound of his guitar and the timbre of his voice. His music takes me back to Argentina, to those vast, empty spaces of the Pampas.

As Juan plays, the mental billboards of my time in Argentina come alive. I can smell the grass, taste the meat, touch the leather, stretch my vision towards the horizons. As he plays his way through a melancholic samba, an upbeat chamamé or a sad tango, nostalgia taps me on the shoulder and I am so happy to follow it far, far away.

'Juan, do you know a song called "Sopla viento"?' I ask, remembering one of the songs Sophie and I learned in Argentina.

'Claro,' he beams, adjusts his position and begins to strum the tune. We sing the entire song, word perfectly, in harmony, bonded across time and space. This is the closest I've been to happy in months and it was music that brought me here. Music. Once such a large part of my life, now totally forgotten.

I look at Juan and ask him, 'If I write the lyrics, can we work on writing a song together?'

'It would be my honour.' He smiles.

I don't feel lonely this evening as I sit huddled by the fire in the main room, wrapped in layers as a shield against the cold. I am missing my boys more than I could ever have imagined. I close my eyes and ask myself, *What do I want to write a song about?* And Reuben's smile fills my mind's eye.

Mandame tu sonrisa

Porque la mía, no la hallo.
Send me your smile
As mine has gone.

The song comes easily to me. I share the words with Juan.
The melody comes easily to him. His talent brings the words
to life. Two days later we have a song.

Send me your smile
As mine has gone.
Don't hide in the shadows.
Don't be gone too long.
Send me your strength,
Mine has all but waned.
Hold on tight – be safe.
Remember what we gained
Because . . .
You're worth your weight in gold.
You're worth more than a star.
Please find your smile,
The trace of you, wherever you are.
Send me your words
As mine no longer flow.
Don't speak to me of sadness.
Happiness I need to know.
Send me your courage
As mine got up and left.
Hold my cold face in your hands.

Life has left me bereft.

Because . . .

You're worth your weight in gold.

You're worth more than a star.

Please find your smile

The trace of you, wherever you are.

The trace of you, wherever you are, trace of you, trace of you.

I write the song for Reuben but, as I sing the lyrics with Juan and we search for harmonies in the melody, I feel as if I could have written it for myself. Reuben and I have both lost our smiles. Our brotherhood is symmetrical.

30

REUBEN

Deep down in the pit of my soul,
Where all the pains are hurled,
I have a pool so deep,
For the worries of the world.

Count Cayetano de Alvear, *Cantares*

FINDING REUBS A HOME IS the largest hurdle in our path.
Could he move back to Spain with us? He doesn't want
to. Could he move permanently to London with Jack? Not
sustainable. We are anxious and decide to contact Social
Services. Norfolk doesn't even answer the phone. London is
oversubscribed. They refer us to Dorset and to our relief, Dorset
Council answers. Following an intense administration process,
a lady from Dorset Adult Learning comes to visit Reuben at
Jack's cottage in Dorset. We enjoy tea and scones together as
she takes us through the options.

245

'We can get you in the system down here, Reuben, if you'd like that. Get you registered and then we'll start looking for a place for you to live.'

'Nah,' Reubs replies with a mouth full of currants and points to the sofa. 'Like it here.'

As we plan for Reuben's future, there seems to be no clear path forwards. It's complicated. What is clear is that Jack needs a break from the responsibility of Reuben's welfare, so I convince him to allow Mum and Dad to take over for a few months.

'We could rent a flat for them down here,' I suggest. 'They can help Reubs through this transition, help him get settled in the town while we wait for a place for Reubs in a home.'

Reluctantly, Jack agrees and says it is one of the biggest regrets of his life. All that work and love, effort and strain, energy and commitment had moved Reuben to a much stronger position. We assumed wrongly that we'd moved the baseline up and that Reuben was protected from regressing again. How wrong we were.

Mum and Dad moved down to the southwest as planned and Reubs let himself slip back at the earliest opportunity. Does he do it in protest or because he can? The ever watchful eye of Samwise Gamgee, who will never let his Frodo Baggins slip back is far away. All the routine and responsibility disappear, and Reubs is allowed to sink back into the passive role of a son who needs to be cared for. Dad baths him. All the layers come back. The walking stick returns. His voice disappears. Reubs disappears, silent, expressionless and lost.

By the time we realise, it is too late. Reubs looks at us through a steely gaze as if to say, 'See? Mummy and Daddy are not as strict as you are, so I can let myself go again.' Jack had been coaxing him out of a negative mindset for months, and within days, he slipped right back to where he was before.

After a few weeks a place becomes available in a residential home.

'These places don't come up that often,' explains the social worker.

Our worry subsides as we realise there is a way out of the spider's web, but explaining the process to Reuben seems an impossible task.

'Why, brother? Don't want go. Want stay you and Samwise Gamgee,' he whispers. 'Or with Mummy and Daddy.'

It breaks my heart. I think it breaks Jack's heart even more. There is no easy choice. Jack and I go to visit the home. It is warm and the staff seem happy. But despite their best efforts to deep-clean the newly available room, remnants of death linger from the previous tenant. Can we really put Reuben here? We want him to be happy. We decide to go for it.

To help Reuben feel safe and peaceful, I organise a total redecoration. He loves Narnia. The Lion, Aslan, accompanies him in his daily meanderings. I order a lion mural from Poland, a lamppost from London, *Welcome to Narnia* stencils from Derby and paint from Bridport. Two weeks later a decorator transforms the downstairs bedroom into a magical, warm, safe space. A magnificent Aslan covers an entire wall, ready to guard Reuben day and night. When Reuben sees it, his face lights up with that rare smile. Just like the old days. Just like when he was happy.

With Mum and Dad down the road for a few more weeks, it seems like the ideal start to Reuben's new life. They can meet for lunch or dinner and spend time together in town. Reubs starts joining them at a little local church that they have become involved with. He has the familiar love he needs on tap. Jack and I both wait with bated breath to see if our plan might work. We both worry about Reubs now that his care is out of our hands.

Winter at The Corner passes by in gentle hues, each day more silent than the last. It feels like the world is in retreat. The land is marked by the absence of change. Everything feels held by a permanent frost and our days are busy with various attempts at keeping warm. As the weeks pass, the pile of logs in the old mule stalls diminishes faster than we'd anticipated. The fires are constantly burning. Will we have enough firewood to see us through until spring?

Part III

31

LOCKDOWN

I T IS MARCH 2020 AND the world is being forced to stop. I've taken Mum to Rome as a treat for her seventy-fifth birthday, and we feel the full force of the early pandemic. On 10 March, we leave Italy's capital on the last British Airways flight out of Fiumicino. Mum orders a Bloody Mary to calm her nerves. I hear Nathan's words in my head: 'Don't you dare take Mum to Rome. It's too risky.'

Too late. It was risky but we had the most amazing time. I have a photo of Mum utterly alone at the Trevi Fountain. She took a photo of me, also alone, on the Spanish Steps. I hug Mum goodbye as I pop her on a train back to Norwich, and she tells me, 'I wouldn't have missed that for the world.'

'Same here, Mumsie. I loved every minute. Keep your mask on all the way home.'

Jack and I fly back to Spain on 11 March. We know what's

251

coming and we call many of our friends to warn them. Debs asks if she can lock down with us.

'Of course you can,' we tell her.

She races to get to us before the travel restrictions in Spain come into force. Nervous energy moves around the world like misfired darts. All is panic. We retreat to our respective homes and are told to stay indoors. It is a mass un-movement of millions. It is anti-migration as humans race no more.

Josh and Rhea only arrived two weeks ago. They are as anxious as we are.

I go around to the riverside of the house to have a chat. They've already rearranged everything and it feels more like a home than it has ever felt. Rhea has a real eye. Josh has an eye for Rhea. They make me laugh. We can look each other in the eye and smile comfortably. After the series of The Corner keepers that have gone before them, I am convinced that Josh and Rhea are the real deal but, then again, I've been wrong before.

'Guys, I'm not sure whether you are aware of the news, but the British Government is advising all citizens to go home.'

They look at each other before Rhea says, 'But we don't have a home to go back to. We gave up our jobs and our flat.'

Josh adds, 'Is there any way we can stay here for the duration?' He sounds posh when he says 'duration'.

'Did you go to private school?' I ask and we all fall about laughing.

'Worst money my parents ever spent!' he adds, cheery-eyed at his own humour.

'Well, I suppose you can stay until this is all over. We'll all have to muck in together, mind. We're not going to sit here doing nothing for weeks.'

'Oh absolutely,' Josh enthuses. 'We don't want to be idle. I have an album to write.'

There is a hung pause, like a two-bar rest in a musical score.

'I've got a book to write,' I say. It feels far too intimate to be sharing this information with people I barely know, but something in me encourages me to take the leap.

'A book?' Josh says. 'About what?'

'About this place and everything that has happened since we bought it. It's a long story.'

'Ooh. Will we be in it?' Josh asks.

I don't bother to reply.

Rhea says, 'I'd love to build a new allotment and get all the planting going with Jack, if that's alright?'

'Amazing,' I say.

So here we are. The Famous Five; Jack, Debs, Josh, Rhea and me, with four dogs, two cats, ten hens, a cockerel, four ducks and a whole lot of space and time stretching before us. How I wish Reubs was with us. And Mum and Dad. And Nathan and Kate and the boys. And Matt and Liz and the boys. I wish I could bring them to the safety of The Corner, out here on the other side of the river.

How on earth is Reubs going to manage in his home? Will he be okay? Will they be able to keep him safe? Should I have gone and got him? I didn't even think. I had been so intent on getting Mum home safely. Could we have gone to Dorset to get him and brought him back to Spain?

Dad is on the high-risk list. Jack offers them the cottage to shield themselves. They can no longer visit Reuben. At best they can drive by, park for a few seconds, toot their horn and wave their love, as Reuben looks out from his bedroom window, trying to glimpse his mummy and daddy.

The Corner has had part of its soul ripped out. Reuben's room is peppered with his props of happiness. They lie there for weeks before I can eventually bring myself to sort through them. I suppose I hope he will return, but as time passes, it becomes clear that Reuben is rejecting the idea of returning to Spain.

I walk into his room one afternoon in the stillness of siesta time and begin to open drawers and cupboard doors. I imagine this is how parents who lose a child must feel. This horrific task of removing memories and relegating them to the past, in the painful admission that they will never have a future. I feel as if I am packing his personality into black bin liners, obscuring him from the light. Handling each item is like a bee sting, an intense emotional pain. As I divide his belongings into piles, I feel a new love for him surging out of control.

I need to get him back here. I want to break the glass case that holds the hammer to his safety exit. Can I steal him away and show him joy? But I cannot reach him.

I hope his carers are sitting with him and explaining away his doubts. I hope they are able to take the time of day to quieten his restless soul. What I really hope is that they are able to love him and not just care for him. For without love, what is Reuben?

I see his stone lion on his windowsill. I hope the Aslan mural we papered onto his wall in the care home is doing a better job of protecting him than I have done.

Jack and I go through his belongings. We have three piles: keep, throw and donate. I feel as if we are meddling with his personal life, breaking his autonomy. Jack pulls the 8-metre-long silver cape out of the wardrobe, the one Reubs wore to reenact his favourite scene from *Priscilla Queen of the Desert*. He asks me, 'Will he ever use this again?'

I hate myself for replying 'Probably not', and plonk it on the *donate* pile. Why am I underestimating him?

It frustrates me daily that my happy place didn't end up being his. I had assumed that Reuben would always be with us. Life has proved me wrong and I am fighting against the stages of acceptance as I sit in his room and type these words, surrounded by all his favourite things. I miss him. My essence is not complete without him.

I call his residential home.

'It's complicated. We're waiting for instructions from Head Office. For the moment, we're keeping everyone in their rooms until we get guidance.'

I can't bear it. I call him but he doesn't pick up. I send him a message to tell him I love him. I don't mention anything about the pandemic. I don't want him to worry. He is confined to 16 m2 while we are free to roam. It's almost as if I can't let myself enjoy it. I am so torn. Thank goodness we put that giant Aslan mural on the wall.

Words from *The Art of Stillness* by Pico Iyer come to mind: 'It is only when you stop moving that you can be moved in some far deeper way'.

Now I am in *nowhere* and I have *nowhere* to go, so I clutch the words to my chest like a family heirloom. I am ready to be still. I am so desperate to get off the merry-go-round.

I take myself on longer and longer walks. I find a new route up to Topknot, cutting through the retama on the slopes of the North End. The dogs have their noses to the ground as they slalom between the shrubs tracking wild animals. It's damp on this side of the mountain because the sun barely reaches these parts.

> *Be, still, be, be, still, still*
> *Still, be, still, still, be, be*

I double-paradiddle myself into a trance, trying as I might to forget everything, to remove all form, to delete structure and to exist only as breath, only as a tiny part of the whole.

I feel nature drawing me onwards, upwards, inwards, urging me to the far reaches of the land.

I plot a tangent up the steep slope that leads to the south side of Topknot. Terraces aid my climb and I see what look like the dried stumps of vines. So, this is where they used to grow grapes! It makes perfect sense: shaley soil on south-facing banks. I squeeze under the overhang of the Pinnacle and look down to the river. It feels as though I am seeing it for the first time. The refreshing gusty energy of new perspective.

'People are the way they are, because . . . ' My mother's words come back to me on the breeze. Am I moulded by my past? Is my reality hewn from the failings of my beginnings? Was there another way for Joe's life to end? I remember his face, his voice, his gait and I refuse to believe his choice was the only end. There was another path, another way.

Early one morning, before anyone is up, I follow the dawn along the river, hearing only my footsteps. The morning is filled with the sounds of birds and animals greeting each other through the low-lying mist that hugs the gorge. Once I reach the Final Fence, I sit. It's so wild here that, out of respect, I fall quiet, like a hushed visitor. Witness. Observer. Friend.

I remember Jillian's rage, Jacob's words about healing, Juan's marvel, Tonia's delight, Chloe's resolve, Anita's tears. I get it. This is not just a home. Perhaps it's the site on which it stands, ancient and sacred. Shards of ceramics and a Roman roof tile weren't brought here from a museum, that much is certain.

This is the River of the Silent Ones and this is where I want to be, where I need to be. I am suspended in a sense of nothingness. I can listen to the beating of my heart as words rise and fall. Clarity. It is a gentle re-introduction to the core of me. I know I am safer in silence. Silence can trigger me away from pain.

I close my eyes and remind myself that light can travel even through the darkest spaces. I want to be brave but there is a tension in me.

Remain silent or talk.

Forget or remember.

Hold on or release.

I want to live in the lighter shades of my memories. I want to unpick the fear and release its sinewy hold on me. I want to renew the old in me, restore the most broken parts, rebuild my walls, tie and mesh the cracks and replaster my facade. Civilise the barbaric.

I decide I can no longer harbour the memories behind a breakwater of silence, so I begin to break the wall of secrecy and imagine the words and how I might commit my pain to paper.

Back in the living room, Jack is salvaging his company from a nosedive. Zoom conferences occur in a constant chain. One ends, another begins. There are voices I have never heard before all over the house. It feels like an invasion. I have the opportunity to retreat. I need a *nowhere* to be my *somewhere* . . . *anywhere*.

I remember the cottage at the back of the house and wonder if I can make it work. I spend the entire morning scraping and sweeping to remove the grime. One house martin nest remains, tucked against a ceiling beam, empty but so perfectly formed. The precision in the curve of the neck before the widened opening is testament to the baffling skill of these tiny birds, like an ancient water vessel on its side. I imagine the opening filled with eager heads protruding, beaks open and expectant. I leave the nest untouched, hoping my presence in the room will not intimidate their return. It's too perfect a home to abandon, ready for house-proud house martins.

Once cleared and clean, the rectangular 6 × 4 metre space appears bigger. Two doors lead into rooms in far worse states, filled with debris from the 2012 flood. I close both against the chaos. There is a third door, bricked-up and cemented closed from the other side, from when the brothers walled each other off. And through the window, recessed into the metre-thick wall, with a low sill of tiles the colour of dried blood, an iron grille criss-crosses the view onto a light-filled patio. A pair of wooden shutters sits battered by the insistence of seasons, scarred and scored, guarding a hint of the sacred.

I envisage the room transformed and begin to walk around the house looking for pieces of furniture, paintings and *objets d'art* to convert this empty room into my writing nook. I want to try to restore it into a semblance of its former self, when love and life and laughter rang out through the walls.

When I lived in Seville, a Cuban painter called Reynaldo Loyola gave me some studies of elements of some of his larger paintings. His *Christ*, *Muse*, *Angel* and *Prophet* tell me where they want to be hung.

I bring down my sculpture of San Roque in his little baroque chapel. I remember the day I bought him from an antique dealer in San Telmo, Buenos Aires. The authenticity certificate (that I seem to have lost) states that he was made in a Jesuit mission up the Río de la Plata in 1670. He is probably the oldest thing I will ever own. I gather a saucer of copper coins and commit to dropping one into his collection box each morning, as a ritual to start the day. I have what I call my 'writing candle' that smells of old leather and parchment paper. I only allow myself to light it at the precise moment just before I begin to write, not when I am thinking or perusing, or reading or procrastinating, but *just before* I begin to write. When I can hear the rush of words.

Jack helps me carry my writing desk down. I had to think where it was. When we moved to The Corner we placed it next door, in the lovely corner room by the river. I can't believe I've been without it all this time. I bought it from an antique shop years ago. Malcolm, Sophie's father, who was a specialist in all things old, approved wholeheartedly.

'Probably English. Oak. Circa 1930,' he told me. 'Love the inlaid leather. Very smart indeed.'

I trace the grain in the wood with my fingers and touch its cold, curved brass handles. The green leather, mottled over time, is always soft and chilled to the touch. To go with it,

Malcolm sold me an 1870s' French writing chair. I find it in a storeroom. I am annoyed that I have spent so long forgetting myself, so long denying the things that are important to me.

After hours of hard graft, I stand back to view the creation. It is just enough: spartan but warm, basic but practical. The floodwater line marks the walls which are as thick as a fighting bull's haunches. Now, all it needs is warmth and the light of candles, so I busy myself hauling firewood and watch as a tiny flame licks logs, encouraging them to let themselves go and become a part of the whole. Two brass candlesticks find their way onto the mantelpiece, flanking the mirror that leans purposefully against the chimney stack.

My new writing nook is born, flickered to life by the prospect of inspiration. If I place my phone on the wall outside, it picks up a slight signal, just enough to bounce Bluetooth to my speaker that sits under the window. *Requiem for My Friend* by Zbigniew Preisner, begins to hum its score amid the dance of shadows. A Polish playwright gave the CD to me in 1999 and it has accompanied me ever since.

I am moved by something rarely felt, something unusually close to perfection. The combination of elements in this little room, past and present, safeguarded by walls built from stones that have always been here. There is a timelessness to the atmosphere – anticipative, at once ancient and fresh. I am held here in the balance of a meeting of the elements. I feel as if I belong here.

Now, the musical backdrop is *Officium* by Hilliard Ensemble and Jan Garbarek. My friend Matt Brown Hair used to listen to it incessantly on Jerry's Denon music system in the living room of our second-year university flat. Soon, I will tell you about Matt Brown Hair. The crisp quality of sound wrapped those crucial conversations, shared by the fire. How music conjures up the past. Each note triggers a word until quietly, as I sit there, basking in my new sanctuary, entire dialogues return to my memory.

Am I about to write a requiem? Matt Brown Hair will play a pivotal role in the telling of my tale, his love for me so vital at a time in my life when my own self-acceptance hung in the balance of love and hate. Will ink create a requiem for Joe? Will letters form words that might lead me away from silence? The words will not exist until I write them.

Some of my favourite books form towers, like crenelations of a fortress, on a support table to form an L-shape of reference, inspiration and support. I am buttressed. I am flanked by coloured spines. Pads, notebooks, old, new and, finally, pens and sketching pencils roll onto the desktop and I am ready. No more barriers. No more excuses. Time is on my side and so I pick up a favourite pen that my brother, Nathan, gave to me for my thirtieth birthday, and notice that the *Let it flow* inscription has started to fade.

Time is my new friend, and as I release myself from the guilt of relinquishing responsibilities around the house, I tunnel into the vibrations of my surroundings.

The warmth wrestles with the chill. I am not quite ready to settle, so I go and make myself a cup of tea. Bugger. We've run out of PG Tips.

Debs has got the yellow marigolds on and is removing everything from the pantry and stacking it on the kitchen table.

'I've never seen anything like this in all my days,' she says. 'It's outrageous. But I will have this kitchen spick and span in no time. You alright? Look like you've seen a ghost!'

'I kind of have,' I reply. 'I need a cup of tea, but I think we've run out.'

'Hang on. Let me have a rummage. I've seen teabags somewhere.'

From amid packets of pasta and about twenty jars of French mustard, she produces a box of Whittard World Teas. Our friend Diana gave them to us for Christmas. Perfect. I plump for 'Russian Caravan' and stare at the cobwebs in the corner of the ceiling while the tea brews, filling the kitchen with its smoky aroma. Just three more minutes. What's three minutes when I've been waiting for thirty years?

'Right, Debs. I'm off downstairs to start writing.'

'Off you go then. I expect nothing less than a masterpiece. I don't know where you find all them words, but if anyone can do it, you can, Manni Moo,' she says. 'I'll ring a bell or something when lunch is ready.'

As I carry my tea down the backstairs and around to my writing room, I notice a portion of wall has dislodged from the back building. A tiny speck of red peeks out from beneath layers and layers of cal. A cross section of years and years, and years and years of layers of quicklime appears like a millefeuille, the passing of time made physical: generational layers, lives lived, births celebrated, deaths mourned, best years, worst years . . . their edges lit by the slanted rays of sunlight.

There it is. Count Cayetano's red, hidden for all these years. The history of this house is beginning to join up. I flick off a flake with a fingernail and place it on my desk.

Many of my earlier layers are hidden from sight, barricaded behind fear. I decide to dismantle the barrier and begin to peel away the second, third, fourth skin of my memories. It's a gradual, careful process. I don't want to let my tea get cold so I finish my cuppa before I begin, like a nurse gently lifting a gauze pad from an open wound.

My desk is tidy. I contemplate the eagle's feather, an empty notebook with a pen alongside. I know there is no fire within me that cannot burn, no rock I cannot overturn.

For years I have dreamed of this.

I want to live in an old house, surrounded by olive trees in the middle of nowhere.

Here I am, living the dream. This is the visualisation of my greatest desire. And yes, the vision has been ripped from me. There have been times when I wanted to run away, sell the house, leave and never look back. I know Jack doesn't want to sell it. He loves it here, perhaps more than I do. But how can I salvage the peace? The house seems to speak to me. The wind whispers its way through the stone walls and the windows rattle their Morse code in their wooden frames. All appears silent but if I listen, really listen, I can hear nature's enduring truth.

Much water has passed under the broken bridge since we moved here almost five years ago. Nothing has changed. Everything has changed. I hope my pen does not run out of ink before I understand.

Perhaps it's okay to live in a ruin, to learn to live with the cracks in the walls and gaping holes in the roof that let the sunlight in. It's like accepting ageing. Why the obsession to stay young? To cover lines and stretch skin so it appears younger? Can we not learn to live within a natural state of the passing of time?

The neighbours ask us, 'Are you not going to rebuild the bridge?'

We don't want to rebuild the bridge. We simply want to accept this place as it is. We may live in a ruin but there is wisdom in its walls – wisdom that I need to understand before it is covered with fresh plaster and new paint. I need to sit with her for a while and learn, listening to the wall's whispers and the secrets they reveal.

Here, in this oldest part of an old house in this hushed valley, I need to restore myself, bring myself back from ruin and remember the whys and the hows. Flanked by mountains, I feel hemmed in without feeling trapped, alone without feeling lonely, isolated without feeling frightened, exposed without feeling vulnerable. The house is at least 150 years old and the cracks are more than beginning to show, the deep wrinkles on a face with a thousand tales to tell. I will lean into the wisdom here, hark after the heritage of this house.

Words are coming like a tidal wave. I have been aware of their approach for a while. It is like standing on an empty beach waiting for a storm to roll in. It's time to paddle out and catch the crest of the wordwave as it crashes onto the shore. I am ready. I want to be trapped by them, pinned down by them, to wrestle with them and battle with them until they untangle the truth.

It's about the way this house makes people feel. I see it as a mirror that shows us the very best and the very worst of ourselves. There are no distractions to take us away from ourselves here, so we are forced to pivot and face inwards. Perhaps Jacob's words were a prophecy. Perhaps The Corner will truly be a place where birds with broken wings will come to heal.

As much as I am not ready to restore this ruin, I am ready to restore myself. Finally, I think I have found a way to return.

'You cannot travel the path until you become the path yourself' (Buddha).

32

THE LITTLE DRUMMER BOY

I'll go back to childhood sweet like a briar rose,
Like a bell which wakes us from a dream.

Hanuš Hachenburg, from 'Terezín', 1944

I AM RICHARD. I AM A child again. Well, strictly speaking, childhood ends at puberty when you're around twelve. Does that make me an adolescent? I am fourteen, but I still feel like a child. I am in a vicarage.

A vicarage is a house of a vicar, I remind myself. And a vicar is the leader of a house of God.

In that house of God, I play the drums in the worship band, attempting to paradiddle my way into paradise. We practise in church on a Saturday evening and as the return journey is 18 miles, it makes sense for me to stay over in the vicarage. That's what the adults decide and I don't disagree. The vicarage is so much bigger than our house and I get my own room. But there is no lock on the door.

Sometimes we're in the spare room, sometimes we're in his room. Their room. I write this now as an almost fifty-year-old man, close to the age he would have been back then. He was an almost fifty-year-old married vicar taking a fourteen-year-old into his marital bed while his wife busied downstairs in the vicarage kitchen, alternating between ironing his shirts and peeling vegetables for the following day's Sunday lunch. The things he said. The things he did. The things he asked me to do. The weight of just how wrong his conduct was pulls my head down towards the keyboard to focus on my fingers as they type. My eyes are downcast as I sit with the dreadful memories.

'We're not doing anything wrong,' he would tell me – my parents' friend, their spiritual leader.

Who am I to argue? I convince myself that it is normal. He unlocks a part of me which, henceforth, forces me to become covert about my own sexuality. I would have discovered it all in good time, as I remember fancying my PE teachers long before all this started. But I would have been able to explore it on my own terms, with my own peers. He robs me of that joy. Every Saturday night he removes another pinch of my innocence. It becomes fuelled. It becomes my greatest secret. I start to find it hard to concentrate on my GCSEs and I go for longer and longer bike rides all on my own.

My parents have no idea. My brothers have no idea. I become an expert in the game we play and it is a long game. It goes on for almost two years.

The last time something happens, he moves just a little bit too swiftly. His approach is just a little bit too decisive, his eyes just a little bit too excited. I feel just a little bit too invaded and something inside me flicks to anger. He leaves the room even quicker than he came in and closes the door. We never speak of it. I never sleep at the vicarage again. I never have to, as my parents decide to move to the village.

In church, I hide behind my drum kit from the man who preaches in the pulpit. If I position myself at the right angle behind my Zildjian crash cymbal, I can't see him. If I leave via the back entrance, I can avoid his lingering kiss as he stands in the front entrance to greet people as they leave.

I bottle it up. I lock it away. I hide it. I don't tell a soul.

I don't tell a soul until I am eighteen and I am sitting in the classroom in the compound of that evangelical Christian organisation on the outskirts of Santa Cruz de la Sierra, Bolivia. I am just starting my Year for God.

I'm learning Spanish as if by osmosis and feel more at home here than anywhere I've ever been. I'm in the training phase of bible school and the teaching is intense. It's designed to act like emotional heart surgery – an early twelve-step programme based on the Bible.

Five of us have been sent from England to complete the school and then help run a day centre for street kids and alcoholics, who live out their lives in the markets and hiding places of the city. Our team is made up of a nurse, a teacher, a civil engineer, an occupational therapist and an eighteen-year-old me. Today the teaching is all about the Father Heart of God. The lecturer is from Germany and is dressed in a pair of funky lederhosen in vivid orange that match her spiky ginger hair. She stands before us with her notes, pushing her glasses back up her nose every second or third sentence, and I feel as if everything she is saying is directed exclusively towards me. How could she know? My heart starts to pump at double, triple speed.

She urges us to analyse our own fathers or anyone who has ever tried to father us, and explains how our own vision of God may have been distorted by those role models of our early childhood. It all makes sense. Her arguments are too convincing. There is nowhere I can hide. The teaching is too competent. Anyhow, I am done hiding. I am done being silent.

Abuse knits you together in the wrong way. I feel like a beautiful scarf. Knit one, purl one.

Knit, purl, knit, knit
Purl, knit, purl, purl

Lovingly crafted. Unique. It's not a perfect knit. It's not a machine knit. It's a human knit. There is loose weave where the sun was shining and tight weave where the storms rolled in. Somewhere near the middle of my scarf, there is a clump of tangled mess. Invasive threads from somebody else's needles, an ugly mistake, a glaring imperfection. It affects the whole.

Weft, weave, weft, weft
Weave, weft, weave, weave

I grab the arm of Suzanna, the lovely Suzanna from Cochabamba, my group leader, and lead her into the garden. She looks at me with her honeycomb eyes of kindness as I tell her everything, the terse grass lawn tickling my legs as we rotate our position every so often to move with the shade of a banana tree.

In the following days and weeks, Suzanna helps me through the healing process. I write the vicar a letter and then take a microbus into the city centre to send it from the post office near the main square. I never see the letter again, but I reference it in my diary.

His reply arrives at our community post box a few weeks later. I find Suzanna in the kitchen doing the washing-up, plastic plates and cheap, bent cutlery strewn over white tea clothes to dry.

'He's replied,' I tell her. She dries her hands on her apron and follows me out to the garden.

'Let's open it together, Richard,' she suggests. (I still went by Richard at that point in my life).

Open, Close, Open, Open
Close, Open, Close, Close

I read his handwriting out loud, buffeting the cracks in my voice. The tone is legal. He was a lawyer before being *called*

271

into the ministry, before donning the dog collar. What a clever lawyer he must have been.

He thanks me for my beautiful letter.

He is highly embarrassed I have initiated contact before him.

I am mature beyond my years.

He admits responsibility.

He asks for my forgiveness.

Finally, he asks me to burn the letter.

Who am I to argue? How am I to know that those flames take away the possibility of a criminal investigation? These flames will fill my parents with an anger that bursts the dimensions of their bodies. Dad will never really express his anger. Mum is different. Years later, she will scream through burning tears: '*Why? Whyyyyyyy did you burn it?*'

Because I wanted to draw a line under the pukey pain.

Because I needed to turn a page.

Because both Suzanna and I agreed it was the best thing to do.

Because I was 6,000 miles from where it happened and finally felt as if I could put it behind me.

Because he told me to.

And I thought I had put it behind me. I really did. But after Joe's death, when I walked by the River of the Silent Ones, the memories came back to bite me. As an adult, I barely remember being a child. A minor is always a minor.

He threw an 'I am innocent' party at the church following a public investigation which was eventually abandoned, owing to lack of evidence. Friends of my parents attended. If he was innocent, what did that make me? A liar? I was far away in Edinburgh, sitting my finals, but this all happened on my parents' doorstep. I can control my own pain, but not that of others. I can't bear to imagine my parents' suffering. I still have a letter from Mum, pouring her heart onto the page, admitting that her devastation led to depression over the whole affair. And this is the key about abuse. It affects not just the victim, but its ramifications are widespread. I hate to imagine my parents' pain, and that is why I don't want to be one of the Silent Ones any longer. I hope that these words might provide them with a key to unlock their own pain.

When we are forgiven, I believe we should honour that generosity and never re-offend. He did the opposite. A new case arose. He was caught masturbating in the showers of a Scout camp and was banned from working with children. After the ban, he appealed the decision, to defend his innocence once again.

A disciplinary tribunal for the Secretary of State in London contacted me to provide testimony. My lawyer represented the Child Protection Act. I entered the court building alone as a grown man: confident, calm, composed. My friends, Fernando and Jose Mesa, waited for me in the pub opposite.

The vicar was there with his wife. I was aware of their shapes but made sure I never looked at them. I was surprised by how at ease I felt. For days I had been dreading this moment but, once inside, I suppose the truth set my fears free. He had plenty of reasons to deny it, but what reason did I have to lie?

I centred my gaze on the disciplinary board that addressed me with pointed questions. My answers did not embarrass me. I hope they made him squirm. I have no idea what was going on in his wife's head. I imagine her sitting there in her Sunday best, hair set, silk collar turned up, pearls on. The saddest part of all of this is that I used to love them both. She made the greatest gravy.

I knew how wrong he had been and I told the court how his actions had affected my life and my relationships ever since. Apparently, according to the report, I was a strong witness. His lawyer made no headway in cross-examining me, and later, my lawyer obtained strong concessions which corroborated my evidence.

I left the room with a heightened sense of who I was. A new confidence began to bloom as I crossed the street to be reunited with my friends who had the first of many pints waiting. Something had shifted in my mind's eye. A misplaced sense of guilt left me. It's weird. I dreaded seeing him again. I never wanted to be back in the same room as him. When I least expected them to, my fears left me. We shouldn't be frightened of returning. Going back to the source of our pain is sometimes one of the best ways to find release, as we work our way back to the centre of the labyrinth.

Yet again, it wasn't to be. Even though the tribunal deemed his 'conduct in relation to you to be misconduct and the type of conduct which placed you at harm or at risk of harm', they upheld his appeal, citing a sufficient passing of time – he was no longer deemed to be a danger. Another witness would not give evidence. I've often wondered who he was. The vicar walked free again, probably holding his wife's hand.

The vicar is dead now. He was never convicted of any crime, so he wasn't a criminal. They would have needed the letter. So, he walked free. And here is why I am breaking my silence – he only walked free because I forgave him, because I burned his letter.

When he died, my Mum called me to tell me the news. His passing was totally inconsequential to me. I felt nothing. Was he a bad man? I think he was a good man who did bad things. I would lay my bottom dollar on the fact that he was damaged and, rather than turn to face his hurt and squash the power of abuse, he gave in to it.

I see the Little Drummer Boy before me, sitting behind his red Pearl drum kit with its brand-new Paiste hi-hat cymbals; his pride and joy. He is small. He is untouched. He is pure. He is a little light. Those fragile flames should have been protected, nurtured, allowed to burn and not blown out. Richard was a child.

33

CAYETANO

I MAKE NEW DISCOVERIES ABOUT OUR count. The information sits with me in my writing room like a long-lost friend.

Some weeks ago, I applied for his records from the National Military Archives in Segovia. I received an email with a sixty-page document – his entire military records, handwritten and painstakingly documented. Sixty pages. The records confirm that he was born in Pamplona in 1850. The fact that I learn the names of his mum and dad makes him immediately more real: Manuel and Gregoria. He was in active service by the age of fifteen and quickly climbed through the ranks: Junior Officer, Lieutenant, Captain by the age of twenty-four, Commander, Lieutenant Colonel, Colonel, Brigadier General, and finally, Divisional General aged sixty-six.

The slanted inked writing is difficult to read. His career took him all over Spain. And then there is a pause in his career, a hiatus. In 1900, when he was fifty, he came to Archidona and spent three years here – 1900, 1901 and 1902. Three years of sabbatical.

The archive also emailed me a photo of him. Kindly and noble, he wears a double-breasted jacket, the lapels stiff and broad. The collar of his white dress shirt is starched into wingtips. His Van Dyke beard and moustache frame an ageing face. Hair neatly parted. Nose long and strong, and a slightly pinched look to his gentle eyes. I stare at his image with an air of nostalgia. Ah, Cayetano. There you are. Every bit the gentleman I imagined you would be.

I cast my eye over the notes on my art pad. Whole pages scribbled, dashed, lined and drawn with the musings of my mind. I light a candle with the last of a box of long cooks' matches that my mum left in my last Christmas stocking and sit with my notes for a while, refusing to be distracted, finding the breath of my imagination. From the low hum of the quietest part of me, I feel Cayetano close. I feel his breath whisper around the stones, through the cracks in the door, through the leaves on the step and along the wooden beams of the low ceiling. Is he here? Is he gifting me words? I remain completely still, focused, rooted. The walls soak up my ideas and store them there, like rising damp.

Count Félix, Cayetano de Alvear y Ramírez de Arrellano, calls me from beyond the river, from his resting place in the Almudena cemetery in Madrid. He raises his head from the earth like Old Man Mountain, gently pushing his nose and face through the earth's crust, just enough to catch a glimpse of me through the olive trees, urging me onwards and beseeching me to walk only with my pen and finish what he started.

I open my eyes. A gust of fresh air skipping off the river flows through the open door and extinguishes the candle's flame. I see his face. I only wish I could ask him the question: 'Don Cayetano, were you a writer?'

34

THE LAYING ON OF HANDS

To live is to suffer, to survive is to find some meaning in the suffering.

Friedrich Nietzsche

O N THE SUBJECT OF FRIENDS, I have my own quiet and particular philosophy: that our true friends, counted on the fingers on one hand, wouldn't like to live without us, nor would we like to exist without them. Our true friends know our soul and I would go to the ends of the earth for those I truly love.

Never one to be part of a group, for much of my life I have been a loner. Isn't that true of many damaged people? That's not to say I have constantly battled loneliness. Much of this digging deep on a personal level is learned behaviour from my childhood.

When I arrived at Edinburgh University, I began to form a group of true friends, to belong to a posse. I would hear them talk of their 'home friends' and I began to notice the foundational values that a strong sense of home places beneath your feet.

Many of them were Christians. They were my most natural magnet. Having just spent my Year for God in Bolivia, I was still a teetotaller, a virgin and a fervent believer as I walked around the university campus wearing my alpaca poncho and an inquisitive smile. I became Mission Secretary of the Christian Union. The committee would meet once a week to plan, study the Bible, pray for direction and set the agenda for the mission philosophy of the Union, both within the university and beyond. They were my tribe.

University was a vast sea of learning. Not only was I learning the academics of my passion in the Latin American Studies course on the thirteenth floor of David Hume Tower (now 40 George Square), but I was also learning about myself and the world around me. I learned that people live in houses with names rather than numbers. I learned that some students drove smart cars and were members of exclusive 'members-only' clubs in the city. I learned that some students owned their own flats in New Town. I also learned that my father fasted on Tuesdays and, with the savings he made on food, he sent my elder brother and me a cheque at the beginning of each term for £100.

One person truly saw me and I truly saw her. Ours was a friendship that left us both unveiled. Ali was the first person I told about my sexual tendencies, on a beach in St Andrews. Neither of us quite knew what to do with the knowledge. It was a painful wedge between us, forcing us to be friends when other feelings might have blossomed. She held that information bravely and alone for so long, and I will always be grateful for her love and unwavering support. I learned that my road was not going to be an easy one.

I also learned that I needn't have gone as far as Bolivia to help children in need, that in Leith there were children from ripped-up home lives who desperately needed a listening ear and a semblance of guidance in their lives. I learned that my life thus far had been very sheltered. I learned that there were other paths people could choose to find fulfilment in religion. I learned there was a Baha'i group. As I read through the booklet of university associations, I also learned there was a Gay, Lesbian and Bisexual community group. Really? I learned of gay bars, gay cafés, gay clubs. I never visited any of them but on my bike rides and runs, I discovered where they were.

There was no way I could venture there, not as Mission Secretary of the Christian Union. Impossible. My mind was a battleground. I kept those thoughts at bay with small prayers pronounced with fervour. No. I must stay strong as a warrior for God and remain within his purpose for the rest of my life. These impulses were surely the work of the devil on my shoulder, whose evil intention was to keep me from the path God had chosen for me. Isn't that what I had discovered in my Discipleship Training School in Bolivia? I pored over my notes.

I busied myself in Christian duties and prayer meetings, and buried my head in my studies. My formidable Director of Studies had told me very early on in the course that I possessed a firm grasp of Spanish grammar, but that I spoke like a South

American street kid. She said that I would have to spend the first year catching up with my fellow students, who had a more classical basis of Castilian Spanish. Eighty per cent of them had studied in the best private schools of the United Kingdom. I had learned on the streets and in the drug dens of Santa Cruz. I spent hours in the basement of the David Hume Tower, in the Visual Arts department, pouring over Almodóvar films and working on my Spanish pronunciation.

One afternoon, after a swim in the public baths, I felt the lure of a direct gaze. The owner of those creamy eyes was a man almost three times my age. I followed as he led me to the door of the sauna. It all happened quickly. It was a rushed and clumsy fumble. I left the sauna, threw my clothes over my hot and sweaty body, and ran home. I scrabbled with the keys. My heart was beating so fast. Once inside the bathroom, I sat on the floor hardly believing what had just happened. I tried to shower away the shame.

But I had followed him of my own accord. There had been no manipulation. No lies. No deceit. I was no longer a minor and I had stepped over into an undiscovered world. Now I knew where to go to find men. There was a public place where I could go without raising suspicion, where men might want me. Where I might want them. The code was cracked. It was the beginning. It was legal. It was exciting. It was frightening. It was my one and only drug.

My addiction was fuelled by the thrill of secrecy. I was oddly proud of my double life. Who knew? Who could have guessed? Drilling it underground forged a duality into my character which I think brewed deceit in later relationships. It would eventually take the natural and understanding love of Jack to gently break those chains. But back in Edinburgh, it felt like a game. Didn't Paul in the Book of Corinthians say, 'I have become all things to all men that I may by all means save some?' (1 Cor. 9:22). I definitely wasn't doing it to save them. Maybe I was doing it to save myself.

I suffered bouts of total confusion. To clear my head, I would cycle Edinburgh's streets or hike up to the summit of Arthur's Seat to cast my plight to the winds and survey the city from its highest point. I continued my double-life antics for over a year. My liaisons with men remained sporadic, anonymous and hidden. It seemed unthinkable to even want to know the names or identities of the men I touched.

In my second year I shared a flat with three incredibly special guys. We were a popular crew and enjoyed a year of fun and friendship in our New Town basement flat. There were two Matts in the flat and a young Reuben named them 'Matt Yellow Hair' and 'Matt Brown Hair' to differentiate them. Those nicknames stick to this day. One evening, Matt Brown Hair and I were alone in the flat. I was drying up in the tiny galley kitchen and he was by the open fire smoking a cigar. Oh, we were so civilised in our early twenties. Out of the blue, he asked me three questions.

'Manni, what's your favourite film?'

'What's your favourite breakfast cereal?'

'What do you think about homosexuality?'

He had me. He knew. I panicked. Matt was a Christian.

Lapsed, he would say. Or struggling. Questioning. His mind was a deep well. He was studying Psychology and in his end-of-second-year exam, one of his answers impressed his professors with its unusual insight and brush with perfection. The department recognised this publicly and a photograph of him hangs in the building to this day.

Matt Brown Hair had the stroke of a genius. I dropped the plate I was drying.

'Don't worry. Leave it,' he told me as I looked at the shards shattered on the black-and-white linoleum. 'Come over here, Manni. Come and sit down, mate. I think you and I should have a chat, don't you think?' He patted the plumped-up cushion of the green high-backed armchair next to him and flashed his cheeky grin.

But Matt Brown Hair was the last guy I would have chosen to tell. He was a lad's lad. He played football and went drinking with the boys. I sat down in stunned silence. I looked towards the door and hoped that Matt Yellow Hair and Jerry wouldn't return for a while. This moment might never be repeated and I didn't want it to end.

'What do you want me to tell you, Matt?' I asked him nervously.

'Everything,' he replied.

His words lifted a burden that had been squashing me for years. My mind took flight and I glimpsed a new freedom: from lies, pretence, fear. As I looked into Matt's eyes, I saw sympathy without condescension, understanding without judgement. He was listening as a psychologist. He was listening as a friend. It was an evening of pure academic insight. It was also an evening of pure love. I had never felt so wrapped up in the arms of a male friend. It was a feeling of acceptance I had never experienced from a man before. I had love from my brothers, but this was different. Matt was a peer.

He made me feel safe. So many friends have been brave enough to ask me if I was in love with him that I have been forced to ask myself the same question. I loved him. Of that there is no doubt, but no, I wasn't *in* love with him. Our friendship was gold-plated, with the rarest and most precious of platonic love. He became another keeper of my secret, a most treasured companion. I am sure Ali was as relieved as I was that she could finally confide in Matt Brown Hair and talk with him about my struggles – a burden shared.

As I grappled with my demons, Matt Brown Hair held my shield. As I languished in confusion, he gave me clarity. We rented a cottage together in the Scottish Borders to revise for our exams away from the city and hiked in the wee hours of the morning. We were mates. He even stood by me when I decided to tackle the problem head on.

My decision went against his principles, but he accompanied me all the same. Greater love hath no man. I had taken the solitary decision to seek out conversion therapy. I felt I owed it to the God I had believed in, to at least try to change. If homosexuality wasn't his plan for my life and would set me on a trajectory far from his blessings, then the fear these teachings had instilled in me convinced me to attempt the power of prayer.

There was nothing contrite in my decision. There was faith and there was hope. I still believed my sexuality was working against my natural state. I knew by this stage in my life that I was an all-or-nothing kind of guy.

We cycled to my local church community building in the middle of the day. Matt waited outside, guarding the bikes and pacing the pavement while I was inside trying to have the homosexuality purged out of me. When I see it from Matt's perspective, even greater is my love for him.

I'd previously shared my predicament with my youth leader and, together with one of the elders of the church, they decided to banish my sexual orientation from me, to denounce it and cast it out in Jesus's name.

Elders of the church were once again laying their hands on me. Looking back, I am surprised that I was willing to go through such a degrading and shocking experience. So earnest was my pursuit of purity. In my heart of hearts, years of learning and devoted Christian practice had convinced me that this was the only way. To empty myself of freewill, empty myself of 'self' and pray the gay away. I quiver at the excruciating reality of it all now. How confused I was.

I want to bundle my twenty-one-year-old self into my own arms, hug him close and tell him how loved and accepted he was. How close to the brink of emotional collapse I must have been. I dread to think what might have happened had Matt not been with me on those bleak, black days. Thank you, Matt Brown Hair.

I stood in the middle of the church while two men wailed in tongues and prayed in confidence that, through their words and their faith, the homosexual tendencies would flee from my body, that I would be set free, that I would be whole, that I would be pure in Jesus's name. They laid their hands on my head and my heart, applying pressure in varying degrees. I cringe at the memory of their faces; they seemed to be enjoying themselves. I suppose they had nothing to lose. I took myself to the altar that day. There is no greater act of humility and sacrifice that any god could have asked of me. I was Abraham laying Isaac on the altar. I clamoured to God that if he was the all-powerful deity, surely he could heal me and take away my chalice of pain? I was pleading for a miracle.

It was in that empty church, listening to the low roar of bus engines as they worked their way along the Lothian Road, hearing the buzz of the city filtering through the stained-glass windows, blending with the beseeching pleas of my pastor, that I lost my faith.

I could no longer invest my time, life and energy in a system, a creed, a church that had led me down a dead end of despondency. I had done nothing to deserve it. It just didn't work. It wasn't true. It made no sense. I saw it all so clearly. I was Paul walking away from Damascus. It was a personal epiphany based only on personal convictions after years of Bible teachings, sermons, bible schools and youth camps. The ship had sailed. There would be no looking back. I no longer wanted to change who I was.

I left the faithful ones behind me, clinging to their hope and strolled out into the street, just as one might leave a cinema after watching a horror movie. The world inside the building and outside in the city had no parallels. Matt was biting his nails. We hugged.

'How was that, mate?' he asked me.

'Well, there's nothing more I can do, Matt, bar electrocution therapy.'

'Do you feel any different?' he asked, already knowing the answer.

We laughed as we peddled up Clerk Street to buy warm doughnuts from the bakery on St Patrick Square.

My self-inflicted dabble with conversion therapy strengthened my resolve to avoid changing the essence of me. I realised how potentially damaging it was to reject a naturally occurring part of me. Matt Brown Hair helped me through the following weeks. I think he was relieved it hadn't worked. He loved me as I was. Now, I just had to learn to love myself.

My own parents have travelled the length and breadth of their own torment. My father flew to Lisbon to be with me. My own mother took a more tortuous road. I received a letter from her which I still have:

'I want you to know now more than ever that I still love you so much it hurts. I've always loved you, perhaps too much. I'm not going to say what's right or wrong in all this', she begins.

She ends, 'All my love, Mum xx'

It took us a few months to find the courage to face it together, but eventually we did, in a Burger King in West London. On moulded plastic seats, we cried and confided in each other until we both reached a place of peace.

Back in Edinburgh, I began to share my secret with my inner circle. Looking back now, it all seems a tad dramatic. A gang of us went to a friend's family's holiday cottage in Badrallach and there in the conservatory, one sunny afternoon, I shared my news. It rather scuppered the buoyant atmosphere. Shocked faces went for walks. It was new to us all. We opened bottles of wine while we worked through it together. My male mates wondered if I'd fancied them all this time. I assured them I hadn't and they seemed relieved. *I* was relieved.

Word was out in the Christian Union, where I had been Missionary Secretary for almost two years. I had to stand proud among the whispers. The hurt came when every member of the committee boycotted my twenty-first birthday party. People I considered friends called with lame excuses. From others, it was simply a no-show. It felt like orders had come down from on high. Shunned. Stunned. So, I partied with my real tribe with a catwalk in the living room. Everyone dressed up in Jean-Paul Gaultier get-ups. Matt Brown Hair wore body art. Matt Yellow Hair wore tartan trousers. I wore a kilt and a blue-and-white stripey top.

University broke for the summer and we all parted ways. Friends with cars crammed them full of belongings and drove home. I didn't have a car, but I did have a dear school chum, Anna, whose grandad lived in Edinburgh, and he kindly let me take over his garden shed. Most of my belongings, boxed and bagged, dominated his shed for the best part of two years. I will always be grateful for his generosity. Another suitcase in another shed.

I headed south to enjoy the summer with my family. In my head something had changed. I was more open to a new freedom, less chastising of myself. Matt Brown Hair was to spend the summer putting up marquees for weddings. We kept in touch by phone.

As a family, we took a rare foreign holiday to Çeşme, in Turkey, a friendly town on the east coast facing the Aegean Sea. I was having the time of my life with my brothers as our escapades took us into the Turkish nights. Our mornings were spent nursing hangovers by the pool, chatting to our parents. One morning, I was the first brother to wake and took a sleepy stroll down to find Mum and Dad lounging by the pool.

'Morning, Mumsie. How are you? You'll never guess what happened last night!' I chirped.

She glanced at my dad who was rising into a sitting position as he swallowed hard and adjusted his sunglasses. He placed his newspaper on the blue-and-white striped mattress.

'Sit down, love,' Mum said, patting the end of her sun lounger. 'Something terrible has happened.' I could feel sadness descending from the crystal-blue sky.

'What's happened?' I pleaded

She grabbed my hand. 'I'm so sorry, love. Tash got hold of us last night with some terrible news. Matt Brown Hair has been killed in a car crash.'

I think I grimaced. I don't think I heard her. I wanted to tell her the funny tales of last night's escapades.

I was a bursting dam. Emotions raged from me in torrents.

She grabbed me and pulled me towards her, but I didn't want her warmth. I didn't want her embrace. I didn't want anything from anybody. My insides vaporised and I became weightless. I remember skirting around the edge of the pool, up the steps to Reception, through the double doors and out onto the street. I needed to be in an open place and ran towards the edge of town, up towards the hills. I ran because I didn't know what else to do. I felt as if a thousand souls were running with me, scuffling and elbowing, as if the gun for the start of a marathon had just sounded and there was a surge for space. And yet I was alone. I felt the wave coming, rising inside me, so I ran all the harder to suppress the pressure. Houses flashed past as concerned faces followed my unusual pace in this town of gentle walkers.

I spotted an empty hill and jumped onto a rising path, up and out of the urban maze. I crumbled into a heap and waited for the bubbles to rise. They erupted and a scream deep in my throat hissed its way through gritted teeth and into the wind. I stayed there until I was cold and slowly made my way back to the hotel where my family was waiting for me with a plane ticket back to London. Ali collected me from the airport and we spent a long week together in her flat waiting for the funeral.

After Matt's burial, when each of us went our own way, I felt totally bereft. Grief is so personal that it can't always be shared.

I simply wanted to coil into my shell and be alone. Matt had been my guy rope and kept me taut against the buffeting winds. I missed him endlessly, and still do. Our friendship was unique. Of course these types of friendships exist, but in their purest essence they are difficult to find. I had lost that jewel, the person who understood the course of my emotions, perhaps better than I knew them myself. I became unhinged. Something in me clicked, triggered by deception, by the insurmountable annoyance that I had spent my entire life serving a religion and answering to a god that had left me adrift and then sunk my life raft.

If Christianity were a company and God were its boss then, when Matt Brown Hair died, I handed in my notice. His death confirmed my decision – I no longer wanted to devote the best years of my life to what suddenly appeared to be a flailing business with a cruel and manipulative CEO.

I don't think I could have been a more committed Christian. I'd towed the line, studied the Bible, prayed. I had been a virgin all the way through my teens. I didn't smoke. I didn't drink. My only vice had been clinging regimentally to the word of God, and I know I put several noses out of joint with my hardline opinions and radical viewpoints.

I looked back at my years of service and realised that I had nothing to show for it. God couldn't have had a more loyal subject. If he wasn't able to utilise my gifts and devotions to his cause, then he wasn't a good boss. Pure and simple.

More importantly, for many years now, I had been denying a part of me that had been pushing its way to the surface, desperate to find its own expression.

I chose me.

I walked away from the physical church and I walked away from the church of my mind. I abandoned the faith structure that I had believed in since my early childhood. It all became crystal clear. If God was a loving God, who knew how many hairs I had on my head and only wanted the best for me, as my omnipotent, omnipresent, everlasting Father, why had he played this cruel trick of nature on me? Why had he punished me further by taking away a friend who had held my hand through my personal struggle?

All the counter-arguments I had learned through days of evangelising came back to bite me: free will, sin, the fall of mankind, God won't test you beyond your own limits, what doesn't kill you makes you stronger, and so on. I laughed at how ludicrous it all sounded now.

The relief wasn't instantaneous. It took me several months, even years, to untangle myself from those cords of creed and coercion, but I eventually stepped into the new me. I stepped into 'me', unfettered, unshackled and free.

I heard the whispers behind my back:

'What a great shame.'

'Don't walk away from God's purpose in your life.'

'Reconsider. I am praying for you. There are some things we simply cannot understand. Only God knows the whole truth.'

'Do not walk away. Jesus is the only way.'

I still have the letters.

'Ask God to show you the way home.'

'There's an evil one prowling around trying to snatch Jesus's children away. You need to fight it.'

'Like the Prodigal Son, you may have spent your inheritance, but your father has a feast waiting for you.'

The arguments were strong and the accusations weighed heavily on me, but I never looked back. I have never been back to the church I once knew. Granted, there have been Christmases when I have indulged my parents and, to show a united family front, have gone to a Christmas Day service. This has been more about tradition than faith. I remember my mum's pleading eyes when it came to Communion and the guilt I was supposed to feel for staying in my pew. If only Mum had understood how every cell in my body rejected the idea of Holy Communion, then she surely wouldn't have asked me twice.

It's funny how I had always assumed, arrogantly, that because 'God is Love', a life without God would be loveless. That is what I preached for years, at school, in Bolivia, during our 'Stepping Out' Mission at Edinburgh University. I was an active part of the campaign to tell our campus pals that they needed what we had.

How wrong I was. I think I have loved more since losing my faith than before. And when I say, 'losing my faith', I use the term lightly. I didn't lose my faith. It's not something I have misplaced and am wandering around my life aimlessly looking for. My faith is not in Lost and Found.

Rather than spending my life celebrating the truth, I prefer to spend it questioning. I enjoy the search, perhaps more than the truth itself. I enjoy the empty space.

After that prayer session in the church in Edinburgh, I simply put my faith down among those empty pews and walked away. When Matt Brown Hair died, the deal was sealed. I gathered up all my faith, all my prayer, all my commitment to intercession, all my worship, all my conviction and bundled them into a tight parcel, bound with string. I then left that parcel in a very open and public place. I didn't hide it. Finally, it dawned on me that I had nothing to hide.

As part of my grieving process, once I was through denial and anger, I felt I needed help to guide me through the 'what if . . .?' stage and the creeping sadness. I knew Matt's mum was a counsellor and a psychotherapist, but would that be too weird?

I suggested it to her and her reply was, 'I can if you can. From the minute you walk in, I won't be Matt's mum. I'll be your therapist.'

We both knew that was nigh on impossible. I remember arriving at Leeds Central Station and feeling nostalgic about my solo trips into Leeds centre for my percussion lessons ten years previously, observing that little boy Richard through a prism of life experience.

My hour with Anthea was balm for my emotional bruises. I found the whole experience oddly thrilling and was filled with a sense of relief that I didn't have to go it alone anymore. She walked me gently through my memories using wise and compassionate questions as signposts. We both felt the privilege of being able to acknowledge Matt's importance and the hole that his death had left. I shared details that I wanted her to know, both as my therapist and as Matt's mum. He was there in that room with us, of that I am certain, grinning from ear to ear, chuffed to bits that his mum and his mate were tunnelling so deeply into the uncharted depths of my psyche. In a way, by analysing the spectrum of our shared grief, Anthea finished what Matt had started. She was able to tie up the loose ends of his legacy in my life.

I hope that hour helped Anthea as much as it helped me. What a beautiful hour, a golden hour of humanity. There was a splitting of dimensions that morning. If pain can be a privilege, then that hour was probably the closest Anthea and I would ever get to that truth. I found the connection healing. I left the therapy room feeling lighter and more secure, as if I'd turned a massive corner. It helped me accept two things: Matt's death and my own sexuality.

Rather than this being a cause for concern, I met my new freedom with a huge sense of relief. I wanted to make up for lost time, pivot, do a 180° about-turn and head in totally the opposite direction. In a house with three brothers that wasn't going to happen. With no means to access the wilds, I took myself to the extreme wilderness of London. I could escape for £2.20 on the fast train from Reading station to Paddington.

I donned a pair of tight blue jeans and a fitted white T-shirt. I had no agenda. There was no plan. I simply walked until I was tired.

It really is astonishing how a world totally invisible to me before this moment – for I did not know it existed – revealed itself on London's streets. Eye-flicks, second glances, a sudden slow in a steady gait, a stare that turned heads here and there, glances at once hungry, compassionate, mournful – and charged. I learned the language as quickly as I'd learned Spanish, as if by osmosis. In the space of a few hours, I became fluent in this underworld of communication. I perfected the codes of cruising.

I remember it was a hot day. Most of London was in the parks, the garden squares, the commons. Sunroofs were open, soft tops were down. My feet took me to Earl's Court and I loitered outside the Tube station until a French man did a double-take as he walked past me. I followed his gaze. He stopped and returned to my spot. We shook hands and chatted with a natural warmth. I had known nothing like it. He invited me back to his hotel. I asked his name. It was my choice, and I chose to go with him.

That experience was like a butterfly that landed on a domino halfway down the sequence of my life's design. Up the line, those dominos remained upright, untouched, but down the line, experiences fell into each other like a sequence of adventures. I could spend days in London and enter a time warp of random encounters. It was like a feast after a famine. I found warmth. I found kindred spirits. There was no judgement. It was my secret universe and I could enter it at will.

Back at home, no one suspected. At least, if they did, they didn't let on. It was a departure and an arrival – a homecoming. I crossed from one tribe to another. I was honest with the men who took me into their arms. They could see that I was damaged and none of them wanted second dates. I missed

Matt Brown Hair with an ache in my soul, but I wasn't alone on this walk to the centre of the labyrinth. I knew that he was somewhere, pencil behind his ear, observing my movements, taking notes and analysing them with his professional psychologist's eye.

'You're gonna be alright, Manni Boy,' he would have said. 'Do what you feel is right. Trust your inner self. That is the only thing that will bring you home.'

35

EAGLES' FLIGHT

I NEED TO GO FOR A walk, to shake off the residue of memories. I don't want conversation. In my search for words, company will hide words from me. I go alone.

Off to the east, flying low, close to the arched backbone of the ridge, I spot them arriving, flying in perfect formation, equally distanced. Mother eagle. Father eagle. Eaglet. The unity is glaring. Mother glides masterfully through the thermals, barely twitching a feather, her approach long and flat, reaching the nest with millimetric precision. Father finds the exact same flight path and echoes the same perfect intricacy, flying through my field of vision, barely moving, stationary in flight. Total dominion. Eaglet follows confidently, but misjudges its line and has to pull up clumsily at the last second. His talons grip the outer edge of the nest and panicked wing-beats tip him into safety.

'Phew!' I exhale. BB pushes into my side to feel me close, sensing my relief.

All three birds remain there, comparing notes. I am barely breathing, just short slurps of air. I have no camera, no phone, only my mind to record this sight. I consciously wipe my mind clean, opening a new folder in the memory bank of my mind. I need to remember every single, last detail.

I remember when my dad took the stabilisers off my orange Playmaster bicycle, the first time I rode solo. I was in Headingley, Leeds, up by the recreation ground. I remember the untethered thrill, the priceless satisfaction in my father's eyes.

Mother and eaglet then commit to a tandem flight. She leads and her offspring follows. She traces their approach in reverse, heads to the east, over the ridge and out of sight. The fledgling hurries after her, flapping his wings ten to the dozen to keep up.

This time his line traces his mother's to perfection and he lands back with a new confidence. He is ready. This is it. This is his moment.

I try not to blink. I don't want to miss this. His first solo flight. He finds the edge of the nest, barely pauses and launches himself into the valley. His wingtips flicker with insecurity and tiny tilts as he attempts to find his lines. His flight is a far cry from the smooth, precise glides of his elders.

I call him by my special whistle. Who knows if it resonates with him? Perhaps I am deluding myself. I repeat it every few seconds to let him know I'm here.

He lands in a tree to rest. It's an awkward landing. He has to lift his wings to readjust himself and find his balance.

I watch breathless as he launches himself into another round of spectacle. He is silent this time, no longer shrieking with glee. His movements are altogether more focused. I become part of his intent.

The steep hillside with the low sun reveals his shadow as he joins it for a dance against the cliffs of the Pinnacle. He tilts and swoops in the muted hues of last light, his shadow calling him back as he disappears and re-enters the scene, tipping his wings against the wind. He is flying. He is playing. I have lost track of both parents, but I know they will be watching. They know their work is done.

36

DUENDE

I WAS LIVING IN SEVILLE WITH Quique, my first Spanish boyfriend, when I met Antonio in broad daylight on a street in Madrid's Chueca neighbourhood. I thought I'd learned my lesson when I left one relationship for another in London, but apparently not. This time I was to learn it good and proper. When Antonio and I walked past each other, it was what they call in Spanish a 'flechazo', an arrow, straight to the heart. Our eyes locked as we passed each other and a tangible attraction pulled between us. He was fiercely masculine with thick, muscular limbs and a warrior torso. Sallow skin wrapped his angular bone structure, and an intense stare penetrated a fringe of silky black hair. Both of us stopped dead just one door down and turned around. Barely three weeks later, I had left a wonderful life with Quique and had been pulled by an inexplicable force into a slow-motion car crash of a relationship. There were many alarm bells that should have and did go off

302

in my brain, but I ignored the vast majority of them. Call it my fatalistic curiosity. When it was all over, my friends flooded me with their previous concerns.

'He had a dodgy eye. Never trust anyone with an eye that drifts all by itself.'

'He had such a peculiar energy.'

'There was something about him that always scared me.'

Why didn't they tell me at the time? I probably wouldn't have listened. I was smitten by this man who could recite Lorca like no other. When he danced everyone stared. I found a flat in Seville for us to rent. I hired a van in Madrid and drove all his belongings down from the capital. Normally I love that drive, leaving the entrails of Madrid through tunnels and barriered dual carriageways, quickly passing all the industrial estates, or polígonos, that wrap it like a no man's land between town and country, before the city spits you onto the sheer, vast tabletop of Spain – the Meseta of La Mancha. Vineyards, windmills, tiny towns and enormous country estates lead into the jagged mountain range of Desfiladero de Despeñaperros, before Andalusia welcomes you calmly from below, beckoning you into her light and oceans of olive groves.

This ride was different though. The car felt unsteady, as if the tyres needed air, but I couldn't bring myself to stop and check. I just wanted to get there. Antonio talked all the way, reciting the minutiae of his life in Madrid and his origins in Andalusia. I was taking him home. As we approached Seville from the northeast, having left behind us the mighty city of Córdoba, he began to sing 'Ojos Verdes', one of my favourite songs. I couldn't believe how well he sang it, perfect inflections of the semitones of flamenco. Some dark recesses of my heart began to flood with duende. I looked at him, smiled and tightened my grip on the steering wheel.

In Seville, Antonio filled me with assurances that he knew loads of famous people who would plug him into Sevillian life. He was a hair stylist and had worked with big names from the Spanish film industry. He had loads of savings. So many friends. I should have known when he disappeared to make long phone calls. I probably should have known when Reuben took an immediate dislike to him and a friend of a friend told me to be careful. I really should have known when he went out and didn't come back until the quiet hours of pre-dawn. But by then, it was too late. I was in too deep. Antonio had woven too many threads, spun countless radials around me. I was a spider trapped in his web.

But oh, when he recited Lorca, I lost all my cares. I was bewitched by him. He was also careful to take great care of me. He washed and folded my clothes like a professional. He would select my outfits when I was in the shower and leave them laid out on the bed. Gradually he took the simplest of choices away. Within six months, I had begun to lose the core of me.

One morning, an unannounced visitor pressed the buzzer for our first floor flat. Jan, recently arrived from Holland, looked deflated by life but forced a brave smile through a face too old for its age. Foolishly, I let him in and he stayed for weeks, sleeping on my sofa.

When Jan was able to talk to me alone, he snatched the opportunity to take me into his confidence. While looking over his shoulder to make sure Antonio didn't reappear, he bore his tormented soul. He had met Antonio, much as I had – a chance meeting and a near-fatal attraction. Seven years later, he had reached a point of such personal derailment, lost in the chains of addiction, not only to alcohol and drugs, but also to the very man who had skilfully ensnared him, that he attempted to take his own life. His attempt failed and that same day, he was straitjacketed, flown back to his home country by his embassy and placed in psychiatric care for six months.

'And do you know the first thing I did when I was dismissed?' he asked me, furtive eyes glancing sideways. 'I walked out of that institution, caught a taxi to the airport and flew straight here.'

The dates tumbled in my head as I tried to steady the free-fall. I had met Antonio almost six months previously to the day. Had that been the day of Jan's attempted suicide? The day before? I gasped at the brilliance of Antonio's duplicity. My shoulders rose in anxiety until my chin touched my chest, my neck disappearing in a gesture of disbelief. I had been duped.

'Why the hell did you come back, Jan, when you had already got away?'

'Because I'm an addict.' He laughed, mouth open wide, a tiny string of spittle linking his bottom lip to his top. 'But I'd rather be addicted to Antonio than heroin.' I noticed his saggy skin where surely muscle used to keep it taught. I saw the yellow in his pleading eyes. He was pleading for my friendship. I refused to befriend him. They were part of the same problem. My problem.

I decided I needed to get out. I just needed to plan my exit, but it wasn't going to be easy to extricate myself.

And still, Antonio lied. Still, I believed. This is where I fully understand how victims of domestic abuse are silenced by their own fears, men too. I should have known better than to remain quiet. Quique did a very brave thing. He was pained by my exit, but still cared for me and wanted to show me the error of my ways, not to win me back, but to help me exit my situation with Antonio.

Friends in Madrid knew of Antonio, who posted adverts in local newspapers and was known in the gay community. Quique was so convinced of his own findings and frustrated by my blinkered blindness that he posed as a client and, through a series of explicit text messages, engaged the services of a male escort from Madrid. He paid for a hotel room on the outskirts of Seville, invited the escort over and one hour later, Antonio walked into the hotel lobby. He was wearing a crisp white shirt, tight jeans and black boots, and a face like thunder when he realised he'd been beaten at his own game. He had walked straight into a trap.

'You can't trick a trickster,' smirked Quique.

Quique's phone call didn't quite give me enough time to gather my most important belongings. Antonio returned when I was packing. The details of what happened are painful to write. The panic. The blind, searing panic. The dangerous anger. There was a tussle, but he was stronger than me and hit me repeatedly. I fought my way past him, gripping my suitcase and scooping up a rucksack with my free hand as I lunged for the door. I ran into the city nightscape and found a quiet space up a dead-end street by the river and howled behind a green wheelie bin. I tried to coordinate my hands. It was like trying to dress after a cold run and an even colder shower, when your fingers will not respond and there is a disconnect between your will and your movement.

I scrolled through my phone contacts until I saw Quique's name blurred by tears and managed to press the green call button. Once I had been seen by a doctor at A&E, he called me with further instructions to get to safety. I spent four days hiding in a hotel room until Quique arranged for me to collect all my belongings and end the contract at the apartment. I can't remember the details. All I can remember is the fear.

I ran away from Seville and checked myself into a five-star hotel on a golf resort near the Portuguese border. I took long baths and wrapped myself up in fluffy white towels. I ordered room service since I had no desire to step outside of those four bedroom walls. I sat still, waiting for my pulse to slow. Cocooned. Safe. Thankfully, I had money in the bank and an avenue of choices ahead of me. I wondered about all those people in abusive relationships who had no exit route and no money to get out. I don't know what I would have done without the support of my friends.

Serendipity knocked at my door the very next day in a delightful way. A job offer from a dear friend who was setting up a new business. As we chatted, I told her I was available and interested.

'Great. You're just the person we need. You came to mind in a brainstorm yesterday. We're not far from Seville, so maybe we could meet up to talk it through.'

'I'm not in Seville. I've gone away for a few days.'

'Oh. Anywhere nice?' she asked.

'Yes, I'm in a hotel near the Portuguese border.'

'Oh, so are we. We have come on a recce because this is where we want to put the office.' Her voice slowed. 'We're in the Vincci Isla Cristina, on the golf course.'

My lips cracked as a huge smile divided my face in two without warning. 'Room 121.'

'No, Room 15. Why? What do you mean?'

'Arabella, I'm in the same hotel.'

She scream-laughed so loud that I swear I heard it from down the corridor.

'What are the chances? This is amazing. I knew it. It was meant to be. See you in the bar in five minutes?'

'Give me ten as I need to jump in the shower and get dressed,' I replied.

In the shower, I couldn't work out what was water and what were tears. I didn't care. I cried because I was happy. I cried because I was sad. I cried because there was a new beginning. But there was still a small part of me that felt I didn't deserve it. Life had delivered me a hard blow, but here was a beautiful and timely lifeline. I dressed in disbelief and looked at my reflection in the huge bathroom mirror.

'You're gonna be alright, Manni Boy,' I told myself, but my voice sounded different. For a tiny moment I saw the reflection of Matt Brown Hair beside me.

Fate took me to a sleepy coastal village, surrounded by marshlands and the stimulating punchy scent of 12,000 hectares of pine forests. I settled down with my new friend duende and began to reread the texts of Federico García Lorca. He helped me heal my sensibility. Duende, when not used for good, can cause us to lose our way. When it is used in purity, it ignites the very core of us, but I will never lose my respect for its power.

I ran ten kilometres five times a week, as a way of distancing myself from the memories of Seville. How ironic that a city I love so much holds such bitter ghosts for me. Even today, there are certain areas of town where I don't like to go, certain streets I avoid and certain bars I refuse to enter.

My running route was always the same and I would attack its gentle slopes and curves with repetitive effort. Slowly the memory of the pain dissipated. I needed to rebuild my emotional stamina. There was no other way. As I write this almost twenty years later, sitting behind my writing desk, it baffles me that I was able to lose myself so entirely. I had almost thought myself a wise old stick, a good head on strong shoulders, but life can succeed in toppling us. How frighteningly close I came to the brink of myself.

My dear friends, Kas Limón and Sophie, prescribed me at least six months of singledom and celibacy.

'You've lost yourself, Manni,' they told me.

All I could do was nod in silent agreement. I had diluted myself, compromised who I was. I was lost. I needed to lay fallow. My new home was a gem of a fishing village called El Rompido, in the province of Huelva. While running the same 10 km circuit every day, I put myself back together. Those months passed gently without so much as a hint of drama. I remember only the sunsets, the pine forests, the long shadows of dawn and the still nights when I learned to trust myself again. Each day, the mechanism of my smile returned more naturally. The pain left me. There was no more fear. After gentle caresses by wind, sea and sand, I knew instinctively that I was whole again. Again. Again.

37

OTTER

IT RAINS ALL NIGHT AND the water spouts running off the roof into the lemon-tree patio are more than white noise. They keep sleep from me and I surrender to a dawn walk. I take a different route, hardly on purpose but because I cannot think, downriver beyond the ford towards the village, but hidden from sight by the rise in the olive grove. The sun has no place in today's molten sky.

Something causes a ripple in the river water. I don't see what causes it at first. I just see the concentric circles rippling from a spot beneath the low-hanging branches of a eucalyptus tree.

I adjust my position just a few metres and then I see them. Three otters, unaware, slinking over the rocks – a silent, united trilogy. So Jack hadn't lied after all. Why has it taken me five years to see them? Maybe I wasn't ready. They were always here. I just wasn't in the right place at the right time. As quickly as they appear, they disappear downriver. The dogs missed them. This sighting was just for me.

I don't really know what to do. A smile starts in my belly and rises through my throat. It almost hurts to release it. But I do. I stand there grinning, the last eight years passing through my mind's eye like a film reel.

As I approach the house, the wind picks up. My thoughts will not stay still. They're swirling around in my head and whistling through my body in time to the rhythm of the banging doors and the slamming of the window shutters. Crash. Whoosh. A surge of wind down the corridor. There is a rasp of hinges, a squeal that makes my shoulders rise and my eyes close to a slit in anticipation. The bathroom door slams with a force that I imagine will be followed by the noise of shattered glass. The kitchen windows blast open into the vortex. The wind outside gathers strength and joins forces.

I hear it circling the house in ever-stronger flourishes. It comes and goes in fits and starts, dancing down the river and returning via the track like a giant dragon in a Chinese New Year parade. The house is brimming with colossal serpents of wind, finding one way in and another way out, bringing with them dust and leaves and flies and noise. The wind is inside my head. For a moment, I breathe in a pocket of silence, only for the wind to re-emerge, striking a new formation up on the olive grove and then attacking the house en masse.

On days like today, The Corner is open to all the elements. The weather is inside the house. The walls do not really exist, they are mere archways to bring the outside in.

As swiftly as it builds, it fades away, the wind a mere memory. Silence is the absence of sound. The word's ancient roots are linked with the wind. Silence happens when the wind dies down. Silence is the stillness that happens afterwards. Silence is slow-flowing water, and we hear it when we stop, when we enter a state of calming stillness.

The River of the Silent Ones flows slowly now, barely audible, a whisper through the branches of the silver birch. The waters seek the Mediterranean. My soul inhabits a new quiet. Old Man Mountain remains in his peaceful repose, the contours of his human face rising through the limestone beyond the olive groves.

There is no cuckoo call. Leaves do not rustle. I am happily hemmed in. I feel cocooned, wrapped up, safe and warm.

38

ON ONE OF LISBON'S SEVEN HILLS

Figure on the horizon,
Who I do long to see.
'Why are you so far away from me?'
I ask. 'What's wrong with me?'

                    Manni Coe, 1986, aged 12 years

'I NEED YOU TO FORGIVE ME,' my father says, as we look out over the terracotta roofs of Lisbon's Alfama neighbourhood.

My father hasn't flown out to Lisbon for a banal chat. Three weeks previously, I finally decided to tell my parents I was gay. I was just about to enter my fourth year of university and I wanted to broach the subject before my finals. I arranged a special dinner for three at a luxury hotel in rural Berkshire, thinking a neutral location might ease the conversation. It didn't go as I'd imagined. Before the end of the meal, Mum turned her chair around, giving me her back, then asked Dad for the car keys and waited for us in the car park. She wouldn't speak to me for three months.

My brothers told me that it was as if I had died. My parents lay awake crying every night, as if they were mourning their son. I am so grateful I never heard them weeping. Mum's silence forced me to Lisbon, where I suffered a nervous breakdown.

My turmoil kept me in bed for two entire days and Andres, my first-ever boyfriend, a go-go dancer and model from Peru, called my parents as he didn't know what else to do. My father, uncharacteristically, did something quite radical. Leaving a note on his boss's desk, he caught the next available flight to Lisbon. The note read: *My son needs me. I am going to Portugal and I don't know when I am coming back.* Perhaps he felt that he hadn't been the best father to me in the past. Here was his chance to step up into the role and he wasn't going to let the opportunity slip.

'And I am going to sit here until you are ready to forgive me. I need to hear the words,' he says, with a clear determination in his voice that I don't recognise.

The visitors are dwindling. We are almost alone in Lisbon's São Jorge Castle. The city sighs with the last upheaval of a busy day, the fine light hazing off the wide, shimmering silver-blue ribbon of the Tagus River. I dare to look my father in the eyes. I know it is now or never. Circumstance and serendipity might not orchestrate a repeat. These moments appear and then slide away. I know that if I choose not to forgive him, he will be crushed.

I remember the years of my father's aching sadness. As kids we used to make fun of him, laugh at how sad he looked. We used to joke with Mum that he looked like a disappointed camel.

'Oh, I was so terribly sad, Richard,' he says. 'Sorry. I still can't get used to calling you Manni. And I have to admit something awful to you.'

'What?'

'I was envious of you. Envious of your ease. Envious of your bright smile. Of the way you excelled in school. When you got into university, it was so hard for me.'

'But, Dad,' I ask him, 'how can you be envious of your own son? I'm only here because of you,' I remind him. 'You created those opportunities for me.'

Here is my father on one of Lisbon's seven hills, emptying himself of pride – the breathing epitome of humility. He is asking his son to forgive him for being distant and absent; for not taking him to his drum lessons at Leeds College of Music or watching him run the 110-metre hurdles for Reading; for the lack of affection; for the love that up until this very moment, he has found so difficult to express. He is also asking forgiveness for not suspecting what went on with the vicar. He recalls odd comments. There were odd gestures he remembers seeing but he didn't clock them at the time. He wants to say sorry for not keeping me out of harm's way. His love for me has brought him to Lisbon. He came to rescue me but, really, he has come to rescue himself. We are rescuing each other. Father and son, old man and young man, sitting on the ramparts of Lisbon Castle, our combined futures hanging over the precipice.

My dad had been absent in my childhood just like his father had been absent in his. Grandad Les Coe returned from Normandy with the 'noise of blood and thunder' in his head and never spoke of his torment. He, like countless comrades, locked his experiences away and they scorched the very core of him. With a strong work ethic instilled in him by the post-war industrial push, he forced my dad to leave school at sixteen and take up an apprenticeship as a butcher. Dad never got to go to sixth form, where he was set to be appointed as Head Boy. He was made to swap his A levels for a blue-and-white striped apron. So many abandoned dreams.

Socially awkward, my father buried himself in sport. He lived for table tennis and reached county level. Not once did my grandad go to watch him play.

There are other things that happened in my father's childhood that are not my stories to tell. He was dealing with his own demons just as I was born.

'It was as if I was metamorphosing,' he tells me. 'The memories crippled me. Everything about me felt barren and hard. It was worse than grieving, like an agonising process of rebirth.'

Little me, screaming little blue me, with a hole in my heart, short of oxygen, began life wrapped in unhappiness. Mum suffered a bout of post-natal depression while her husband struggled, but she loved me deeply and still does. This explains the incredible bond we have enjoyed and suffered all our lives.

Twenty-two years later, my dad wants to break the chains of generations of emptiness. It takes a brave man.

The longer I wait, the harder the task becomes. They are

three words. I. Forgive. You. Four, if I want to add 'Dad'. A mortifying embarrassment swells within me. My mind drifts to coffee and dinner. I know I need to put my dad out of his misery. No, wait. That's not the right sentiment. I have the opportunity to lance a wound. I am struck by a strange sense of power and know I cannot walk away. I am already gleaning the pernicious nature of unforgiveness. I focus, follow my breath inside my body, down through my airways, into my heart cavity, attempting to identify what forgiveness might feel like. What does it look like?

I find it there as I gaze at my father's pleading eyes. I give it a name. It has a shape. They are the hardest words I have ever had to utter. As they rise and form in my larynx, a physical pain rips through my vocal chords. The words scratch and tear on their way through. And then they are here, at the back of my mouth and all I need to do is speak them forth, to release them.

'I forgive you, Dad.'

There is only silence. We are totally alone on the ramparts. The day is about to end. I feel suspended in time and fading light. His body crumples like a puppet whose puppeteer has just dropped the strings. His limbs fall into a pile of bones and tears. My prodigal father. There is no space for my feelings. There is no physicality to our embrace. We are outside of ourselves and it feels entirely otherworldly. I crouch down on the bare stone of the terrace and take him in my arms. He is my son. I am his father. My father's father. I hug my forgiveness into him until he can weep no more.

My dad always says that's the night his life began.

39

WRITE A BOOK

—

CAYETANO SLOWLY BEGINS TO REVEAL more of himself to me. There is a trust developing in this odd bond through history. He is an old soul trying to get through. I print the photo of him and have it propped up on my desk. His honour stops me in my tracks. How he did the right thing and stepped down from ownership of this house he loved so much. It feels like the ultimate sacrifice. He had to wait for twelve years until he held the keys in his hands again. The fact that he returned brings such sweet meaning – our count, our captain, our considerate gentleman.

How I would love to speak with him. History affords us a peculiar magnifying glass to pry on someone's very private affairs. Death gives us licence. The joy of discovery and explanation is the motivation that plummets historians to the depths of archives and dusty documents, unearthing their meaning. I am in touch with historians now and they hand me more nuggets of gold. It becomes a communal dig and I am handed tools unfamiliar to me, but I soon learn how to use them. They delight selflessly in my delight. It's an odd form of virtual, historical connectivity in these strange times.

I discover that Cayetano was a writer. Of course he was. I find references to published works not only in Spain's National Archives, but further afield. A copy of one of his works sold for next to nothing on a second-hand book website in 2017. There is a 'How much they paid for it' window on the website. A mere 36 euros. Who are *they*? Why on earth do they want his book? Where can I find it?

I find a copy online and it's a parable called 'A Story of Flowers' about a tiny flower vying for light and smothered by foliage from other plants that keep the sunlight from her. Finding his works becomes my lockdown drug. I uncover reference numbers, fill in online forms to order copies, await the confirmation, together with an apology that in 'these unprecedented times, it may take longer to process your order'. I imagine civil servants in the National Archives handling precious books with white gloves as they scan relevant sections to create digital files.

Little by little, Cayetano's words trickle into my world and my suspicions are confirmed. He was a man of romantic substance, a poet, a raconteur with a passion for the natural world. The Corner was his portal into the recesses of his creative soul. He spent those three years here after suffering an accident in one of his military postings. Three whole years convalescing here. What a dream. I imagine him rebuilding his life after trauma, healing his broken wings. There is nothing like the ebbs, flows and cycles of nature to retune the soul.

'We have said that the duende loves the edge, the wound, and draws close to places where forms fuse in a yearning beyond visible expression,' wrote Lorca.

Count Cayetano felt it here too. He retreated here to heal his wounds. Whether his 'accident' caused physical or emotional wounds matters not, as you can't have one without the other.

I feel a kinship as I sit down to get to know him through the words he wrote almost 130 years ago. I let them linger, like a fireside chat with a treasured friend. I wonder where he used to work. Was it here, in this room? I am struck by how the structures of the natural world remain steadfast in areas where humans have not interfered with its fragile balance. He would have listened to the same birdsong. Did he let the river accompany his thoughts? Did he throw his pain into the same gorge? He was warmed by the same winter sun on cold days, shaded by the same trees in summer. We were both witnesses to this spectacular fold of the earth's crust that unleashes so much blessing and understanding.

El Rincón is a time warp. I read a collection of verses Cayetano wrote in 1886, dedicated to his beloved sister. I find a scanned copy in the Biblioteca Digital Hispánica, Spain's National Library. Cayetano signed it, brown ink from a wide-nibbed fountain pen scoring his eternal signature into the paper. I wonder how long it took for the ink to dry. I cannot believe

I've found him. I trace the letters to reenact the flow of his pen. I sit for a while staring at my writing pad. The barrier of time and space disappears, and I sit with him like that for a while.

Since living by your side
You are all I see.
I no longer live with you.
Rather, you live in me.

Count Cayetano de Alvear, *Cantares*

Cayetano was a man touched by the mighty power of love, the deepest emotion of all. I imagine him clinging to the wild wonders of The Corner as his escape into barbarism, a foothold in both worlds. It speaks to me that he spent the last years of his life here and yet he died and is buried in Madrid. I am yet to visit his grave. When I am able to travel, I will take a copy of this book and read to him from it, in the hope that my words might reach him, as his have reached me.

'I want to live in an old house, in the middle of nowhere, surrounded by olive trees' are the words I uttered that led us here, and now I sit in a room in the oldest part of our old house, in the middle of nowhere, surrounded by olive trees. I am aware of those ancient trunks anchored into life-giving Andalusia, bearing their presence on the house and sharing with me their invisible connectedness. I am welcome here. I allow my mind to wander. Have these walls always cradled creativity? Have they ever caressed another searching soul and held the world back to allow the still passage of time, ensuring enough silence to access hidden words and the disentanglement of ideas? I am given over to the possibility that they have. There is an inert stillness in this spot by the river. I prick my ears to listen to the gurgling waters and they slip by the house whispering their secrets.

We live by the River of the Silent Ones, but I will remain silent no longer.

40

A LONG WALK

I shout, 'Everything!' and the echo says, 'Nothing!'
I shout, 'Nothing!' and the echo says, 'Everything!'
Now I know that the nothing was everything
and everything was the ash of nothing.

José Hierro, from 'Vida', translated by the author

I SEE BATTLE SCARS AND COURSING wounds under the polished plaster reflection of my face.

I'm inside out and back to front before sunrise.

Darkness plummets by my side. Hold on or let go?

Made of broken pieces, held together with smiles and sadness, laughter and tears. Gone are the days of early Eden for we have learned to fear. Forgotten are the days of heady summers for we have learned to hate. How I would love to repeat my hay-bale ponderings, stare at the shallow waters of an autumn brook without thinking of December.

It is time to pin ourselves together with ties and mesh, quietly beg of our future to mend our past.

Today's sun may warm our skin, but it is the promise of next year's rain that will hold our mind's gaze. Pain must flow if we are ever to reach our ocean of yesteryear. The River of the Silent Ones knows the way, but must we follow? Memories will be a guide in the valleys. Light can cross even the darkest of spaces. Midnight caves of winter are no match for the smallest candle. The deepest abyss of shadows cannot stop the dawn, neither can the sun hush the wind.

For we all have little ruins inside us. It is me and it is you. Together. One. All. Broken parts of the whole. Gaudí takes your shards and makes everlasting art. I am not afraid of cutting myself on the sharpest edges of my soul and yours. Our mind and theirs.

It is possible to restore a ruin. This house, if we ever manage to restore it, will still hold its cracks and fissures. We will be able to bracket them away from harm and render fresh cement and plaster on top, but they will persist, hidden but present. We are so used to its decrepit state that we must be careful not to modernise it beyond recognition. We need to restore what is here. We should never forget its past. I have grappled to understand it and will have little say over its future, past our time here. This book is my only lasting word. I wonder if, 130 years from now, when we are long gone and our mark on The Corner is being slowly erased by wind and water and the inevitable passing of time, might a middle-aged person stumble across it and find within its walls and under its arches a place of solace for their questioning soul.

I tread lightly, not wanting to hear the crunch of the earth beneath my feet, careful not to interrupt the discourse that begins in me. The dogs linger back intuitively once we reach the alberca and let me continue alone.

Joe came to visit me in my dreams last night. He has been close all morning. I cannot get him out of my mind. I often think of him, but today is different. It's as if he has hold of me and won't let me go. It's a gentle, persistent feeling following me around, like a shadow on a beach.

The lapis-lazuli sky is as still as can be, barely a rustle in the trees, the river almost silent in its perpetual glide. Everything aligns and I think I am ready. Do we stay or do we go? It's time to make a decision.

I leave Thyme Point brushed with doubt and walk straight on to the Final Fence. All the miles I have ever walked pull at me from behind, in a kind of counter-intuitive drawback, inertia reversed. Time to let go. It only lasts a moment, an aerial view of the entire journey, and then it short-circuits. I have the Final Fence in my sights.

I take the invisible parts and begin to build a wall of words, hoping for all this to be over, to be able to finally turn the page.

I scramble up the sloping edge of a colossal boulder by the Cove and stare in wonder at a tiny oleander that clings to a fissure in the rock. The count's tiny flower, refusing to give up. Something growing out of nothing, defying nature.

A mother's plea to 'Please don't forget my son'.

A father's desire for forgiveness.

A vicar's instruction to burn a letter.

A friend's assurance that, 'You're gonna be alright, Manni Boy.'

Joe's assumption that I would understand if . . .

A little boy Richard, playing his drums.

If I were to gather all this suffering like freshly fallen snow and squeeze it into a ball, it would only last as long as the heat in my hands. Nothing is permanent.

This home, this gorge, this river, these mountains, these meadows with their perfect miniature flowers is home only for as long as we are here. It's clear to me that our true home won't be about restoring something that is falling down, mending what is broken, but rather, learning to live with the cracks and imperfections. The Corner has taught me light and shade, love and the lack of it, smiles and tears.

'We lived our best and worst times in that house.'

Please believe me when I tell you there is a force of nature here. Jack may call it gobbledegook, but I know he feels it too. He misses it when he's not here, that ability to slot into invisible mechanisms. When we are far away, The Corner visits us in our dreams. It affords our souls a rare freedom.

Finally, I am ready and so I climb. Not a route I have ever taken before but a new track, surely cut by the ibex and deer. I weave upwards in gentle switchbacks, finding old vines for footholds, all the while scouring for shards of ceramics, broken vessels of the past. By the time I reach the summit, I am clutching a dozen pieces in my hand, gripping them so tightly they almost pierce my skin.

I hear a melody and then lose it. It rakes my insides. An echo. Fighting its way back.

Time echo time time
Echo time echo echo

I start to cry and I don't know why. Those are the best tears. Now? Not yet. I drop the shards, give up the fight in an attempt to empty myself. I face west. A mid-November sunset is blocked by a bank of gun-metal grey sky. There are no individual shadows. Everything is shade. Flat. Dull. Undefined.

As I stare west, alone among the retama grasses, as still as them, rays burst through, a torch in the fading light, spotlighting the entire scene with fingers of gold. I gasp. I'm not sure where to look. So I look inward. I don't want any part of me to remain in the darkness. I don't want to be one of the Silent Ones: the silent father, the silent mother, the silent friend, the silent brother.

It all comes back to me as if this moment is passing me the code to crack the safe of suffering. I know I have to do it. One more time. There is no other way. I cannot turn back now.

The rutting season is over and one lonely stag is intent on making himself heard. The bellow comes from an invisible place, beyond the bend in the river, past Otter Pool. I am not quick enough to seek the source, but it doesn't matter as the sound swiftly fills the entire valley, touching everything I can see and then ricochets along the river, bending with its shape. It lasts long enough for me to know I will never forget it.

Me, sunlit, drenched in a primal scream. I have to say the words. It is no easier the second time. I cannot see him but I think he is here. I think I can hear him as the last wave of sound peters out. It is the end of the road. This is the lauburu facing clockwise. I am in a hall of mirrors of forgiveness. There is an infinity to this moment as I see myself in reflection. I am ready to forgive: others and myself.

'I forgive you.'

It's like an avalanche and I am in the middle of it, but I know I will not be harmed. It's a soul slide. An opening and closing. I am hot and cold. Inside and outside. Here and far, far away. I am on the edge, staring at the blazing light.

I stand there as long as I dare, until the clarity brushes me no longer, until all is without light. I can see him: that little guy who wandered around in wide-eyed wonder without that bruise in his heart; that young man whose smile was never far away before the world took it from him. I can see the version of me, before the pain.

I reach into the nothing to catch the arrow on the wind,
Snapping it in two on the nearest boulder of blackening limestone.
It hit its target and I can now find my way home.

I leave the pile of fragments of times gone by at my feet, turn around slowly to face east and head home, to the lauburu facing anticlockwise, to the beginning of time. I am in the centre of the labyrinth and now I can work my way out. Healing is not linear. Like water, it trickles its way from source to sea.

I give the wind my songs.
They are snatched by the wind's intents,
Then the echo returns them,
Converted into laments.

Count Cayetano de Alvear, *Cantares*

Detained quite by accident in this house, in this beautiful part of Andalusia; with the calm this place affords my health and spirit, I rejuvenate, I finish this body of work and I dedicate it to you.

If anything within it keeps your attention, if it gives you the slightest delight, if it teaches you something, if you gain from it anything that is not easily destroyed, ephemeral, insignificant . . . keep it with you, together with the memory of my love for you.

Dedication to his daughter-in-law, Count Cayetano de Alvear, *Cuento de Flores,* Archidona, 15 January 1900.
Seconded by Manni Coe, Archidona, 2 March 2024.

POSTSCRIPT: THE BEGINNING OF THE END; THE END OF THE BEGINNING

THE LIGHTS IN THE HOUSE lead me down. I traverse down the mountain, never losing sight of home. The Corner sits quietly, timeless by a long straight section of the river. She looks perfect. I can hear Beau barking for his dinner and the last birdsong before our winged friends turn in for the night.

A message pings into my phone. I hesitate before reading it.

'Hello, my darling,' I say as I enter the kitchen, where Jack is rinsing rice to remove the starch.

'Oh, hello,' he replies. 'Did you have a good time?'

'I had an amazing time,' I say. 'Amazing in every way.'

'Good,' Jack says, looking deeply into my eyes.

'That's a look of love if ever I saw one,' I jest. 'Never get attached to a boyfriend.'

'Too late,' Jack says. 'Now come and sit by the fire.'

331

Over dinner, as the not-quite-dry-enough olive wood crackles and spits in the hearth, I say, 'My darling, Reubs just sent me a message and I don't really know what to do.'

'What does it say?' Jack asks.

I read him the message: 'brother. do. you. love. me.'

We gaze at each other for a paradiddle, a double paradiddle, flicking from one eye to the other, our dinners resting on the coffee table that sits between us.

We both know.

We both know this is a cry for help.

We both know I can now go to rescue my brother.

We both know that I am ready.

ACKNOWLEDGEMENTS

My agent, Dotti Irving, has seen *Little Ruins* through each and every draft, believing in the story from day one. Her infallible guidance has been my tonic. My friend Adrian from Little Toller gave me early words of wisdom and then Simon Thorogood from Canongate took the baton and has been the book's torchbearer. It has been a joy to share in his finesse and vision. The exemplary and fun-loving Claire Reiderman helped me get the manuscript over the line at the very end.

To the entire team at Canongate: Jamie, Jenny, Alice, Amaani, Kate, Lily, Lucy, Stephen and Vicki. Thank you for giving this book its own stall in your stables. My office visits were a real treat. Thanks to my cover designer Luke Bird and my proofreader Jo Mortimer. My copyeditor, Gale, was as skilled and as focused as anyone I know.

To Alan Wilson, the late Bishop of Bucks for our all-too-brief friendship. I hate the fact that we never got to enjoy that beer in Spain. To Rosie Harper, Louise Whitehead, The Bishop of Oxford and the Rev. Donna McDowell. You have all been a source of true comfort and support. Thank you.

To Anthea Green, Matt Brown Hair's Mum – for your love & support.

To our volunteers and housesitters at The Corner – the good ones! Thank you for holding the fort through thick and thin.

To Angel Snow for your musical artistry. Your song 'Arrows' accompanied me on my journey home.

To my Dorset tribe & Bredy Bunch for your fun & friendship. Jason for truth talks with brandy, Nikki for fearless encouragement.

To my Spanish friends for teaching me how to live well.

To our neighbours and community in Archidona; for your stories, your advice and friendship.

To those individuals and families who have given me their blessing and permission to write about their lives, even though the memories are still painful.

To my late dad. It makes me sad that he is not here to see *Little Ruins* carve its path when he helped me carve mine through life. I will always love you, Daddio.

To my family for being the reason I know who I am. Kate, an early reader and encourager. Nath, my creative inspiration. Matt & Liz, for your love & support. Mum, there is so much of you in these pages. I love you.

To my friends for helping me find my own emotional pulse and celebrating with me; especially Ali, Paul, Matt, Anna, Tash & Oli.

LLL – for asking the right questions at the right time.

My phone trilogy 'Los Chalchaleros', with Kas, Limón & Sophie, is my yardstick and my compass – I love you.

Boobalish – your truth is how I found my own.

Andrew – the beginning of my everything.

Count Cayetano de Alvear – for loving The Corner like I do. I am yet to visit your grave in Madrid and am waiting for the right time to pay you my respects and gratitude.

The Corner – for your delicate beauty and your timeless wonder. You are the portal to my Narnia.

Clare Milford-Haven and James' Place. To Clare for your guidance, advice, support and friendship. What you have achieved in memory of James is a testament to your love and generosity.

James' Place offers free, life-saving therapy to suicidal men. They have testimonials from hundreds of men who consider that their support and advice saved their lives. If you'd like to know more about James' Place, you can find their website at jamesplace.org.uk.

If you feel triggered by any of the themes in this book and would like to talk to someone for support, there is help available.

For a 24/7 Crisis Textline: text SHOUT to 85258

Prefer to talk? Call Samaritans on 116 123

Need NHS help? Call 111

REFERENCES

Alvear, Count Cayetano de. *Cantares*, E. Runiños, 1886.

Alvear, Count Cayetano de. *Cuento de Flores*, R. Velasco, 1901.

Foster, Ruth. In: Sophie Turbutt, '"How can life go on?" Reflections on the Holocaust and its Aftermath.' The York Historian, 27 January 2017. https://theyorkhistorian.com/

Güiraldes, Ricardo. *Don Segundo Sombra, Shadows on the Pampas* (trans. Harriet de Onís), Constable, 1935.

Hachenburg, Hanuš. 'Terezín', September 1944. In: Hana Volavkova (ed.), *I Never Saw Another Butterfly: Children's Drawings and Poems from the Terezín Concentration Camp, 1942–1944*. Schocken, 1994.

Hierro, José. 'Vida'. In: José Hierro, *Cuaderno de Nueva York*. Hiperión, 1998.

Lorca, Federico García. 'Theory and Function of the *Duende*' (trans. J.L. Gilli, 1933). In: Melissa Kwasny (ed.), *Toward the Open Field: Poets on the Art of Poetry 1800–1950*. Wesleyan University Press, 2004, pp. 197–208.